PENGUIN BOOKS

Tall Tales (Some True)

GW00779038

Greg McGee

Tall Tales (Some True)

PENGUIN BOOKS

PENGUIN BOOKS
Published by the Penguin Group
Penguin Group (NZ), 67 Apollo Drive, Rosedale,
North Shore 0632, New Zealand (a division of Pearson New Zealand Ltd)
Penguin Group (USA) Inc., 375 Hudson Street,
New York, New York 10014, USA
Penguin Group (Canada), 90 Eglinton Avenue East, Suite 700, Toronto,
Ontario, M4P 2Y3, Canada (a division of Pearson Penguin Canada Inc.)
Penguin Books Ltd, 80 Strand, London, WC2R 0RL, England
Penguin Ireland, 25 St Stephen's Green,
Dublin 2, Ireland (a division of Penguin Books Ltd)
Penguin Group (Australia), 250 Camberwell Road, Camberwell,
Victoria 3124, Australia (a division of Pearson Australia Group Pty Ltd)
Penguin Books India Pvt Ltd, 11, Community Centre,
Panchsheel Park, New Delhi – 110 017, India
Penguin Books (South Africa) (Pty) Ltd, 24 Sturdee Avenue,
Rosebank, Johannesburg 2196, South Africa

Penguin Books Ltd, Registered Offices: 80 Strand, London, WC2R 0RL, England

First published by Penguin Group (NZ), 2008
1 3 5 7 9 10 8 6 4 2

The excerpt from 'Howl' on page 70 is from *Selected Poems 1947–1995* by Allen Ginsberg
(first published in *Howl & Other Poems* 1956, Penguin Books, 1997) copyright ©
Allen Ginsberg, 1956, 1996. Reproduced by permission of Penguin Books Ltd.

'I'm an Odd Fish' on page 204 is from *Dancing to My Tune* by Denis Glover
(compiled and edited by Lauris Edmond, Catspaw Press, c1974) copyright ©
Pia Glover. Reproduced by permission of the Denis Glover Estate.

Cover photograph: Claudio Bonazzon

Inside front cover images, from top left: Detail from *Whitemen* promotional poster by
Dick Frizzell, author's own collection. Reproduced by permission of Dick Frizzell.
Middle left: *New Zealand Listener* cover (27 August 1988) reproduced by permission
of New Zealand Magazines. Middle right: Author and Roy Billing burning the Junior
All Black jersey in protest at the Auckland–Springbok game in 1981. Photograph
from the Roy Billing collection, reproduced courtesy of Roy Billing.

Inside back cover images, from top left: From the 1982 Mercury production of *Foreskin's Lament*,
with Philip Holder as Foreskin and Roy Billing as Tupper, from author's own collection. Top right:
New Zealand Listener cover (27 August 1988) reproduced by permission of New Zealand Magazines.
Middle right: Photograph by Claudio Bonazzon. Bottom: Detail from *Whitemen* promotional
poster by Dick Frizzell, author's own collection. Reproduced by permission of Dick Frizzell.

Designed by Vivianne Douglas
Typeset by Pindar NZ (Egan Reid), Auckland, New Zealand
Printed in Australia by McPherson's Printing Group

ISBN 978 014 300913 9

A catalogue record for this book is available
from the National Library of New Zealand.

www.penguin.co.nz

Contents

one

Giving Voice

In May of 1980, I left Auckland and puttered south to Wellington in my Austin A40 Farina bought with $400 I'd borrowed from a Domestic Purposes beneficiary who was moonlighting as a waitress on K Road. I'd been sent a free air ticket by the organisers of the first Playwrights' Workshop, but had cashed that, bought gas and pocketed the balance. The winder on the driver's side window had given up the ghost. I had torn the lining of the door off and propped the window up on a block of wood, but the vibrations kept knocking it askew and the window would crash back down, so I left it down. There was early snow on the Desert Road, and by the time I got to Wellington I had a head cold that stayed with me through one of the defining weeks of my life.

In late '79, I'd seen a poster calling for full-length plays to be submitted for a Playwrights' Workshop to be held the following year. I just happened to have one handy. It was called *Foreskin's Lament*.

7

Earlier that year I'd slipped a copy into Raymond Hawthorne's letter-box in Picton Street. He was Artistic Director of Theatre Corporate, which I'd been going to a lot since I got back from overseas. Impressed with the intensity they brought to their productions, I dreamed of my play being done there, on that little stage with the audience so close. I heard nothing back from Raymond, so I plucked up my courage and rang him at Corporate. He asked me to come in and see him.

We sat together, knees almost touching, in his shoe-box office in Galatos Street, across the road from the Old Golds social club. A general strike was being mooted by the unions and Raymond told me his actors had threatened to go out in sympathy. Good on them, I thought, but I was immediately glad I didn't express that sentiment as Raymond launched into a diatribe against his 'fucking actors', saying the 'silly cunts should realise that Art and the Theatre are above all that'.

We eventually got around to talking about my play. He was mainly puzzled by it. He said he could see how Act One would work – it was powerful and reasonably straightforward and stageable – but Act Two . . . It wasn't that he didn't like it, he just couldn't quite figure out what it was or how it would work. He encouraged me to go away and have another think, though he didn't really specify what I should think about.

Shortly after that, I'd seen the poster for the workshop and sent the play to Playmarket, the playwrights' agency which was running it. Playmarket had three readers for the 100-plus plays they received. The first reader, venerable drama critic David Dowling, had to plough through all of them, separate the wheat from the chaff, and make a short list of 20, which went on to be read by two other readers. Dowling, I heard later, ranked *Foreskin's Lament* 16th, so it only just made the cut. The second reader, Adrian Kiernander, a young academic at Victoria University, was more impressed: he finished reading *Foreskin's Lament* about one in the morning and immediately got on the phone to the third reader. In Auckland, Mervyn Thompson, well-known playwright and director, was woken by the phone and listened blearily to a voice on the other end yelling, 'This is it! This is it!'

Mervyn, who was going to be running the workshop, obviously agreed with Kiernander when he read it, and sometime in early 1980 I was told my play had been chosen as one of the four to be given a full workshop by professional directors and actors at Victoria University in May.

A couple of weeks before the workshop, I went round to an address in O'Neill Street, to meet Mervyn, or Proc, as he was known. Proc wasn't in the main house but in the basement flat round the side and down the back. I remember being quite reassured when I shook his hand – he was wearing a blue flannel shirt rolled up at the sleeves to reveal working-class biceps. He told me I looked exactly as he'd imagined. I wasn't quite sure what that meant, but took it as a good sign. He told me straight up that *Foreskin's Lament* was the only play he'd ever read that he wished he'd written, that it was going to have a wonderful reception and that it would be produced throughout New Zealand. Jesus.

Nevertheless, as I drove south to Wellington, I was nervous about the upcoming week. I had never been to a rehearsal, ever, let alone to a rehearsal of my own play. Worse, I'd been warned that there were going to be 10 or 20 observers at every rehearsal session – theatre professionals and academics and others with a particular interest in theatre who had paid for the privilege of watching the genesis of these plays. I was worried that, under all this scrutiny, someone would ask a question which would open a black hole of illogic or mistaken motivation which would then swallow the play whole.

I was made very welcome but I was unsure quite how to behave, what the ground rules were. To begin with, that wasn't a problem because Proc made it clear to the cast and observers the huge goodwill he had towards the work.

The actors were supposed to have read the script before they turned up, but of course most of them hadn't. As they edged into the first read-through, I could see them quickly making guesses as to what sort of beast this was. They quickly latched onto the fact that it was a rough-trade sort of a play, and most of them brought out their standard rough-trade accents – Cockney. With Proc's encouragement, they went Kiwi, but, again – and this was also true of Proc in his demonstrations to the cast – they went very broad initially but then gradually relaxed into a more natural vernacular.

In that first reading, listening to the actors struggle to render their own accent on stage, I began to understand why the play was going to have such an impact. Later, some academics would say that here, finally, was 'our voice' on stage. And though I thought that was overstating it – there were so many other Kiwi voices, just as valid, who weren't in that play – I began to understand that in my innocence, and ignorance, of New Zealand drama, I'd done something innovative by giving voice to these characters.

My secondary school, Waitaki Boys' High, like most New Zealand schools of the time, had studied playwrights and authors who were either dead or overseas. We did have an innovative

English teacher, Derek Bolt, who had come to Oamaru from England to paint 'the clearest light in the world', and who had studied at RADA and went on to do one-man shows throughout New Zealand (and set questions for *Mastermind*). Bolt was daring for Oamaru, and for the nation: he would discuss *Lady Chatterley's Lover* with me and gave us *One Day in the Life of Ivan Denisovich* to read. But the school play, which I reviewed for *The Waitakian* in 1968, was nevertheless *Journey's End*, rather than *The Pohutukawa Tree*. Similarly, we learned about the history of the Whigs and the Tories, rather than, say, the epic forced march of the great chief Te Maiharoa down our own Waitaki Valley in the brutal winter of 1879, when the government bowed to the runholders at Omarama and threw him and his tribe off their land. Or we studied the rivalry between Gladstone and Disraeli in the late 1860s, rather than the contemporaneous and much more exciting clash of wit and force between Titokowaru and McDonnell at Te Ngutu o te Manu up in Taranaki.

My family, like most in the working class north end of Oamaru, didn't go to the plays and musicals put on by the local repertory and operatic society at the opera house, one of the grand Oamaru stone buildings then falling into disrepair. We thought that sort of carry on was for the nobs up the South Hill. When we went to the opera house, which we called the rat house, it was to boo Nikolai Zugendoff, the nasty Russian wrestler, or to cheer Alf Cleverly, the local boxer. So my interest in drama had burgeoned late, while I was in London, and I'd just assumed that back in New Zealand we had our own *Changing Room* and *Look Back in Anger*.

I no longer remember the changes I had to make during that week in Wellington as we worked our way through the play.

There must have been quite a few, because every night I'd go back to my room at one of the student hostels and work on them, nose streaming. At one stage I must have expressed a degree of tiredness or frustration, because I remember David Carnegie, my dramaturg for that week, saying to me, 'If you can't hack it, give it away!' Fucking hell, I thought, I'm being beaten over the head with my own words. I took it as a compliment, as he and Proc were both incredibly supportive.

The rehearsals went well, with the cast geed up by Proc, and I didn't feel at sea in front of them or the ever-present observers, until, during one session, Proc was having difficulty with a bit of dialogue and threw it open to the cast to improvise.

I wasn't quite sure what improvising on the script really meant, but I quickly came to understand that it really meant improving the script. The cast duly cast about without much added value that I could see, at which point Proc opened the forum to the observers, most of whom were playwrights, or would-be playwrights, or theatre practitioners or academics, full of good intentions and Good Ideas, who seized the opportunity to make a creative contribution. As Proc worked his way through some of the suggestions, trying them out, dutifully asking me what I thought of them, I felt myself sinking gradually in a quagmire, with my play on top of me, forcing me deeper. Were some of these suggestions useful? Were they better? Were they worse? If they were worse, was I allowed to say so? Was I just being overly defensive?

At my worst moment of indecision, I got a folded note from the back row of the observers. I opened it and read the handwritten words: *Plays are not written by committee. Cheers, Roger Hall.* I slipped the note into the pages of my script, took a deep breath and told Proc that I wanted to go back to the script – I had an idea for a change that might help. We were back on track.

Mostly, I felt privileged to be there, spending all day discussing the view of the world which the play represented, through the characters I'd created. These talented people were bringing their interest and intelligence and craft to bear on my words – that seemed to me to be the essence of rehearsals – and what writer wouldn't like that? It felt like life lived on a different level of intensity, inquiry and engagement.

By the end of the week, we were ready for the reading in front of all the observers and an invited audience of theatre practitioners, including the artistic directors of the professional theatres who, it was thought, might take a punt on a play if they liked it enough. 'Enough' would have to be a lot, because, despite Bruce Mason's pioneering efforts and Roger Hall's success with *Glide Time*, home-grown plays were regarded as hugely risky. Proc was intent on making the reading as good a sell as possible, and had pushed the actors into incredible progress, given they'd only had three or four days of rehearsal. They had some basic blocking in place and some were even partly off the page – they knew their lines without reference to the script. It was a strong cast with, most notably, Grant Tilly playing Tupper, a role he was to reprise the following year at Circa with great success.

That night, there was something naked and vulnerable about the actors – even though they were fully clothed during the first act – in the sense that they were without props and costumes and sets and all the usual subterfuge which helps them to create a different world, to suspend disbelief. Maybe it was because they had only the words to connect them with the audience that the reading attained an intensity which some people, myself included, reckoned was never repeated in production, despite the play's later great success.

The audience that night seemed as charged as the cast; many of them had been part of the week, as observers or actors in the other plays being workshopped, and had become bound up with the energy and excitement and the claustrophobic focus. Whatever the cause, the play seemed to crackle and burst upon the audience. And when it finished, after a long, seemingly stunned, silence, they got to their feet and applauded.

The evaluation session was held the following morning. I got to sit up front and deal with the brickbats and bouquets from those who had an opinion – observers, cast, audience. I wasn't looking forward to it, but my training as a lawyer at least gave me some confidence in being able to deal with it. When I saw how many people had turned up, however, my confidence drained away, particularly when one of the first speakers, Wellington critic Ralph McAllister, stood up and said he loved the play, but what a pity about the bit on the end. He was referring to the lament, a long monologue which Foreskin addresses directly to the audience. I had half expected this, and had taken a deep and anxious breath in readiness to parry the criticism, when Professor Don McKenzie leapt to his feet and launched into an impassioned defence of the lament – a far more eloquent and persuasive argument than I could possibly have mounted. That's how the rest of the session went – the audience argued enthusiastically with each other, while I sat up the front doing noddies, grateful that I had to say nothing. I thought that was appropriate really: I'd already had the stage for more than two hours to make my case with the play.

The other thing I realised during that session, as these strangers argued over the meaning of my play, was that it had gone – it was no longer mine. Already, though a hell of a lot more work was needed to make it stageable, it had wrenched itself away from me and staggered off into the welcoming arms of these strangers. I didn't realise until some years later that this phenomenon is the sign of success, that it doesn't always happen, that if you remain the sole guardian of your work it probably means little to anyone else.

On the Sunday, I drove back up the island in my draughty A40, hoping that my life was about to change. I was buoyed by the reception for the reading and by the generosity of Proc and the cast. All I could think of was that wonderful exclamation from the Venetian dialect, 'Ghe'sborromi!', which signifies amazement, delight, surprise and incredulity, and is used by men and women alike, despite its literal translation as giving the exclaimer a small ejaculation. It seemed the perfect response to what had happened that week, given the Italian genesis of the play.

That reading in May 1980 was five years almost to the month since I'd left Dunedin to try tailoring my life so that I could write. On the face of it, my Five-Year Plan seemed to have worked with Stalinist precision. The truth was quite different.

two

Galileo Galilei & the Prophecy of Doom

Wanting to be a writer wasn't something I shared with many people. It seemed such a pretentious aspiration, given my background. I was the first of my family to go to university and though I had managed an LLB with a wide variety of grades, from the odd A through to much more numerous Cs, and had been asked by the dean to do honours (I thought it would take too much time out of my rugby), I had no connections within the legal fraternity. Except for Iain Gallaway, of Gallaway Son & Chettleburgh, the firm started by his father.

Iain, who moonlighted as a rugby and cricket commentator, must have seen something about me that he liked, amidst the mud and blood of Carisbrook on those wintry Saturdays when I was playing for the University As or Otago. At the end of '72, I played an All Black trial in Wellington and missed out, but just before that door closed, Iain Gallaway opened another for me. He gave me a start at $32 a week, explaining that, really, I should be paying him for educating me. He had a point. In those days the LLB course was less practical than it is now and though, after four years' study, I might have been able to argue a fine point of law in the Supreme Court, I had only the vaguest idea what a mortgage was. I rapidly found out. Iain became my mentor, giving me enormous responsibility for my age, mainly in corporate law, as well as allowing me to dip my toes in the courts, where I mounted epic defences for the likes of my team-mate, Anton Oliver's uncle, who had been arrested for streaking.

By 1975, I knew I had a partnership with Gallaway Son & Chettleburgh if I wanted it, but when I looked at the chair in which I might be sitting for the next 50 years, something inside urged me to run while I still could. I needed to write.

I tried to rationalise it: I was 24, I had enough experience in the law to come back to it if I wanted to; I had no dependants, not even a pot plant; I was running out of excuses for not doing what I had always wanted to do. I thought trying to write and failing miserably would seem better when I was 70 than looking back and knowing that I'd never tried.

I put together the vaguest of five-year plans – change my life so that I could write. From that moment, I resolved that everything I did for the next five years was going to expedite my becoming a writer. If, after five years, I'd crapped out and found I couldn't write, I could go back to law.

Leaving Dunedin was the first step, and a wrench. When I told Iain I was leaving, I bullshitted him about wanting to see the world. It was sort of true, but I couldn't tell him I wanted to write and didn't think I could do that if I'd stayed in Dunedin. So I fibbed and fled.

It was a pity I didn't tell Iain what I was up to, because a quarter of a century later I read his autobiography, *Not a Cloud in the Sky*, where he described himself returning from the Second World War desperate to become a writer: wrong time, wrong place, and the line of least resistance led back to his father's law firm. There was no doubt he would have understood my need to write if I'd had the guts to tell him. He wrote me a generous reference nevertheless, saying if I ever returned, there was a partnership waiting for me.

As a preliminary step to my OE, I'd arranged to do a locum in Henderson for a sole-charge solicitor, Milan Kostanich. I was too young, according to the Law Society, to run a firm by myself, but Milan arranged several experienced practitioners to act as 'trustees' to guide me – my mate Paddy Finnigan, who had organised the job for me, was one, along with the likes of John Sparling and Jim Kingston – and the Law Society relented.

Milan made the terrible mistake of letting me stay in his cliff-top house at Te Atatu while he was away. He had a wine cellar. 'Help yourself,' he said as he departed. I hadn't drunk a lot of wine in Oamaru, nor in my seven years in the student ghetto of North Dunedin, but I soon developed a taste and in the six months that Milan and his wife Shirley, sister of Peter and Joe Babich, were overseas, I and my very few Auckland friends cleaned out the cellar. I learned later that it contained a vertical tasting of damn near every vintage the Babiches had made. Milan, to his credit, didn't say much. In my own defence, I'd been desperately lonely out there in his big house, and had gravitated towards Ponsonby, where the girl I'd chased north lived.

Ponsonby was funky, a bit like North Dunedin, only warmer. Like Dunedin, and unlike the cul-de-sac in Te Atatu, there were people on the street. My girlfriend flatted in what is now a mansion in Hamilton Road owned by the guy who made millions from vodka.

In '75, it was gloriously shabby and louche and hip. Downstairs, at one stage, lived Roger and Mel Donaldson, and bits and pieces of early Hello Sailor were drifting about. Ponsonby still belonged to students and old Catholic working class families and Pacific Islanders and hippies and musos and halfway house incumbents. When I rode my trail bike down John Street to the Progressive Youth Movement vege co-op in the old hangar at St Paul's College, I got chased by dogs. When the back tyre blew out and I canned off in Ponsonby Road, there wasn't any traffic to run over me. It was right in front of what is now SPQR, but in those days it was a motorbike garage and I could just wheel the bike over the kerb and get the tyre repaired.

Gradually, the further details of my five-year plan began to crystallise: my girlfriend had researched an Italian language course at Perugia, which sounded terribly romantic, and I also heard about Ken Carrington, All Black winger and hero out west, who was playing rugby for money in a small Italian village.

The idea of using rugby to finance my writing seemed like the answer to my dreams, so I got Ken's address from one of Milan's clients and wrote to him, asking if he knew of other Italian towns which might want a player. He wrote back, saying he was returning to New Zealand next year and did I want to take over from him at Casale Sul Sile? Ken said Casale was a bit under-resourced and this time around wanted a player-coach rather than just a player. I looked up Casale on the map. It seemed very close to Venice. I could go to Perugia, learn to speak Italian at L'Università per

Stranieri and then head up to Venice where I'd be supplied with a house and a car and enough lira to live on. That seemed like one hell of a plan: run a couple of practices a week, play a game at the weekend and spend the rest of the time writing the great New Zealand novel – how difficult could that be?

In March of '76, after a year in Auckland and a sniff of Ponsonby, I boarded Lloyd Triestino's *Galileo Galilei*, bound for Genoa. I knew then that when I returned to New Zealand, if I was still writing, Ponsonby was the place I would come back to.

I'd decided it would be better to travel to Italy by ship, to savour the experience and pick up some Italian, rather than be instantly delivered par avion. My little red portable Olivetti was in my suitcase and I could see myself cruising across the Pacific, liberated from all earthly worries, tapping away at the beginnings of my novel whilst watching the sunset over the forequarter or afterdeck or whatever those bits of the boat are called.

I'm not sure what I imagined an economy cabin would look like, but the sweat-pit down in the bowels of the ship just above the engines and next to the crew quarters had very little romance about it. There were six single bunks and the other five denizens didn't speak English, so conversation was limited. So was sleep, because Bender, an elderly rotund German, had an unusual ability to snore on both inspiration and exhalation. Except when he stopped breathing altogether. Then I would wait, increasingly anxious on his behalf, ears straining against the constant background thrum of the engines, until an explosive snort signalled he'd dodged another heart-arrest bullet. Bender looked like Friar Tuck, with a halo of fine white down that began at the edge of his bald pate and ended at his toenails. I knew this, because when he wasn't strutting about the afterdeck in his black Speedos, crinkled to a small pouch under his massive belly, he was naked.

Since the cabin was too claustrophobic to spend time in during the day, and hauling the Olivetti out on the afterdeck was a statement I wasn't prepared to make, very little writing got done until after Acapulco, where I got involved in a 'mutiny' and, almost inadvertently, got published.

In the mid-Pacific the ship answered a mayday call from someone with a broken leg on a yacht, apparently, and lost time doing so. I must have been below decks at the time. As we steamed towards Acapulco, the passengers were informed that the Acapulco stopover, instead of being a couple of days, would be four or five hours, from about eight in the evening until one in the morning. Many passengers were incensed – Acapulco was one of the most anticipated stops in their round-the-world cruise and their chances of seeing the famed cliff-top divers, for instance, in the dead of night, looked slim. Plus there was no wharf at Acapulco, so everyone who wanted off the ship had to be taken off by smaller craft, which ate up another couple of hours.

Much of this debate passed over my head – I was one of the few who thought four hours in Acapulco in the dead of night was better than no hours. I disembarked and was ferried across the harbour to the city. Tino, a well-dressed middle-aged Italian who collected dolls and who had been teaching me a few Italian phrases, seemed to know his way around and offered me a ride in his taxi to see one of Acapulco's 'piu belle viste'. We ended up in what he called a bar overlooking the bay, where I discovered that the lights of Acapulco weren't the beautiful views Tino was referring to. The bar was full of gorgeous and scantily dressed

Mexican women and, miracle of miracles, many of them seemed to want to have a drink with me. Raymond Hawthorne once said I had a wonderful innocence – knowing Raymond, he would have meant it as a euphemism for ignorance – but I was 25, not 15, and had no idea, until several very unambiguous moves later, that I was in an extremely well-appointed brothel.

When Tino and I made it back to the *Galileo*, we found the large purser's foyer occupied by about a hundred very angry passengers, mostly middle-aged. They had prepared a petition asking for the stay in Acapulco to be extended to a full day, so they could at least see the sights. I was keen to do that too, because so far I'd seen only Tino's 'belle viste'. The petition had been signed by hundreds of passengers, according to an English couple who seemed to be prime movers, along with a German guy in his 30s.

I had come across this German a couple of times: he was arrogant to a cliché and an Italian barman I'd got to know told me he was a captain in the German army, and that he was very unpopular with the Italian crew. According to my friend the barman, the German's father had been a panzer commander in the Second World War and didn't have a high regard for his Italian allies, an opinion his son seemed keen to pass on to every Italian he met.

The English couple and the young German insisted that the petition be presented to the captain. They were taken away, but returned ashen-faced a little later, saying the captain hadn't shown, but a lesser officer had ordered them and the German off the ship. They were to pack their bags immediately and be taken ashore by a waiting boat. The German was furious, but the wife of the English couple broke down in tears, saying they had no money left, this was their trip of a lifetime, they had no way of getting home from Mexico. This didn't seem fair, so we took up a different petition, asking that if these people were to be thrown off the ship, Lloyd Triestino, the owners of the *Galileo*, should at least pay their airfares back to Europe.

There was an announcement on the PA, repeated in Italian and English, that the ship would sail as scheduled in half an hour. Because there was a strike at the Panama Canal, passenger ships were given priority, provided they kept strictly to their booked times. The *Galileo* had lost time answering the mayday call and if it had further dallied in Acapulco we would lose our priority booking and would have to sit out on the Pacific side of the Panama, waiting in line with all the cargo ships and oil tankers. Why hadn't the passengers been told earlier?

The announcement told the passengers in the purser's foyer to disperse to their cabins. I noticed Tino disappeared quickly, but no one else moved. We made it clear that we wouldn't disperse until the ejectees were guaranteed air tickets from Mexico back to Europe. When some officers in uniforms came to say that the boat to take them to shore was waiting we placed the English couple and the German in the centre of our throng and repeated our demands.

There was another announcement, this time only in Italian – and my Italian wasn't good enough to know whether it was a message to the passengers to disperse or a message to the crew to congregate. Very shortly after that, the doors at both ends of the foyer burst open to reveal a dozen crew at either end. Being taller than most, I could see that these weren't the bar staff and waiters and officers in their white mocker, these were tough-looking men in T-shirts and jeans. Some were carrying short lengths of rope.

There were no announcements or further palaver – they put their arms out elbows first and launched themselves into the crowd of passengers.

I guess they were trying to get to the English couple and the German at the centre, but as they concertinaed the crowd from both sides, the crush forced some people up off their feet and others down to the floor. The ones on the fringes were isolated and beaten. I saw a young Aussie bashed backwards onto the floor; as a couple of crew went after him, he managed to save himself by slithering through the double glass doors into a passageway. I saw a middle-aged Italian woman whacked with a rope, an Australian girl's breasts were violently pulled, several women got punched in the face. At one stage, as the panic and screaming set in, one crewman seemed to be offering a group of mainly women an escape route to the outside promenade. But as they staggered towards the opening doors, a fire hose operated by a crewman out on the promenade bowled them back into the mêlée.

I tried to get my back against a wall. As the crewmen reached me, I had two or three women behind me, between me and a bulkhead. I was no shrinking violet. Having been worked over by the brutal Canterbury pack of the early '70s and marked Grizz Wylie in Ranfurly Shield challenges more than once, I was reasonably certain I'd never again have to confront anything quite as disconcerting as Grizz's baleful glare from under those trapezoidal eyebrows. But I'd never seen anyone as out of control as four or five crewmen who confronted me, screaming and gesticulating. I said nothing. My fledgling Italian deserted me and whatever I uttered would have been misunderstood so I just watched the eyes of the guy closest to me so that I could intuit when he was going to swing and trusted my peripheral vision to pick up the others.

I was scared: I might have taken out one or two of them, but I had a strong feeling that if a punch was thrown they'd be all in, and it wouldn't stop until I was down and seriously out. I remembered a terrible old story I'd been told by a returned serviceman I worked with at the Oamaru Fire Station. One hundred Germans are marching towards a lone Kiwi soldier whom they know has one bullet left in his rifle. The Germans keep marching, calculating the odds logically at one hundred to one that they'll be the one who collects that bullet. The Kiwi soldier perishes. One hundred Italians are marching towards the same Kiwi with the one bullet. Instead of calculating the odds logically, the Italians begin thinking, It'll be me! And they turn and run. It was the kind of racist crap that the German army captain would have been proud of and, funnily enough, as the split seconds stretched out and the men in front of me calculated the odds, the German saved the day by bursting from the middle of the crush and sprinting off down the nearby passageway. The guys in front of me saw him and took off.

The German was caught and he and the English couple were taken off the ship before we put back out to sea, as scheduled. I understood that our efforts weren't entirely in vain and that the three of them were flown back to Europe, courtesy of Lloyd Triestino, but there was a very weird atmosphere on board for the rest of the trip.

I was incensed at what I'd seen and made it clear to any Kiwis involved that they should insist on getting their injuries recorded by the ship's doctor, and we should put together statements about what happened. One New Zealand woman who'd been 'physically assaulted and verbally insulted' was afraid they'd throw her off at Cristóbal to stop her taking things further and gave me a letter to pass onto the New Zealand consulate in London if that happened. It didn't, and I still have her letter.

My activities did not go unnoticed, and being put off at Cristóbal was no longer the issue for me after my friend the barman told me to be very careful – that if someone disappeared off the afterdeck in the middle of the night, it wouldn't be the first time it had happened on that ship. I had none of the evidence that is now available about the number of passengers disappearing mysteriously off cruise ships – over 30 between 2003 and 2006, by one report, not including known suicides or those, under one influence or another, known to have deliberately jumped – but the barman's advice had the ring of truth.

I'd seldom felt more vulnerable. There were no police on board. These guys had my passport and my money and they determined what I ate and drank. Moreover, my cabin, down in the bowels of the ship, was very close to the crew quarters. I resolved not to take any risks, so I stayed in the bar for the next several nights, where the lights were never doused, and slept during the day out on the afterdeck near the swimming pool. All this for the price of an economy fare.

In Cristóbal, at the Atlantic end of the Panama Canal, I posted a letter, detailing what had happened. My girlfriend back in Auckland gave it to a friend who worked on the *Auckland Star*, where excerpts from it were published. My very first published work.

'I'll Never Forget Crew's Sheer Hate, Writes Passenger on Galileo!' read the banner headline on the front page of the 22 April edition. It wasn't the title I would have chosen, but then I wouldn't have chosen 'Auckland Solicitor' as my pseudonym either, as in 'The Auckland solicitor has asked to remain anonymous at least till he leaves the ship, for fear of reprisal.' No wonder. My purple prose deserved severe punishment. The *Star* reported me verbatim:

> 'The savagery of the crew was incredible, and many of the women were petrified. Finally, the foyer was cleared, leaving the crew, bloodlust whetted, walking up and down, laughing and replaying their favourite punches. The sheer hate was something I'll never forget, although I remember the head bar steward crumpled against the wall sobbing throughout the whole spectacle. But most of the crew took a frightening delight in carrying out their orders.'

You could certainly see the aspiring novelist trying to get out from behind the anonymous solicitor. But my efforts were prosaic compared with the inspirational creativity of a '21 year old New Zealand girl' who was quoted on the front page of the following day's *New Zealand Herald*.

> 'Two hundred people collected in the lobby by the purser's office,' said the girl, 'after they heard that they were not letting people ashore return to the ship. People were throwing chairs overboard and swearing in the most terrible language at the crew . . . Suddenly fighting broke out . . . It was like something out of a movie with people hitting each other with chairs. They even had flick knives . . . The beds in the infirmary are now overloaded with the wounded

from the fighting and with the sick.' . . . One crew member
. . . told her that some of the passengers had been highly
abusive and had started most of the trouble. There was a
crowd of rough New Zealanders on board. 'I was ashamed
to call myself a New Zealander after them,' she wrote. 'I'm
sure we are doomed and will never see Genoa.'

Forget the movie fight – I'm not sure where we got all the chairs
to throw as most of the furniture was nailed down – what about
that last line? Barbara Cartland would have been proud. I couldn't
compete with that; clearly there was too much of the solicitor in
me, far too much respect for the facts. Or maybe I was keeping
company with the wrong crowd.

The same girl had been quoted in *The Press* on 17 April, complaining that 'many people were sick with a type of virus sweeping
the ship . . . possibly being the cause of the death of one woman.'
Not only that, but 'the air conditioning was not working and . . .
the bed-sheets had not been changed.' When the passengers got
wind that the stay in Acapulco was going to be foreshortened,
she'd heard 'talk of hunger strikes and boycotting meals'. In my
own defence, and on behalf of the other rough New Zealanders, I
strenuously deny any allegations that I boycotted meals, caught a
virus or complained about dirty bed-sheets.

Concerned family tried to get in touch with the ship, according
to the *Herald*, but were alarmed and infuriated by 'radio silence'
and a 'cloak of secrecy' around the ship as it made its way across
the Atlantic to Spain. 'One Auckland man desperate for news
of a friend on board the liner tried to get in touch with the ship
by ringing Spain and contacting Spanish radio. He was told the

ship was not accepting calls of any kind. "I'm getting extremely annoyed about this – it is just not right," he said last night.'

On 23 April, the *Herald* was reporting on the front page that 'Acting Prime Minister, Mr Talboys, had asked the Ministry of Foreign Affairs to begin immediate enquiries into allegations that New Zealand passengers on board the Italian liner *Galileo Galilei* had been maltreated.' Talboys was also Minister of Foreign Affairs, so presumably the chain of command was reasonably short. Their inquiries certainly were.

As the *Galileo* staggered mutely from Cristóbal to Curaçao and then across the Atlantic, the news of the 'mutiny' was broken in Europe by the English couple and the German. When we got to Malaga, a couple of new German passengers boarded and between Malaga and Naples, our last stop before Genoa, they surreptitiously revealed themselves to a few of us as reporters for *Stern* magazine, after the story of 'the mutiny on the *Galileo*'. After speaking to a few of us, however, they found that the facts didn't seem to fit the story they wanted to write – no mutiny, not even a riot, just some dumb passengers being assaulted by the crew? After a day or two of covert interviews, they simply enjoyed the sun and the beer.

By 21 May, the Ministry of Foreign Affairs seemed to have come to much the same conclusion. The *Herald* was able to report that Talboys had confirmed an inquiry made by the Italian Ministry of Merchant Marine had revealed only 'a collision between crew members and passengers blocking the gangway . . . There was nothing in the report to substantiate allegations that New Zealand passengers . . . were maltreated.'

That was it, really. My first published piece seemed to lack both credibility and longevity. Disbelief was barely suspended. The lingering disappointment was that neither Foreign Affairs nor the Italian Ministry of Merchant Marine got to the bottom of the air conditioning problems and the dirty bed-sheets. Neither of which would have been helped by the New Zealand Maritime Union's threat not to service the ship next time it came to Auckland. I needn't have worried: there was no next time. In 1977, the *Galileo* was withdrawn from the round-the-world service and continued her chequered career under several different aliases, suffering a continuation of the accidents and failures that had always dogged her until finally, as the *Sun Vista*, she sank off Singapore in 1999 after a fire broke out in the engine room.

The *Galileo* episode coloured my view of Italians for a while. As rumours flew about the reasons for the incident, I was no longer sure that Italy was where I wanted to stay. However, an incident in Naples persuaded me that any plan was better than no plan. One of the Kiwi girls was leaving the ship there, so a couple of us helped her to get her bags from the ship to the railway station. She'd had a riotous affair with a beautiful Italian barman, but even so, we'd been on the ship for six weeks, which meant a hell of a lot of time between roots, I would have thought, to plan what one was going to do when one got to Europe. Just before I headed back to the ship from the station, I asked her what she was planning to do next. Drawing deeply on a fag, she said, 'Finish this cigarette.' I looked at her, stunned. Her eyes filled as she admitted that she had no idea what she was doing here or where she was going. It was too late for inquiries as to why she'd run away from New Zealand, what she was running from, what she'd thought would happen at this point – some sort of transformation?

I was glad I had a plan and decided to stick to it, although, having felt watched for some weeks, I was a bit paranoid about Italians. It didn't help that I travelled down from Genoa to Perugia with an Australian woman who believed the Mafia was after us. It might have been easier to dismiss Madam Oz as a paranoid drama queen if she hadn't also been a gifted fortune teller.

We were doing the same classes at Perugia and most of the students ate at the Bar Ferrari or one of the other cheap eateries on or just off the Corso Vanucci, the beautiful main street of the old town. Madam Oz began reading the palms of other students, then quickly gained a reputation. It wasn't unusual to see, late in the evening at whichever bar Madam Oz was frequenting, a line of local Italians, not just students, drawing their chairs into a queue to wait patiently to present their palms. Whatever she was telling them seemed to them to be the truth, and her reputation grew.

Madam Oz wanted to read my palm, but I, professing disbelief and rationalism, refused to let her, even in fun. I felt that letting her read my hand was akin to taking LSD. I'd briefly squatted in Bondi once during the university holidays and a friend who was dealing in acid wanted me to take a tab, gratis, but made the mistake of telling me that the only people who had bad trips were those who were scared of the drug. I was terrified and knew, like those Italian soldiers, that whatever tab I took would mean a bad trip. I believed that the same might happen if I let my palm anywhere near Madam Oz.

She stayed on in Perugia and visited me in Casale some months later, before she went home to Melbourne. In Piero's bar, I watched her read the palms of some of the locals, people I thought I knew reasonably well by then. The first one up was one of the dirigenti, the committee who ran the rugby club. Madam Oz, without any questions, told him he had three children. I knew that to be true. Then she told him two of them were not by his present wife. I knew Domenico's wife and knew that could not be true. As I smiled and shook my head, Domenico said, 'Si.' Madam Oz then told him what had happened to his first wife and other details of his life which I could not possibly have told her because I didn't know. It wasn't Q & A, with Madam Oz reading the signals. She just read this guy's hand as he sat there passively – and the other denizens of the bar immediately recognised genius when they saw it and pulled their chairs into a queue.

Later that night, impressed and drunkenly reckless, I let my superstitious guard down and she read my hand, 'just for fun'. As I'd suspected, it wasn't a fun story. Madam Oz told me I should abandon writing and go back to law. And, by the way, I was going to die young.

Next day, after Madam Oz had gone, I attempted to rationalise what she'd told me of my future. I thought part of her negativity might be put down to her disappointment that our relationship hadn't developed as she'd wanted. She'd also been pissed at the end of a long night on the palms – maybe she'd misread a few wavery wiggles here and there on mine, or seen a few extra lines – but her prophecy stayed with me for some time. I'd never considered the prospect of dying young, apart from some vulnerable moments under the stand at Lancaster Park, before going out to play Canterbury, when, if I'd been a Catholic, I would have asked for the last rites. At that stage, a couple of months into my tenure at Casale, abandoning writing and going back to law seemed not so much prescient as logical: making any progress on my novel was proving so difficult that I was quite prepared to believe that part of the prophecy. I eventually worked Madam Oz's words around to my advantage, figuring out that if I was going to die young, there was bugger all point in going back to law. I might as well live life to the full and do what I wanted. And that included writing, whether it worked or not.

three

The Witches of Sicily

While I continued in Casale to cling to whatever life I had left, Madam Oz's negative writing portents seemed on the money. Coming to grips with the language and my responsibilities in Casale took pretty much all I had to give and there wasn't a lot left over for writing.

Six weeks in Perugia had given me a working knowledge of Italian, but though the course was Italian immersion, life as a student in Perugia wasn't. There were students of many different nationalities at the Università per Stranieri. For many of the Europeans, mastering Italian was a necessary precursor to studying medicine in Italy, where the entry qualifications were so much softer than in their home countries. Nevertheless, in the bars and pizzerias after hours, the lingua franca was English. The Swiss, Germans and Scandinavians could almost all speak several languages and would have preferred to use Italian, but I think they found the Poms, Aussies and Kiwis so laborious and slow to learn, despite Italian being the easiest and most phonetically logical of languages, that it just wasn't worth the trouble.

As a result, by the time I took the long train ride up to the Veneto, my Italian was still pretty rudimentary. In Casale Sul Sile, I discovered that hardly anyone spoke English: suddenly, speaking Italian wasn't just a cute, romantic method of self-improvement, it was an absolute necessity if I was to do the job I'd been contracted to do. And it was only after I got there that I divined how important my job was to the people of Casale.

Casale was – is still, though the fields which used to separate it from Treviso are pretty much built over now – a tiny village on the banks of the Sile, which runs down into the lagoon around Venice. The Sile was a vital transport route, with barges delivering produce from the hinterland of the Veneto to Venice. When I saw the size of the place, I couldn't understand how this tiny village with no footpaths had got a team up through three divisions into Serie A, the first division of a national competition, in which most of the teams had more familiar names, such as Roma, Milano, Torino or Padova. Rugby might have been a minority sport, with the results hidden away on page 16 or whatever of *Corrierra Dello Sport*, but there was Gasparello Casale, up there in type with the big boys. In this way, the team gave the village a national identity, and the whole village got behind the players. A couple of years later, when I wrote Tupper telling Foreskin that 'the town is the team', I was thinking as much of Casale as any experience I'd had in New Zealand.

One huge advantage in previous years had been the local rugby field – it was very close to the river and had a water table just under the grass. When it rained, or when the river was up, the field became a swamp. Even in summer, training there was a risk because the mosquitoes took exception to their habitat being invaded. Visiting teams hated playing on the bog, which guaranteed that Casale always won its share of home matches. They were generally low-scoring affairs decided by a lucky kick or a penalty given by incompetent referees. In the wet that surface became a great leveller and Casale were always a chance in midwinter, whoever they played.

Unfortunately, the dirigenti, in their wisdom, had decided that Casale needed to resurface the field, to prove they were serious Serie A contenders for the long term. The new surface had the opposite effect for the couple of months that it held the water at bay. Instead of bringing visiting titans down to Casale's level, the new playing surface exacerbated the differences in talent, skills and fitness. Visiting teams could now play rugby at Casale, rather than get bogged down in an unattractive war of attrition in the mud.

And so it came to pass that, under the stewardship of the ace stranger who'd been brought in and given a house and a car and a monthly stipendium, the team lost every game from the beginning of the season in September right through to Christmas.

No matter what we did, we lost – by a try in the last minute, by a dropped goal in extra time, by some refereeing meltdown that gave the opposition a penalty kick in the dying seconds of the game. If there was a way of snatching defeat from the jaws of victory, we found it. Game after game, we traversed the many and various ways a team could lose. And as much as the Casalese tried to have patience in their new coach, and as much as I tried to explain that we were playing increasingly good, constructive rugby and just needed one win to change the team's losing mentality, they found it hard to hide their frustration.

Monday was market day, right outside my house. After the inevitable Sunday afternoon loss, I would flee from the village to Venice, where my Auckland girlfriend had landed a job as an au pair in the palazzo of Peter and Rose Lauritzen, later hosts to John Berendt while he was writing *The City of Falling Angels*.

There, I would catch a glimpse of a different world. An aged and arthritic Peggy Guggenheim, in a huge caftan, would be assisted up the stairs by her current gigolo for morning tea with Lady Rose, who was a Keppel, daughter of a viscount and related to Violet Keppel, whose celebrated relationship with Vita Sackville-West was immortalised in Virginia Woolf's novel *Orlando*. Or Venice's propensity to sink would be discussed with visiting American Fulbright scholars whom Peter, a blue-blood Bostonian, would enlist to help in the Save Venice Fund. Peter and Rose knew everyone who was anyone in Venice and it sometimes seemed as if the city was the final refuge for the preterites of the world, people whose time had passed, like exiled Greek and Russian royalties, and others like Peter and Rose, self-exiled aristocrats.

Or I would visit Chicco, my second five-eights, who was a part-time gondolier when he wasn't working in the vegetable market below the Rialto. Chicco would take me fishing out in the lagoon, then take me home down the labyrinthine alleys behind Academia to the small house where he lived with his sister, who'd make us pasta fagioli.

Whatever the attractions of Venice, I'd have to be back in Casale for Tuesday practice: to face the disappointment of yet another loss and the need to try for a win the next weekend.

I had some excuses for my lack of coaching success. A lot of my time went into teaching, not coaching. I had to teach a young guy the art of hooking who had played rugby for two years and hooker never – in Italian. In New Zealand, I had played as a loose forward and regarded front-rowers as rather like the Ku Klux Klan – practitioners of weird mysterious rites in which nobody with half a brain would want to be involved – but in Italy I had to put on the hooded cape and take up the burning cross and try to teach an 18-year-old the arcane secrets of the tight-head. I came to regard the ability to teach as a precious gift, a gift that my experience in Casale confirmed I did not possess.

I was lucky in the sense that I had my coaching Bible with me, *Meet the Lions*, wherein the '71 Lions gave detailed technical analysis of each segment of their game, and in the process demonstrated why their collective IQ got them home against the All Blacks. But *Meet the Lions* was in English and I had to translate what I wanted to use of it into Italian. Moreover, because my Italian was so raw at the beginning, I couldn't risk getting out there on the training field and improvising. There weren't many suitable words in Italian that came to me readily under pressure, so to begin with I had to learn by rote virtually every word I was going to use in every two-hour training session. Each took an interminable time to prepare.

That gradually became easier as my Italian improved. Italian is one of the romantic languages, but it's also wonderfully logical, economical and phonetic. If you see a word once, you know how it's pronounced, or if you hear it pronounced, you know exactly how to spell it. I began to really enjoy it, and I remember magical signposts in my understanding of it. There was the first time I answered a question without mentally translating it – I had replied before I realised I'd understood the question. And there was the time I woke up and realised I'd been dreaming in Italian.

A more important linguistic moment was the time I 'got' my first Italian joke. The relief on the boys' faces, that I actually had a sense of humour! But Riffi, who'd kept my Italian lessons well oiled with huge bottles of his own merlot and pinot grigio, so big they'd have to be carried in slings of knotted rope, had to act out the ending of the joke in slapstick, because the punch-line was never in Italian but always in Venetian dialect, which is much more earthy and descriptive and funny.

It was only after I began to become fluent that I realised why I couldn't understand what the boys in the team were saying to each other: it was because they weren't speaking Italian, but Venetian. They would speak careful Italian to me when they wanted to be understood, but between themselves they would speak dialect, which wasn't just a rapid-fire Italian with the suffixes cauterised, but in many ways a completely different language, with strong elements of French and Spanish. The more Italian I understood, the more I realised that if I really wanted to communicate with the team, I needed to grapple with the dialect. And therein lay more problems.

I soon picked up that they would say 'mi' instead of 'io' (I), and 'h' would often become 'g' and they would eat some of the suffixes of verbs, so that instead of saying 'Ho già mangiato, io' (I've already eaten), they would say – phonetically, because dialect is oral – 'Mi go jar munya'. That was straightforward enough, as was the way they'd turn a double 'l' into a 'y', so that 'bella' became, phonetically, 'beya'. But other translations were fraught with potential misunderstanding.

'Lui' in Italian means 'he' or 'him' but in dialect they'd turn that 'l' into a 'y' and say what sounded to my ears like 'you'. So

I'd be standing there having a conversation with someone who seemed to be talking about 'you, you, you' which I thought, some might say typically, was all about 'me, me, me', but which in fact was about a 'him, him, him'. In time, I discovered that I'd passed on some controversial opinions about certain third parties and volunteered myself for several entirely unsuitable roles. But that wasn't the worst of it.

I thought I heard the boys calling each other 'fiori'. I did think it strange that these macho rugby players should be calling each other flowers, but when in Venice . . . So I began using it myself. In my team talk before the game I would use the term in my exhortations to the players, as in 'Get out there, flowers, and climb into them!' I couldn't understand why the longer my team talks went on, the worse we played. On the field, in the heat of battle, I would exclaim 'Forza fiori! Die fiori!', which I thought meant 'C'mon guys! Get into it, guys!' I did note that the opposition seemed to take more encouragement from my shouts than my own players, who looked embarrassed. I put that down to Italian sensitivities about being yelled at by a stranger.

Finally, Piero, one of the dirigenti, an avuncular figure who owned the local bar where I ate most nights, took me aside after a number of glasses of prosecco and politely inquired whether it was the custom in New Zealand for players to call each other flowers, because he didn't think it was helping much here in Italy. Turned out they were calling each other 'feeoyee' – 'guys' or 'boys' in dialect.

Using dialect was a political statement too. The local kids played a kind of a hop-scotch, where they'd describe circles in chalk on the street. Each circle, a landing place, would be a country

– 'Gli Stati Uniti' or 'La Francia' or 'L'Inghilterra' – but home base was never 'Italia', always 'Il Veneto'. It was a reminder of how recently Italy was unified and of the derivation of what came to be known as the Italian language, which was basically a development of the Florentine dialect. Interestingly, when Venetians mimicked Florentines and dropped their own idiosyncratic pronunciations, they sounded a bit like Kiwis trying to mimic the English, as if they had plums in their mouths.

I quickly learned that everything was political in those times. I'm not sure why that should have been a surprise to me. I'd been in Perugia during the run-up to the June election that year, and there'd been political rallies up and down the Corso Vanucci. The hammer and the sickle would be flying brazenly on the street as the communists rallied in one piazza and the neo-fascists in the next, separated by polizia of different persuasions armed with Uzis. In the final vote, Enrico Berlinguer and the PCI (Communist Party) finally won a measure of power and the Historic Compromise between the Christian Democrats and the PCI seemed finally about to become a reality.

When I was fresh to the job in Casale, it was a political maze. I was the sole selector of the team, but various people wanted various players picked for reasons that were difficult to fathom. And even within the boys in the team, all nominal socialists, there were political gulches. There were so many shades of red in Italy, from the blood-deep crimson of the communist 'extremists', who might or might not have terrorist affiliations, to the lightest shade of pink, where socialism was more or less a fashion statement, like the stovepipe jeans and winklepicker shoes which were in vogue that year. And all those shades of red were in my team, which was drawn not just from the local landowners and contadini (peasants), but also from players bought in from Venice and Padova and Bologna. These outsiders were mostly students, from universities where protests were endemic and where faculties and even the university registries were being occupied. In Bologna, the Historic Compromise was sorely tested when a communist mayor ordered police to shoot and kill a communist student.

One of the Casale dirigenti, who spoke a florid, orotund English and pronounced himself to be an Anglophile, owned an agricultural grain and implement store and referred to 'my friends, the peasants' with ill-concealed contempt. On the other hand, I understood that two of my boys were possible extremists who disagreed with the whole idea of a communist government working with the Christian Democrats. The extremists wanted a 'true' communist government and believed that could happen only by revolution, not by constitutional evolution.

One potential extremist was lock Dal Cin, a huge bear of a man with wild hair and beard, who was rumoured to have done time for unspecified political activities. The other was a bought-in player, Renzo, a student from Venice. A powerful, dashing centre, Renzo looked a bit like Che Guevara, with black curly beard and long hair, which he would tie back with a red bandana when he played. His one weakness was a reluctance to pass, which had nothing to do with any lack of ability. Running with the ball and dying with it was a necessary political statement of his courage, passion and commitment. Team strategy didn't seem to come into it.

Renzo was an intellectual and, it was rumoured, a theoretician for the hard-core communist cell in Venice. On the bus to the away games, we would all sing 'Bandoliero Rosso' and I quickly learned the words, but Renzo just as quickly divined that I was a political innocent. He would sometimes sit beside me and try to explain some of the realities and complexities of the Italian political situation, which he felt that someone in my position of power within the group needed to understand. My ability to follow his beautiful but complex Italian foundered quite often, but instead of getting angry or frustrated, Renzo would flash his wonderful smile, the broad white teeth appearing from within the black beard like a bolt of lightning in a storm.

While respecting my sole selecting role, the dirigenti would gently push me towards this player or that player, often for reasons other than playing ability, which I sometimes understood in terms of the urban/rural parochialism I'd encountered in Otago: the bought-in scrum-half might be a better player, but he was a smart-arse student from Padova and the local boys didn't like him. We were fortunate that Renzo and Dal Cin were both indispensable stars of the team, otherwise there'd have been more pressure to drop them.

In the run-up to Christmas, when we couldn't get a win, things were becoming very tense. None of this – the demands of my position in Casale or the close acquaintance with Venice, where I'd have to flee every Monday – helped me with my writing. Instead of relaxing and enjoying the privilege of being involved so intimately in an endeavour in another culture, I was silly enough at times to be irritated by the way this life was overwhelming my 'art', a prosaic novel set in New Zealand. And something else was happening inside my head: the more I immersed myself in Italian and dialetto Veneziano, the more New Zealand colloquialisms I lost.

By that time, a couple of months into the season, the other

imported foreigners, Kiwi Bruce Munro and his wife Marie, were no longer living with me. When they moved into their own apartment, the occasions when I spoke English were limited to my visits to Venice and a little with Bruce at practices and games. On other occasions when I did speak English it was always to people for whom English was a second language, so I couldn't speak colloquially if I wanted to be understood. I remember, during a phone call home, my brother Peter declaring that I'd developed a Pommie accent.

Bruce – Broochay – presented another problem. He was a beanpole like me, but even taller, at two metres. He was a natural mimic and, unfettered by formal study of Italian, he quickly picked up a smattering of dialect and sign language. In return, he taught the locals some New Zealandisms, including that old standard Kiwi greeting, 'Fuck you'. He was a commanding and extremely funny presence. He would walk into Piero's bar, yell 'Fuck you!' at the top of his voice and receive a chorus of cheerful 'Fuck you, Broochay!'s in return from the locals, then have them howling within seconds by a combination of hand signals: he'd saw his hand laterally against his belly to indicate he was hungry, pull his cheek down below one eye to indicate he was a fox, then poke his forefinger through a circle of fingers to indicate he'd like to fuck Perio's wife, Nini.

Broochay fitted in wonderfully well at Casale and was super-committed on the field. Unlike me, he saw a career for himself as a professional rugby player and realised that, to compete with the big South African and English locks who'd been imported to Italy, he needed to bulk up. I'm not sure when he began taking steroids, but within a year he went from beanpole to behemoth. I'm equally unsure whether it was the steroids that gave him such a short fuse on the field, but Broochay kept hitting people and getting sent off. Every time this happened, the judiciary would penalise him by making him stand down for more games. Once he got a name, he was targeted, sometimes unfairly, but the upshot was that for most of the season I was the only foreign 'star' fielded by our team.

I use the inverted commas advisedly, because by the time I got to Italy, I was decidedly second hand, even though I didn't have many kilometres on the clock. I was playing with a loose ankle from a bad dislocation which the Accident Compensation Commission had reckoned was a 5 per cent permanent partial disability, and a knee with a torn anterior cruciate ligament which had never been diagnosed or reconstructed, not to mention a finger which kept dislocating during games, so that il dottoro had to stand on the sideline throughout the games to pull it back into place from time to time. Despite not being the player I had been, I took on more and more responsibility as our crisis deepened: I called all the moves, I was the main lineout target when Broochay wasn't there, I took the kicks for goal and, finally, the kicks for touch. None of it helped: we played quite well but kept on losing.

Finally, in the shadow of Christmas, the dirigenti called me in and sacked me. They said they'd like me to stay on as a player only, at least for the next game, an away match in Catania against the Sicilians. I already knew that this game was a big problem for them, so I agreed to play but told them after that I'd move on to London, where I had some friends I could hook up with.

By the time I was sacked, my writing had virtually petered out, overwhelmed by the pressure of the present, and the prospect of being able to walk away was something of a relief. Broochay was disqualified yet again, and the game in Sicily was shaping as a real headache for several reasons. The first was that we had to go by plane rather than bus, and some of the boys, two brothers in particular, said they wouldn't fly. One of the brothers wore a hat which he never took off, until the last moment before a game – a complete mystery because he had a fine head of hair. The other was, unusually, blond, and they were both good forwards, hugely strong in hand and forearm from pruning grapes and absolutely fearless, except when it came to flying. And Sicilians.

Before I was sacked, I had been out to their farm to try to per-suade them to make themselves available for the Sicilian game. That visit had been an eye-opener. The two brothers shared a stone hovel with a dirt floor. The pride of place in their reception room was one of those glass-topped display cases from the fairground, the sort you put a coin in and an arm sweeps across and knocks some worthless trinket into the pocket. The wallpaper was a riot of beaver – blonde, brunette and redhead – culled centrefolds from *Playboy* and *Penthouse* pasted up. I drank some home-made grappa, which would have incinerated my tonsils if I'd had any, and tried to persuade them to come to Sicily. They wouldn't budge and it wasn't just the flight down there they were worried about.

They told me that Sicilians weren't Italians, they were 'terroni' and 'Arabi'. And what would happen if either of them got injured and had to spend the night in a Sicilian hospital? I gave up – what would happen? 'Sicilian women are streghe – witches,' they told me, surprised that I didn't already know this incontrovertible fact, 'and while we are lying defenceless in the hospital the Sicilian nurses would be able to put an evil spell on us from which our lives would not recover.' There was no winning that one, and on further inquiry I'd learnt that it was a view shared by many of the boys: Sicily was not part of Italy and they didn't want to go there.

This was a group of people who were not exactly world travellers. Italy had huge economic problems and many contadini, the peasants who lived off their land, really struggled before the EEC and later the European Union kicked in with assistance and agricultural subsidies. It's very different now, but back then some of them hadn't been far out of Casale, before we started travelling to away games. When we had to stay overnight in our first hotel at Milan, some of the new boys got lost in the atrium, gob-smacked at a huge chandelier. When they discovered the mini-bar in their room, they assumed it must be presents for them, the guests, and it would be rude not to polish off the lot. They also assumed, sweetly, and because they hadn't seen anywhere else, that they lived in the best place in the world which I, having experienced it, would never want to leave.

Once I was sacked, getting a team to travel to Sicily was no longer my problem. But the dirigenti cajoled and banged heads until they mustered the bare minimum number of bodies onto the plane to Catania. The game was on a Saturday and we arrived quite late on a Friday night. By the time we'd checked into our hotel, it was getting on to 11 p.m. Despite the late hour, the boys insisted on a meal, so we all traipsed off to a ristorante near the hotel and tucked in.

Public drunkenness is frowned on in Italy and I'd never seen my boys more than mildly pissed by Kiwi standards, even after a game. Mind you, we'd had bugger all to celebrate. But this night in Catania, they hoed into the vino. It was clearly 'Eat, drink and be merry, for tomorrow we may die' and the new coach, one of the dirigenti, seemed reluctant to do anything about it. In fact, if anything, he seemed to share the team's powerful sense of foreboding. In their cups, many of them revealed the same fears as the absent brothers – of being injured and left lying defenceless in a Sicilian hospital, powerless against the wiles of the Sicilian witches.

By the time the team got back to the hotel, it was, collectively, legless, as was the coach. On the way through the foyer, someone noticed a particularly beautiful couple of women at the bar, wearing mini-skirts and revealing tops. Someone else discovered they were prostitutes and that, wonder of wonders, they were available on room service. Once the coach had collapsed on his bed, what was left of the night was, for most of the team, lost to a panicky, riotous, bawdy party, with much singing, slamming of doors, laughing and fornication.

By 10 next morning, when the team gathered for a late brunch before the game, it was clear that the Sicilian witches had already cast their spell and we were fucked. Red, streaming eyes, sore heads, tender tummies and that traditional coach's nightmare, depleted gonads. The general lassitude was gradually replaced by fear as we were bussed to the ground. I recall a very weird atmosphere in the dressing shed before the game – a kind of fatalistic acceptance of impending doom. The coach held his head with one hand, gesticulated with the other and gave us a desultory pep talk, while a couple of backs, still pissed, played a game of pat-a-cake.

Out on a stony field, with the Sicilian crowd caged behind a wire fence, the referee whistled for kick-off and shortly after that we managed to scramble the ball out and a lineout formed. I'd decided the best course of action was to simply do my best in my last game and play out my contract honourably, so when a Sicilian pulled my jersey as I jumped for the ball, I did the usual and gave him a whack. In New Zealand that used to be standard etiquette – your opposition number would try something on, you'd have a swish at him, just to indicate that you wouldn't be intimidated and then you'd both settle down and get on with the game. Not in Sicily. The guy I'd had a swish at took umbrage and the Sicilians went for me en masse, whereupon my freaked team-mates stepped back about 10 metres, to get out of the way. The only reason I wasn't killed was that there were so many of them crawling over me, none of them could get a decent shot.

The game, predictably, was a disaster. We'd lost every game leading up to this match, but had never been beaten like this. I was the only one taken to a Sicilian hospital, with suspected broken ribs that turned out to be contusions. When I rejoined my somewhat shame-faced team, I told them I'd kept my eyes peeled at the hospital, but hadn't seen any witches. I said they must be still buggered from last night.

I went directly to Venice to recuperate and prepare for my departure for London. By the time I got back to Casale to pick up my gear a couple of days later, I found I was a bit of a hero and had been reinstated as coach. After the débâcle at Catania, London was looking pretty good to me and I wasn't sure I wanted to resume the burden, but I liked the boys and felt I'd be letting down some of the young guys who'd done their best for me, so I stayed. I'm glad I did.

First game of the new year, we got a draw against the Lions

of Brescia and, having broken the losing mentality, we lost only one more game that season – to Rovigo, the eventual champions. We beat Milan in Milan, Rome in Rome, Torino at Turin. It was a glorious finishing run, of Kiwi's Melbourne Cup proportions, but we'd been so far behind that we still only barely made the promotion/relegation series at the end of the season.

When we won that and Casale was secure in Serie A for another year, the town was closed for three days for a celebratory festa. I was feted and it was assumed that I'd stay on for another season. I was tempted. I'd formed strong bonds with Piero and many of the players and felt that a lot of the basic work I'd done that season would bear fruit in the next. I could have stopped playing and stayed on as coach, kept the burgeoning Broochay and bought, say, a kicking fly-half from Wales. But . . .

Despite my success in the latter half of the season, I doubted that I was cut out to be a coach. My face was too pointy. It was too easy to read, like wind on water. If I was anxious or lacked confidence, I couldn't hide it. I was of the opinion – still am – that the best coaches, like politicians, should have faces like cliffs, inscrutable and immoveable, even in storms, subject only to the forces of gravity. If you have to be all things to all men, or at least to the 15 to 30 diverse individuals who make up your team squad, you're best served by a face like a blank screen, so that those individuals can project whatever message they need onto it. Graham Henry has an ideal face for his vocation. Duncan Laing had a great coach's face. Jim Bolger would have been a good coach, and Helen Clark and Jenny Shipley. I was more the Jim McLay of coaches. And there was something else, nagging away like an unconsummated love affair: the writing.

Being in Casale and coaching rugby was supposed to have been a means to that larger end, but I'd written next to nothing. Worse than that, when I was sitting at the Olivetti, I found some Italian words came more easily than English. A word like 'magari' would come to me, and I'd then have to think long and hard about what the English equivalent was. Sometimes I couldn't think of one with precisely that meaning or vitality.

The endless political dimension was wearing too, and never diminished even after we started winning. I'd ended up having to drop one of the extremists, Dal Cin, and not because of the dirigenti's intervention.

The huge bearded lock had come to me before the home game against Calabria and said he wanted to jump at seven in the lineout. I told him that's where I jumped, because I was mobile and could change position – and I could jump. He jumped at two because he was so huge he could hardly get off the ground but he could get by at the front of the lineout with sheer power and timing.

'No, no, Gregorio,' said Dal Cin, 'you don't understand. It is a necessity that I jump at seven because that is where that bastard of a Calabrian captain will jump and I must mark him.'

'Why must you mark him?' I asked.

'Perche voglio ucciderlo,' he said with calm earnestness. 'I want to kill him. He's a fascist.'

I dropped him from the team, and this time the dirigenti were only too willing to agree. But during the match that Sunday, Dal Cin and his mates barracked the Calabrians mercilessly from behind the wire perimeter with taunts of 'Terroni!' and 'Fascisti!', which didn't help the atmosphere on the field.

We were winning the game narrowly, with five minutes still to play, when isolated fights broke out across the pitch. The referee despaired of bringing any order back to proceedings and blew the whistle to end the game. I was happy enough to have the points for the win and picked my way carefully back to the dressing room, between groups of players belting each other with fists or trying to strangle each other on the ground. The crowd was in an uproar and Dal Cin and his communist mates were climbing up over the barricade. My immediate thought was that once the final whistle blew, my contractual obligations ended: this was a very Italian affair and I shouldn't presume to intervene. I put on my best shit-eating smile, held out my hand and yelled 'Grazie!' in as broad a Kiwi accent as I could muster at every Calabrian who showed the slightest interest in me. The Calabrians' bus had to be escorted out of town to the airport, after Dal Cin and his mates were apprehended closing on the Calabrian dressing room with hunks of wood.

I felt I was well out of this sort of stuff and I was right. That game had an unfortunate sequel the following year when Casale had to play the Calabrians away, at Reggio Calabria. Ness Toki, an Auckland loose forward playing where I would have been playing, got seriously injured by a Calabrian, who booted him in the head while he was lying defenceless on the ground well out of play. That kick finished Toki's Italian sojourn and his rugby career – he suffered long-term impairment and never played again.

So at the end of the three-day festa, I said goodbye to Casale, stuffed my stack of Swiss francs and German marks down my undies (it was illegal to take that much cash out of Italy), loaded the Olivetti into my pack and took off to meet my girlfriend in Greece, where I had to be very careful where I dropped my trou.

four

Howl

In Greece, my girlfriend and I continued our on-again off-again pas de deux. I wanted her to come with me, but she wanted to go home. She returned to Auckland while I continued on to London where, over the next year, I wrote 70,000 words of a novel that went nowhere, other than to an Irish woman in Shepherd's Market who was going to type it up properly if I could find the wherewithal to supply her with gin.

London was expensive. I'd been living off the proceeds from Casale, mixed with occasional work as a mini-cab driver, as teacher of English to visiting Italians and as Honeywell's credit controller for Scotland and the Northern Regions, where I would ring British Steel and ask them when last month's million quid was coming in. Like British Steel, I was rapidly going down the gurgler financially, had run out of gin and thought it might be time to abandon the novel and London and move on to pastures new. I had a mate in Washington DC who said the George Washington University rugby team needed a coach. So I put aside my reservations about my pointy face and said I'd be there for the autumn season in a couple of months' time.

I'd promised Casale that I'd come and say goodbye before I left Europe for good, so in the northern spring of '78 I travelled back down to Italy, partied for several days and took my leave properly, singing songs and drinking copious quantities of Riffi's merlot and grappa. After that, I decided to go back to London via Sardinia, partly to dry out.

I ended up on the west coast of Sardinia at a little fishing village called Fertilia, just north of the old Moorish town of Alghero. There I sunned myself on the rocks, dived into the Mediterranean and ended up eating in a bar down by the wharf. One evening, the local fishermen were having some sort of celebration in another part of the bar. Later, they began singing songs which I found myself singing along to: Venetian songs with dialect inflections, like 'O che beya Venessia, non posso andar' via, m'hai fatto 'namorare!' – O beautiful Venice, I can never leave you, you've made me love you. I joined in and when we finished singing they told me they were originally Venetian families who had been relocated there by Mussolini because of overcrowding. That further night of wine and grappa meant I had to stay another few days to get over it, which was fortunate, because several things began to gel, there in the aptly named Fertilia.

My year in London had been spent flatting with Kiwi mates, particularly Murray McIlwraith, Mac, who'd grown up a couple of blocks away from me in North Oamaru, and was in the process of abandoning his MA in anthropology and his job with the Archeological and Aboriginal Relics Office in Melbourne to master jazz piano and vocals. It had been comforting, during a long London winter, to have him banging away at the ivories at one end of the flat in Brondesbury Park, while I bashed the keys of the Olivetti at the other. The others in our flat and adjoining flats were mates from Otago University, and I was delighted to be immersed again in Kiwi vernacular. I valued it so much more after missing it in Casale, but also because my acquaintance with the colour and vitality and humour of Venetian dialect had shown me how precious our own version of English was.

That winter in London, as I gradually added to a novel that still showed no prospect of reaching an end, something else did come to a resounding conclusion – my rugby career.

One Saturday I was asked to turn out for a social rugby team called London French. I must have been caught at a weak moment because after my experiences in Dunedin with a social team called Fallopian Tube & Steel, I believed strongly that social rugby was an oxymoron. I had played a couple of games for the notorious Fats when I was recovering from injury, and I'd found the experience quite confusing. When I went soft and 'social' and got knocked over, people laughed and I felt like a fool. When I went in hard and other players fell over, I got booed. I resolved at that point that social rugby was a complete contradiction in terms and I'd never play it again. But, when in London . . .

There wasn't a Frenchman to be seen in London French, just Kiwis, Aussies and Poms. They were all fairly overweight and cuddly, as were the opposition, apart from one lean, hard bastard, a Scot, who thought he was playing at Murrayfield, or possibly Culloden, and started biffing and banging our guys around. I waited until they were awarded a penalty. They took the tap and

I knew that whatever the dummy moves were, this jock would end up with the ball, so I lined him up and hit him with everything I had as he received the ball. Predictably, he objected to being tackled and we ended up swinging at each other.

The ref stopped play and got out his notebook. Pen poised, he asked for our names. I thought 'Bob Dylan' was a bit of a risk, even back then, and the best I could come up with at short notice was 'Gene McDaniels', who at least had the right initials. The ref clearly wasn't up on his black balladeers, 'Tower of Strength' or 'Chip Chip', and carefully wrote the name down and the jock's, then sent us both off. When we got to the sideline I asked the jock if he wanted to finish it and he declined, so I wandered over to the next field where the London French B team was playing and finished the game with them.

I told Paddy Finnigan, my mate the barrister from Auckland, who was staying with us at the time and who I thought needed a bit more excitement in his life, that I'd given the ref his name instead of mine, because he was about to head back to New Zealand. Paddy was worried he might be arrested at Heathrow and is probably still waiting for a letter from the English Rugby Union.

That was it, my last game of rugby, completed under a cloud and a pseudonym. A fitting end for a niggly old (I was 27) crock whose best days were well behind him.

All these elements seemed to coalesce in Fertilia. By the time I got there, I'd been away from New Zealand for a couple of years and the time and distance seemed to give me some perspective on what had been an intense, almost lifelong sporting aspiration. I also needed some sort of anodyne for the novel I'd been struggling with: something colloquial and something that presented me with fewer choices than a novel. In London I'd been going to theatre for the first time in my life, and I wondered if I limited myself to dialogue and the three dimensions of a stage I just might get something finished.

In Fertilia, on the terrace of an old stone building that served as a backpackers' hostel, I pulled out some computer printout paper I'd nicked from Honeywell and brought with me – why? – and started writing in longhand. The paper, which had lateral stripes in white and brown and holes for the printer wheel on either side, was meant for spreadsheets and was twice the width of ordinary paper. I began writing what was happening on stage between a player, Seymour, nicknamed Foreskin, and a masseur, Larry, using the left margins, and off-stage voice-overs from the coach, called Tupper, using the right margin.

Their voices just seemed to be there, writhing to get out. I got through about a third of Act One before I took the ferry to Genoa and returned to London. It was the beginning of what became *Foreskin's Lament*, though at that stage it didn't have a title or an ending. I had no real idea where the rest of it was going, but I did know that what I was grappling with had to do with the end of innocence, and with disenchantment and anguish. I worked on the play over the summer in London, before I left for the States in the autumn.

En route to Washington DC, I had a brush with greatness. I was standing in front of the Van Gogh self-portrait at the Museum of Modern Art in New York, the one where he's got a bandage over his partially severed ear, when a middle-aged American woman came and stood beside me. I had a close-cropped beard and I was wearing my old black pea jacket, which had served as a sleeping blanket and life support in various trains, stations and boats around Europe. She gazed long and hard at the Van Gogh, then at me, then at the Van Gogh, then at me, then earnestly congratulated me on the likeness I'd managed to achieve in my self-portrait. I thought she had to be taking the piss, so I turned towards her, held out both ears like flaps and said, 'Look, both ears!' She fled in mortification, leaving me feeling like a smart prick.

I stayed with my cousin Sue Markham, who by night took me clubbing and pubbing with her friends to the likes of Studio 54 and Costello's. Sue worked for the United Nations, and during the day I was left to my own devices. One day, at a loose end, I thought I'd go and have a gander at Harlem. Just like that. I took the subway up to 125th Street, then started walking. Harlem wasn't the gentrified place it is today, full of condos and middle class whites buying up cheap brownstones to renovate. It was like a war zone, with gushing fire hydrants and buildings that looked as though they'd been hit by fire bombs.

After half an hour of walking, I realised that I hadn't seen a white face since way before I got off the subway. By then I was trapped by my own arrogant naivety – there was no way out but to keep walking. I was being trailed down the street by black guys who were asking what I was doing there, where I thought I was going and did I want to buy their dog, the mongrel snarling at my calves. I might have been saved by the fact that I looked scruffier than most of them. Also, I found it helped to tell them from time to time that I was from New Zealand. None of them had any idea where that was but clearly it was another planet, because why else would this crazy honky be walking among them? It took all my self-control to keep walking, not to break into a panicked sprint.

Eventually I saw the tops of the trees of Central Park, turned down Lenox towards them and finally made it to the reservoir end, only to be completely freaked by the sight of a group of black guys wandering down the path towards me. I cracked then, and took off into the bushes and ran for all I was worth towards Fifth Avenue. I emerged from the bushes, crossed to the canopied entrances and liveried footmen and looked back disbelievingly to where I'd come from. Did these Richie Riches have any idea what sort of world existed on the other side of those trees? I found it almost incredible that two such diverse worlds could co-exist so closely yet so discretely.

In Washington DC, my friend had arranged for me to coach the George Washington University's men's and women's teams. In the States only a small percentage of the top athletes get to play gridiron so there are a hell of a lot of fine athletes left over who are looking for a contact sport. Rugby fits the bill, because you don't need a lot of gear or time.

Rugby's also got a rep in the US as a big party sport and it certainly delivered on that. With men's and women's teams on tap, every practice night kicked on into a pub or club. American women seemed very direct about what they wanted. What passed for moderately risky behaviour in the 1970s looks like lunacy now. On one occasion in the wee small hours I ended up in a yellow Mustang with two whisky-swigging women who ran most of the red lights between DC and Baltimore.

I also had a day job as a janitor at the Australian Embassy, where I could disappear and get a couple of necessary hours' kip in a broom closet. Despite this, the extra-curricular demands of the coaching job were a bit disruptive to the young family of the friend with whom I was staying. I often didn't get home from practice before dawn, and tended to fall asleep during conversations, so I moved out to Silver Spring and stayed in the airy attic of one of the players, Jimmy McPherson and his wife, Pat. There, with Willie Nelson ululating downstairs, and with pleasant autumnal American suburbia right out the window, I pushed on with the play, which still didn't have a name. The US rugby season is divided in two, autumn and spring, because winter's too severe, so by November the first part of the job was at an end and I decided to head home.

I had a lot of fears about coming home. While you're planning and executing your OE, there's an appealing freedom and you can put aside many of those things that otherwise press hard on you – the pressure to conform, to be building a career, to be in a relationship, to be thinking about starting a family, to be fulfilling the expectations of family and peers, who might now be in partnerships and driving flash cars. I was returning with no money, did not want to go back to law, and although my girlfriend seemed to want me to come home, we were close enough to have known better, to realise that getting back together was probably just the product of a temporary lack of a better option.

But two factors drew me back. I knew that there was a place, a haven, Ponsonby, where being different wouldn't matter, and I must also have had a lot of bedrock confidence in the play, which by that time had a first act, and the beginning of a second – and which I knew could only be staged in New Zealand.

I arrived back on a stunning early summer day and my girlfriend took me up to the Waitakeres, where her sister was married on a viewing platform, with Auckland laid out like a beautiful blue-green platter in the distance.

My younger brother Peter rang and told me I had to come home to Oamaru for Christmas. I told him I couldn't: I had no money to get down there. There was a stunned silence for just a moment – 'He's been away for almost three years all round the bloody world and he can't get from Auckland to Oamaru?' – before he kicked in with a loan for the airfare.

When I got back to Auckland from Oamaru in the new year, the beginning of '79, my relationship imploded, finally and completely. It really hurt, despite all the practice we'd had at breaking up during the seven years we'd been together and not together. It had been my first really significant relationship and she'd been unfailingly supportive of my ambition to write.

One of the dangers of this sort of memoir is that you can retrospectively impose a narrative on what were random events, and seem much wiser and more single-minded than you were at the time. Yes, I did have a Five-Year Plan to become a writer, but I also loved this woman and I know that I'm not particularly strong or brave: if she'd wanted to settle down and have babies, I might still have been a solicitor in Dunedin. At critical points in my career as a writer, I've been very fortunate to have people close to me who supported me in that aspiration, or at least didn't gainsay it. In keeping with that support, even in the death throes of the relationship, my girlfriend did me a huge final favour in finding an ideal place for me to finish my play.

No. 6 Bayfield Road was a great home for someone who had few friends in Auckland: people came and went at all hours, under the benign administration of Sue, a solo mum. It was a kind of backpackers' refuge, before 'backpacker' became a tourist category. There were always visitors, dropping in for a cup of tea, a drink, a roll-your-own, a toke, a bed. Parties just seemed to self-generate, almost by osmosis, with no notice given or even real intention expressed. We were all at the fag end of our 20s or the beginning of our 30s; we were worldly, well travelled, well read, mostly partnerless and disillusioned with relationships. Some had children. We were happy enough to take a bit of comfort where we could find it.

As well as Sue, there were Janine and Flynn and James, a charismatic Englishman who was de facto social director, and bubbly Doctor Di, also from England. One of the denizens, Mike, a model train nut, ran the scow *No Big Deal* out to Great Barrier, servicing the communes out there. When the scow was fully loaded with building materials and sacks of muesli and lentils, Mike had to stand on top of the wheelhouse to see, and steer with his bare foot poking down through the hatch, toes working the helm. Navigation was pretty basic. Coming back from the Barrier one night, Mike was surprised at the lack of light coming from Auckland. When dawn broke he found the scow motoring down the Firth towards the lights of Thames. *No Big Deal* sometimes brought passengers back from the Barrier, so No. 6 Bayfield also seemed to be the Auckland base for any communers who needed a bed for the night.

During '79, I had a room in the basement at the back, facing out to the garden, where in summer Janine would dig her vege patch in just a pair of boots, sun glistening off her broad shoulders and muscular legs. If I wanted to be part of what was going on upstairs in the main body of the house, it was easy enough. But the room downstairs, bare kauri sarking and a double-hung window, gave me the separation I needed to forge on with the play I'd brought home.

The Ponsonby of that time – and I mean greater Ponsonby, including the wilds of Grey Lynn through Freeman's Bay, St Mary's Bay and Herne Bay, which were all pretty seamless back then and hadn't yet become enclaves for the rich and trendy – was a great place to abandon a conventional career and try to write. If I'd lived in a suburb where the men drove off to their offices at 8.30, I would have felt like a freak. But in Bayfield Road, there was always a door or window to knock on any time day or night, and someone sympathetic and interesting available for a cup of tea or a toke or a bit of social and, quite often, sexual intercourse. The only freak in the street was the guy with the long red hair who three mornings a week trimmed his beard and crept out of No. 6 in a pin-striped suit (made by Mr Bhana, who had a shop beside the funeral parlour towards the K Road end of Ponsonby Road – both now gone) and headed up to the bus-stop on Jervois Road at the top of Clifton Road to catch the 005 into town.

I'd wait in dread at that bus-stop three mornings a week to be transported to a windowless office in a law firm on Customs Street. I was grateful that All Black great Bryan Williams and his partner Kevin McDonald had given me the job, but I'd lost any desire to do law: I was a backroom boy earning peanuts, using the job to fund four days a week of writing. Before I got that job, I was working part time, courtesy of a friend of my ex-girlfriend, for an engineering firm, Beca Carter, poring through car magazines at the public library, transcribing statistics about the number of cylinders and cubic capacity for some survey about God knows what.

By then, my writing sometimes seemed an excuse for failure,

rather than a rationale for the way I was living my life. Back in the law, even on the periphery, I felt more adrift than I ever had while I was overseas. The few people I knew in Auckland outside Bayfield Road were mostly professionals who were doing well by all the conventional measures. They were kind and generous, inviting me to the pub and to parties, games of tennis and barbecues, but I felt like I'd switched at some junction down the track, and couldn't get back on line with them.

I recall having a beer in the back bar of The Gables tavern with the guy I'd stayed with in Washington DC, who was about to join a lucrative medical practice in Sydney. He told me, with a deadpan certainty, that he would shortly become a multi-millionaire. Maybe he was keeping his emotions in check out of deference to my continuing impecuniousness, but there seemed to be no joy or adventure in it for him, and he told me to stick to my guns, that he'd loved to have done what I was doing.

Nice of him, but at times I was so choked by my own frustrations that I couldn't talk to anyone, even at Bayfield Road. I'd get an attack of what I called 'the voids', empty out, lose my steer on my life, lose my nerve, lose my faith in what I was doing and become trapped in my own misery. I remember leaving a party in an old house at Symonds Street after becoming despondent at my inability to make small talk to anyone there and wandering back down across the Newton Gully flyover, feeling like a visitor from Mars. It had happened occasionally in London too: I remember one Sunday afternoon Mac pleading with me to say something, anything.

When the voids came, I would feel disconnected, then become unsure whether that feeling was precipitated by writing, or was one of the reasons for writing. Did the compulsion to write come from the same reptilian part of the brain that determined our sexual proclivities, deep, inchoate, atavistic, beyond intellect, beyond rationale, and sometimes beyond reason and caution? Whatever, I would regard the need to write as a curse – this compulsion to constantly scratch away at my own experience, trying to create another reality in words. At those times, because words as often failed as enlightened me, writing seemed like a process of reduction, something inevitably less than life itself. It depressed me then to think that this never-ending attempt to impose narrative on the random, significance on the meaningless, to fix and render a nebulous reality, make life itself the simulacrum, would condemn me to being forever once removed from my own life. Though writing often gave me insight, it seemed just as often to interpolate another consciousness between me and my immediate experience of the world.

There's a reference in the play to this kind of mood, where Foreskin says, 'Always the other, where the hell was I?' That line comes from the lament, in the midst of a host of literary and cultural references and is usually, I suspect, interpreted as a questioning of identity on a number of levels, but it's also a cri de coeur from a writer driven to despair by his own compulsion.

The frequency of the voids might have had something to do with the looming end of my Five-Year Plan: time was soon up, and I was about to turn 30. I would stand at that bus-stop in Mr Bhana's ill-fitting suit (not his fault, I have shoulders like misshapen bows), staring down Clifton Road towards the water of the inner harbour, dreading the arrival of the 005, wishing instead to be sitting on the steps of the grandly named Ponsonby Wharf, a little wooden jetty at the bottom of Wairangi Street – long before the Sultan of Brunei bought out the neighbourhood – where I used to look out across the water at the warm pink of the Chelsea Sugar factory, have a quiet toke, and try to divert myself from thoughts about what the fuck I was doing with my life. I tried not to think about what would become of me if the writing didn't work. I'm fortunate I didn't have to answer that question, because I still have no idea what the answer would be.

Whenever I feel unhappy with my lot, I drive past that bus-stop, which has become my personal plimsoll line. In '79, the corner shop behind it was a smelly dairy run by a fat woman who bickered constantly with her surly husband. Now, 25 years on, it's been painted a trendy green and offers holistic services, Aura-Soma, Orion technique, Jin Shin Jyustu, colour coding and organic teas. I'm sure that shop's in a happier place than it used to be, and so am I, albeit not quite so fragrant or enlightened.

During that year, while finishing the play, I also wrote a short story and sent it to Robin Dudding, the editor of the literary quarterly *Islands*. Six weeks passed and not a card or a letter. Desperate for some validation as a writer, I gave the story to Sue, the matriarch of the house, who was a real bookworm. Late the following night, when, admittedly, we were both pissed and/or stoned, she told me that not only could she not understand why anyone would want to write a story like that, but why on earth anyone would be bothered to read it. My first review. Instant sobriety.

After a sleepless night, once again castigating myself for being such a pretentious fool as to even think I could write, I rang *Islands* first thing and shamefacedly asked the secretary to please return my story. Instead, she put me through to Robin Dudding, who apologised for not getting back to me sooner, and told me he loved my short story, found it vivid and funny and beautifully written, and wanted to publish it in the next issue. 'Out in the Cold' was published in *Islands 27*, alongside an excerpt from Maurice Shadbolt's *The Lovelock Version* and a short story by Yvonne du Fresne. I wonder if Robin Dudding knew what a lifeline he'd thrown me. I wonder whether, if *Islands* had simply sent my story back, I'd have had the guts to finish the play and send it to Raymond Hawthorne, and then ring him up.

It wasn't Sue's fault that she didn't like my story – until then, in the abstract, she'd been very supportive of my writing – but since then I've tried not to show work in progress to friends and acquaintances. If you want to write professionally, show your work to professionals. That's probably an overreaction to what happened to me, but the danger is that friends and acquaintances will find it difficult to separate you from the writing, and may bring to it a whole heap of intimate knowledge and agendas that get in the way of objective appraisal.

The failure to finish the novel was fresh in me, and rugby and middle distance races had taught me that there is always a moment, a fulcrum upon which everything turns. You've got to recognise that moment for what it is and go for it, devour it, because if you miss it, you can't retrieve it: whatever you do after it passes is just damage control. Better to grab it and find out you fall short than miss it and live with another 'If only'. With *Foreskin's Lament*, that moment came somewhere in the autumn of 1979. I had to find a way to finish it, to capitalise on what I'd set up, to summarise and extend the significance of everything I'd written to that point. I had ignorance on my side and a bit of arrogance in believing I could do it. If I'd had an academic appreciation of what I was attempting to do, I'd probably have become paralysed and never embarked on it.

I can recall a mad moment where I embarked on Seymour's final monologue, the lament, in that garden bedroom. I'm not sure where the idea of using proper nouns as verbs came from – 'kerouracked into speed/keseyed into acid' – but at that stage most of my literary influences were American. I had deliberately stayed away from New Zealand authors because I didn't want to be constrained by what had been done here. I don't think this was so much a manifestation of cultural cringe as an indication that I didn't feel strong enough to wrench away from that material and plot my own course. Much of the New Zealand stuff I'd read didn't speak to me. I thought, for instance, that the little Sargeson I'd read was flat and constrained, and I much preferred Mulgan's *Report on Experience* to his dull, depressive *Man Alone*. I liked the Maurice Duggan of *Along Rideout Road That Summer* but I loved the verbal pyrotechnics of the Thomas Pynchon of *Gravity's Rainbow* and Allen Ginsberg's great poem, *Howl*, which more than anything else inspired the lament.

> I saw the best minds of my generation destroyed by
>   madness, starving hysterical naked,
> dragging themselves through the negro streets at dawn
>   looking for an angry fix;
> Angel-headed hipsters burning for the ancient heavenly
>   connection
> to the starry dynamo in the machinery of the night.

I loved the sheer ambition and scale of the thing, the attempt to sum up a generation, freeze a nation at a point in time, and the existence of that poem gave me the courage to attempt the lament, itself something of an anguished howl.

That monologue poured out of me over a feverish couple of days and nights. I can't recall for certain, but I suspect I wrote the lament before I wrote the means of getting there, the final conflagration between Tupper and Seymour and Clean and the smashing of the television set. But after eight minutes of monologue and six 'Whaddarya?'s, I knew I was there. I was done.

five

Pricks, Prepuces & Premieres

Five months after the workshop in Wellington, *Foreskin's Lament* debuted at Theatre Corporate in Auckland. A couple of weeks before, I'd met an old friend from Otago and moaned defensively that 'probably no one would come'. June rustled up 20 or so friends and acquaintances, got in early and block-booked for opening night. With a week to go, someone from Corporate rang her and tried to get some of the tickets back – there were only 120 seats in the main auditorium. The word was out in the small world of theatre aficionados, but I knew none of this and in the last few days before opening, if I'd had the money, I would have paid Corporate to cancel the season. I felt exposed, a sensation I later recognised as pretty common for playwrights just before opening. Even Maurice Shadbolt, an experienced author and no spring chicken at the time, tried to sabotage his Gallipoli play, *Chunuk Bair*, the week before it premiered.

How, in the penultimate moments before my triumph, having

worked towards this moment for the past five years, could I suddenly get cold feet? I desperately wanted to make a career out of writing but I didn't want my name out there? Get your hand off it. I didn't tell anyone of my doubts, because I would have got short shrift from those at Theatre Corporate who had put their hearts and souls into making it work.

Corporate's Artistic Director, Raymond Hawthorne, had been at the workshop reading in Wellington and, though impressed, he also saw problems in the practicalities of staging the play which the reading had disguised. If I'd thought my job with the play was finished, Raymond quickly dispelled that misapprehension.

In his shoebox office we spent, to my memory, about four hours a day for two weeks going through every word of the play. He didn't have too many problems with Act One, which is set in the team's dressing room, but told me there was a lot of work to make the second act stageable. When I looked doubtful, he told me he wanted this play to be performed everywhere, but if the second act stayed as it was, set in a number of different rooms in Larry's house, with a party going on in full view of the audience (imagine the props!), with too many characters and a child in the cast, it would present so many obstacles to the fledgling professional theatres around the country that they'd shy away from doing it.

With Raymond driving me, I made major changes to the second half of the play. I got rid of the child, Clean's son; I conflated a character called Prick, the manager, with Larry, the masseur; and the different settings were given the boot, to be replaced by one set, Larry's deck or verandah, where all the action took place, with the after-match party becoming carefully choreographed voices off. This was Raymond's idea. The change of setting made the second act much more of a series of duets, as various refugees from the party enter and exit the deck, but it was a wonderfully elegant solution to those other more pressing problems. Raymond was right and the changes he suggested and drove made the play doable.

I'd been wary of Raymond to begin with. I'd heard stories that painted him as a moody and dominating martinet. I'd heard he deliberately worked his actors mercilessly for such long hours that they had to abandon any other outside life, so that theatre became their whole world. I'd heard he liked to break people down with scathing criticism, then remake them in the image he wanted. I'd heard that one of his actors was so desperate to get out of his Theatre Corporate contract that he tried to seriously injure himself by jumping off a roof. With me, Raymond was relentlessly intense but charming and I grew to admire him for his breadth of knowledge and the generosity and fierce intelligence he brought to the editing process. As he drove the changes which made the play a practical piece of theatre, I began to wonder whether the stories about him were just bitchy luvvy stuff or whether I was a privileged outsider. I found out at the end of the first week of rehearsal.

Roger McGill, the nominal director, had blocked Act One right through and brought Raymond in to view the result. I'd heard a few bollockings in my time – Tupper was the evidence – but I'd never heard anything like the broadside Raymond gave Roger that afternoon, in front of me and the cast. He told Roger that virtually everything he'd done was uninspired shit, absolute total crap, that he was fucking useless. Roger was a big guy, and rumour had it he'd been a sergeant in the Australian army, but he took everything

Raymond gave him. He didn't once try to defend what he'd done, the decisions he'd made. When the tirade ended, late on a Friday afternoon, Raymond stormed unchallenged out of the rehearsal room.

I was utterly gobsmacked, but I was the only one there who was. Roger and the actors had clearly heard it all before. As we walked back up from the rehearsal room in Cross Street towards the theatre in Galatos Street, where the actors had to get ready for an evening performance, I got alongside Roger to offer my commiserations. I expected him to be suicidal: I would have been. But Roger was affable enough, saying that Raymond was right and we'd have to do better come Monday.

Come Monday, Raymond reblocked Act One and from then on kept a close watching brief on everything: so close, that to my mind he really directed the rest of the rehearsal, with Roger acting as his assistant. Roger deferred to him constantly, without, it seemed, any loss of self-esteem. I don't know how he did it. On further acquaintance I think Roger did suffer and was suppressing a hell of a lot of anger, which came out later, when he succeeded Raymond as Artistic Director of Corporate and became similarly domineering but without quite the same leavening of talent and charm.

I remember crossing Roger at a Playmarket Workshop in Auckland some years later, when he was leading Theatre Corporate and I was one of the prime movers of a revised production agreement giving playwrights more power. We argued, and it became quite heated. He raised his voice, then stood on a step to be at the same height, trying to physically intimidate me. He was wearing a leather jerkin and looked quite tough. The bullied become the bullies.

Years later, I saw Roger at Antonio's restaurant, Il Colosseo, on K Road. Theatre Corporate was gone and I asked Roger what he was up to these days. He said he was living off his wits. I told him there couldn't be a lot of money in that. He didn't see the joke, which was fair enough. And I was wrong: apparently he was doing very well as a motivational speaker. For all our later antagonism, Roger did the donkey work for Raymond on that first production and, as I subsequently learned, it's much easier to come in and change something that already exists than it is to bring it into existence. Nevertheless, whatever the official credits say, to my mind Raymond Hawthorne was the director of the premier production of *Foreskin's Lament*.

In the run-up to opening night, I wasn't the only one with misgivings about the play's public reception. I'd been told by various people at the workshop that I should change the title, that *Foreskin's Lament* would be a marketing disaster. Some people thought that it was the perfect title for those who'd seen the play, but for those who hadn't – the people to whom you're hoping to sell tickets – it came across as vulgar and smart-arsed. Elric Hooper of the Court Theatre said that his audience, his 'ladies' in Christchurch, wouldn't be able to bring themselves to actually ask for tickets if they had to say the word 'foreskin': that they might ring the theatre and ask for a ticket to 'that play', or they might end up booking for the studio production instead. At the Wellington workshop, David Carnegie and I had even made a list of alternative titles, mostly dreadful puns, like *Against the Head*.

Then Raymond or someone at Theatre Corporate told me they were having trouble getting the *New Zealand Herald* to accept the advertisements for the play. Someone at the paper felt that they couldn't or shouldn't be printing the word 'foreskin' in the entertainment section of a general circulation daily. It was a preview of the later clash with Patricia Bartlett and the Society for the Promotion of Community Standards – a similar exercise for verbal pedants. 'Foreskin' was certainly more vernacular than 'penis' but not as vernacular and rude as 'cock'. What were we going to do, rename it *Prepuce's Lament*? If we didn't change the name, what were they going to call it when they reviewed it? 'That play'? It seemed to be becoming 'that play' anyway and, in the end, someone senior at the *Herald* got a life and the advertisement was accepted.

By the dress rehearsal, which for *Foreskin's Lament* always meant undress, there was no way out. For me and the *Herald* and everyone else involved the truth was waiting on a small stage in a narrow brick building in Galatos Street, which was going to be packed to the gunwales.

On opening night, I crouched below the seating supports at the back of the theatre underneath the lighting box and watched my play unfold in front of its first paying audience. I couldn't see the stage very well from down there, but I had a great sense of audience response and when bums were moving on seats. Not very much, I thought, even during the lament. They seemed to have laughed at all the right places too. Roy Billing playing Tupper was the rock upon which that ensemble was built. He got the laughs right from the start and relaxed everyone in the cast and the audience, then built the pathos, anger and understanding of his character, playing, he told me later, his father. He was also totally at ease in his nakedness and created a reality around Tupper that anchored everything else.

When it finished and the 'Whaddaryas?' rang around the theatre, and the last spot faded on Chris White, playing Seymour, there was absolute silence for what seemed like some time. I was unsure what that meant. Did they like it? Did they hate it? Was everyone now going to get up and make for the exit in disgust without even applauding the cast?

After an agonising wait, which was probably only a matter of several seconds in sane time, the applause began. And as much as a group of 120 souls could create a cacophony of sound, they did – precipitated no doubt by June and her cheerleader mates. As the brave cast took their bows, I was so relieved . . . until the audience started calling 'Author! Author!' and the cast joined in, looking back to where they knew I was hiding. I'd never heard that call before and was unsure how to respond, when someone in the lighting box behind me told me to get my arse down there on stage and take a bow or we'll be here all night. So I stumbled down the wooden steps to the stage and did my awkward best to take a bow, then fled backstage behind the screen in a euphoric daze. There, as the audience continued applauding and cheering, Roy told me he'd never been part of anything like this before – 'Did you ever in your wildest dreams imagine . . .?'

'No,' I lied.

Of course I said no, then and subsequently. How immodest and vain would it have been to admit that I, 'a hairy playwright from the bush' as Elric Hooper had described me, neither unkindly nor inaccurately, could have dreamed of this sort of reception for my first, my only, play? But wild dreams are sometimes all we have to sustain us in passionate pursuits which are close to our hearts. One of my earliest and most persistent dreams had been to become an All Black. That one hadn't worked out, but had been gradually replaced by another, perhaps even wilder, dream which, in among all the anxiety nightmares and self-interrogations about my pretensions had played out *exactly* like this – an intense performance of my own play in that auditorium at Theatre Corporate to a rapturous reception.

It had happened. On the evening of 30 October 1980, eight days after my 30th birthday, I was given that moment – one of the greatest of privileges and clichés – of living my dream.

six

The Golden Pond

The reviews for *Foreskin's Lament* were almost universally fulsome and generous.

'First play a winner,' said the *Herald*. 'Enthralling, impassioned,' said the *Auckland Star*. 'Make no mistake about it, this play makes a quantum leap forward in New Zealand drama,' said the *Listener*.

On the back of the reviews and the full house signs at Corporate, not to mention the ker-ching! of the cash register, the other professional theatres around the country lined up for the rights. During the next few years, *Foreskin's Lament* was in production up and down the country, to similar acclaim. Even from Bruce Mason, who carried more weight than most and might have had more reason than most to resent this upstart's success, after so long carrying the banner himself for so little reward:

> I had heard so much of the play since its workshop here last
> year and the tumultuous premiere at Auckland's Theatre

Corporate . . . that . . . my expectations were somewhat
blunted by this chorus of praise. So let me now go right out
of my tree and declare that *Foreskin's Lament* is all that has
been said of it, and more.

Heady stuff, but the small taste of public affirmation I'd had ten
years earlier as a rugby player gave me some perspective, as did
my belief that the play's success was as much about timing as
talent.

When a cultural action of some kind – whether it's a play or
a song, a novel, a movie or a mountain being climbed – splashes
down in a society, the spread of ripples is as much about the pool
as the size and weight of the stone that lands in it.

The New Zealand that *Foreskin's Lament* landed in was an
extremely receptive little pond – apparently stolid and unmov-
ing, but full of red-hot magma underneath. Robert Muldoon, the
Great Interventionist, had managed to keep a thin film of calm in
place on the surface, almost as an act of will. Wage freezes belted
the workers and price freezes and import controls and tariffs
constrained business, as did a tightly controlled money supply
and foreign exchange. David Lange later famously described the
New Zealand of the Muldoon era as a Polish shipyard, a metaphor
with which Lech Walesa might have had a problem. Urban liberals
felt held to ransom by the rural marginal electorates which, under
the first past the post electoral system, had returned Muldoon to
government in 1978, despite National polling a minority of votes.

Under sufferance Muldoon had signed the Gleneagles Treaty
to commit New Zealand to a Commonwealth plan to isolate
apartheid South Africa, but the Great Interventionist in matters

economic became Monsieur Laissez-Faire on matters moral, and he had interpreted the terms of Gleneagles in his own idiosyncratic way to mean the New Zealand Rugby Football Union was free to do as it wanted. Thus the Springbok rugby team toured New Zealand in 1981, before a general election, and many of the disaffected decided to vote with their feet and take to the streets. The tour provided a focus for deep feelings of frustration and disenfranchisement, and to some extent my play became part of their public expression.

Many of the protesters – particularly the urban liberals and intelligentsia – also saw rugby as the enemy, as the embodiment of a value system they loathed: rural, misogynist, red-necked and National. It's easy to forget now, when corporates buy boxes and the game at the top end is part of the entertainment and celebrity matrix, how truly unfashionable rugby was back then. It was difficult to have aspirations in the arts or indeed to have any pretension to an intellect and also be a rugby player or fan.

For many people, *Foreskin's Lament* was a theatrical extension of what became known as the Days of Rage during the '81 tour. The play covered a lot of the bases. It could be seen as an impassioned plea for rugby to change, or as a rejection of everything rugby stood for. It could be seen as anti-apartheid, and was both colloquially earthy and artily literate. Even having a policeman as the villain – which sometimes caused a credibility problem for the middle class theatre audience in 1980 – suddenly seemed prescient once the urban liberals were out on the streets rubbing up against the long batons of the Red Squad.

'Whaddarya?' became a rallying cry for the protest movement, and was thrown at police and rugby spectators and even carried as a banner at the front of a huge march in Wellington, where a formidable Circa cast performed the play to full houses at the opera house. Ken Gray, the All Black icon of the great 1960s era, posed with the cast for publicity shots. That gave me particular pleasure because back in 1970 Gray had retired rather than tour South Africa. One of my best moments was watching from one of the unused private boxes at the Opera House as Grant Tilly's Tupper manoeuvred his way through a super-sized stacked plate of saveloys and pavlova. Hearing well over a thousand people roar with laughter was as fulfilling as the engaged, sometimes baffled, silence at the end.

I had huge respect for the actors from all the productions who had to drop their strides on stage and convince themselves that the 'fourth wall' was firmly in place, instead of an audience. Ironically, the full dress rehearsal was the point where the actors had to undress. I remember the courage of Roy Billing at Theatre Corporate, who led the cast out of their pants for the very first time, and did the same on stage, becoming so completely at ease in his nakedness that he seemed, utterly in character, to keep getting sidetracked from putting any clothes on. There were others who believed they had something to flaunt, and did so. One actor, notable for a splay-legged stropping act with the towel about a metre from the audience's noses, later blamed me for the break-up of his marriage. I told him he hadn't needed to write his phone number on his foreskin for the benefit of the women in the front row.

It wasn't that easy for everyone. Backstage, as the actors prepared to return to the stage from the off-stage showers, there was a lot of furtive manipulation so that everything could be seen at its best advantage. During the Circa season, one actor got a bit carried away at the Sunday matinée and the stage manager swore he saw, as the guy made a sudden turn, a droplet projected from the glans across the footlights into the audience, where it hit the powdered cheek of a Karori matron. Probably sweat.

There was priceless publicity for Circa and subsequent productions when Patricia Bartlett, the national secretary of the Society for the Promotion of Community Standards, described the play as a disgrace and laid a complaint with the police to try to get the play banned for 'its gratuitous male nudity, simulated sodomy, and non-stop verbal barrage of obscenities and profanities'. She reckoned that if the offending words were deleted the play would be all over in 30 minutes. She became more incensed after the Governor-General, Sir David Beattie, attended the Opera House and described the play as 'brilliantly produced'.

'After all,' said Patricia, 'the 1936 Olympic Games in Berlin were brilliantly produced. I shall write to Her Majesty the Queen and convey my amazement and deep concern that a play which required five male actors to say their lines with their pants off is considered "brilliant" by Her representative.' Her Majesty's response to the indignities of the pant-less actors is unknown, but Bruce Mason wrote an open letter to 'Miss Bartlett – Lamentable Archery, Madam'.

Meanwhile a vicar, the Reverend Rod Murphy, caused an upset at the Wellington Anglican Synod by rising to speak wearing a *Foreskin's Lament* T-shirt. The Reverend T. Chisholm of Eketahuna took umbrage, saying the garment insulted those who took the Gospel's call to holiness seriously. 'Foreskin's Lament Flaunted', said the headline. The T-shirt featured in photographs in the *Evening*

Post and precipitated an editorial, which in turn precipitated letters to the editor from 'Concerned of Karori' and 'Keep It Clean' of Kilbirnie and, probably, 'Whaddarya' of Wainui.

At Dunedin's Fortune Theatre it was reported that 'an irate and articulate citizen stopped the performance in its dressing room tracks with an outburst of his own, a diatribe on the slump of standards in that city . . .When the splenetic fury abated, the audience was asked if they wanted the play to continue. Applause rang out the answer.'

At the Court Theatre's production, Christchurch's Bible Lady, Renee Stanton, 'attended the opening night as she promised she would. From the front row of the stalls she quietly intoned biblical passages (from Ephesians?) to counteract the evil influence of the effervescence onstage.'

There were more human responses. My landlord's elderly widowed mother at Bayfield Road told her son she wanted to see what I'd been up to. He sat very tensely through the first act and when the interval lights came up, waited with some trepidation for the old lady's response to the display of penises. Was she traumatised, catatonic? Finally, she collected her thoughts. 'You know, son,' she said, in a tone of what might have been wonder or relief, 'I never thought I'd see any of those again . . .'

As the play swept around the country, riding its own wave of controversy and publicity, I felt much as I had at that first evaluation session at Victoria University, where I sat up front nodding as the pro and antis went at it hammer and tongs. I was gratified, but even more removed in a way, as many different people clasped the play to their hearts and took from it what they needed. As people told me about the many and various meanings they'd taken from the play, I never disagreed with them or told them I hadn't meant that. I took the view that they'd paid their money, it was their play and they could take what they liked from it. Even Patricia Bartlett. I did respond in print to her at one stage, but more as a protest against her attempts at censoring others and as an endorsement of theatre as social catalyst. However, as *Foreskin's Lament* became a central part of the social catalyst of '81, the anti-tour protests, its author was exhibiting far more ambivalence.

At Hamilton, as Mary and I marched with a long column of anti-apartheid protesters towards Rugby Park, one of the protest marshals came back and told us they were going to try to break into the ground, and if we wanted to be a part of it, to come closer to the front. I wanted no part of that: I believed in our right to protest, but equally in the spectators' right to watch the game.

This wasn't as principled a stance as it might have seemed. I knew my rugby lore. I knew that Waikato's defeat of the Springboks in 1956 had set the tone for the tour and made revenge for 1949 possible in the later test matches, which culminated in Peter Jones' great try at Eden Park. The protester in me didn't want the bastards here, but since they *were* here, the rugby player in me wanted the bastards beaten. I could see Waikato putting the first worms of doubt into those arrogant Springbok boneheads. Also, there was self-preservation: after my experiences in Italy, I couldn't believe that an occupation of the ground would be achieved without some split heads, at the very least.

But the protest leaders walked the column straight past a phalanx of police at the main entrance and, 100 metres or so later, veered left, ripped out a flimsy wire fence and climbed up a small rise which took them onto the embankment at the Tristram Street end of the ground. The thinnest of blue lines scarcely impeded their progress. When the ease of the breach was seen, excitement overtook my reservations and Mary and I sprinted with the rest for the hole in the fence.

About 300 people scrambled up that rise and charged down the embankment on the other side onto the playing field. The few policemen at the perimeter fence seemed to redirect their energies to developments on the playing field, leaving the hole in the fence pretty much unattended. There would have been at least another thousand protesters on the field, but for a couple of large rugby fans who took it upon themselves to stem the breach. They stood shoulder to shoulder at the street edge of the embankment, hurling protesters back. The charge lost momentum, the breach was sealed and those on the field were isolated from the rest of us and left to an uncertain fate. The two colossi at the top of the rise were Maori – one of many ironies and paradoxes that prevent easy analysis of the political dynamics of the time.

For all the talk of families divided, there was a kind of innocence along most of the protester/rugby fan divide, or perhaps it was just the two sides demonstrating a profound ignorance of each other. At Hamilton that day, while the few hundred protesters occupied the playing field, we several thousand diverted ourselves and the police by attempting to ram sheep and cattle trailers into the back of the main grandstand. When the game was finally called off, the cheer was huge. Tim Shadbolt led the triumphalism on a loud-hailer. I cheered with the rest, then had a very disturbing thought – that those 30,000 furious rugby fans would shortly be let out. This reality didn't seem to impinge on anyone else. The protesters seemed blissful in their ignorance of what might shortly be descending on us. I grabbed Tim and said something along the lines of 'For fuck's sake, get us out of here!'

We did, jog-trotting back to our assembly point at the city centre, men on the outside, women and children on the inner, escorted by a thin blue line of policemen who only just prevented the fans from getting among us. I remember thinking, as I looked at the hate in their eyes, what a desperately ugly bunch of people those angry bastards were. No doubt we looked the same to them, only wimpier.

I sometimes shared the rugby fans' contempt for the protesters. Before the Auckland–Springbok game at Eden Park on 5 September, we marched with the main group of protesters, but I became very pissed off with the earnest, fresh-faced marshals, who seemed never to have been in a fight and to have no idea of the dynamics of violence. These military geniuses would form us up in long columns of six abreast and put the guys with the helmets and protective padding at the front and rear of the column and all the defenceless non-padded men, women and children in the middle. The column would march forward to the police lines, and the helmeted ones would go 'Boo sucks!' or whatever. The police would take a step forward with their long batons and go 'Move! Move! Move!' The padded protesters up the front would step back, then shout 'Fascist pigs!', the police would take another step forward – 'Move! Move! Move!' – to more verbal insults from our brave troops up front. Once this little pas de deux had *really* stirred up the cops, the marshals would order the column to march away, doing a huge conga-line U-turn right in front of the cops, who would wait until the soft centre was nicely exposed and weigh in. Brilliant. It was like being ordered over the top by some pimply-faced lieutenant who'd just arrived at the front.

When the third and final test took place a week later, I'd decided we shouldn't put ourselves at risk with the main groups and Mary and I went with Artists Against Apartheid, a loose-knit group with no leaders which floated around the various protest venues outside Eden Park as the whim took us. We got a much better sense of the whole battlefield and almost walked into the cop lines as they were besieged in Marlborough Street.

I was carrying my Junior All Black jersey stuffed with straw on a wooden cross and at one intersection we set it on fire with diesel carried by Mary and matches courtesy of Roy Billing. I'd jammed it into the grass verge across from an intersection where a hard core of protesters was threatening to breach police lines. As the jersey went up in flames, one of the guys with a full-face helmet wrenched it from the ground, ran across to the confrontation and hurled it like a flaming brand at the police lines. I don't think it quite made it and landed on the heavily protected backs of the front row of protesters.

After I'd made my protest statement, I abandoned the AAA and raced back past the rocks and burnt-out car to Bayfield Road, where I pulled the curtains closed, hoping that the others wouldn't get home in time to catch me at it, just in time to see Alan Hewson kick the winning goal. I rejoiced in that kick, reasoning that the least the All Blacks could do for the trouble they'd caused was give the bastards a hiding.

We tend to regard '81 as such a cataclysmic political event in New Zealand's modern history, and I suppose it was. But it was still, in terms of body count at least, a peculiarly New Zealand phenomenon. I was sure someone would be killed in Hamilton that night. No one was. In this peculiarly New Zealand 'civil war', as some commentators have called it, no one died. I wonder if that is partly why '81 has not gestated any great literature or drama, to date; that two clowns in Auckland came closest to martyrdom. In Italy, there were students in my team from Bologna, where one of their fellows had been fired on and killed by police for attempting to occupy the university. The 1981 Long Baton Shimmy – two steps forward and one back – seemed gentle, even polite, compared with carabinieri holding Uzis.

We were also politically naïve. We thought after Hamilton that the tour was over, but the occupation of the Waikato Stadium guaranteed the Springbok tour would be completed, come hell or high water. It became, if it wasn't before, a law and order issue, a test of will that no government could afford to lose. It also guaranteed something else: Muldoon had his rural marginals in his back pocket once again and duly won the election a few months later, with another minority vote.

In retrospect, I'm struck by how perfectly the occupation at Hamilton suited Muldoon's purpose in an election year. I can't help recalling the relative absence of police at the point of breach of the perimeter fence, how the massed police at the entrance just watched us march past them, our intent surely patent. We had undercover policemen among us who seemed reasonably well informed about other protest targets, but apparently not this one. Maybe it's just another irony from '81, that the protest movement's most tangible success secured Muldoon's power for another term, and guaranteed another three years of frustration and anger for urban liberals.

Muldoon's re-election probably helped *Foreskin's Lament*, as the urban liberals who provided most of the patronage for live theatre had to wait another three years for deliverance and the play – the smashing TV set at the end etc. – went, in the course of 18 months, from being prescient to period piece. It was published in 1981 and shortly after that Auckland University included it in the syllabus for English I, where Sebastian Black's lectures on it became celebrated. One of my regrets is never seeing Sebastian in full flow – he would have beaten the hell out of some of the productions I saw.

Bruce Mason had taken me aside at one point and said that sooner or later I would see a production of my play which would reduce me to tears. He said it was inevitable as different theatres, some of them amateur, attempted to produce it. He told me when that happened, I had to dry my eyes at the end, suck in a deep breath and go down to the green room and thank the cast 'for a sincere performance'. At the time, every production I saw had elements I treasured, and I thought, Oh yeah.

Several years later I was sitting alongside John McDonald, a mate from Otago Law School, watching an amateur production in a provincial centre. He's now a respectable judge, but at uni Johnny Mac was a legendary point guard for the Tall Blacks. As we watched the actors race through Act One in a kind of terror, I cringed. Patricia Bartlett would have been delighted – it was over in about half an hour, whereas usually it took 45 to 50 minutes. The kindest thing you could say about the cast was that they remembered most of their lines. There were no pauses for laughs, or meaning or . . . The terror of being on stage and naked meant they just hurled the lines out there while they lunged out of and into their clothes. When the lights went up for interval, Johnny didn't say anything for a while, then turned to me and said, 'It was funnier when I read it.'

When the 'performance' mercifully ended, I remembered Bruce Mason's advice and it seemed like the right thing to do, because acting is like sport: no one goes out there to deliberately fuck it up. I thought the cast must be feeling dreadful, particularly since they knew I was there. So I steeled myself, took a deep breath, went down to the green room and thanked them for a sincere performance. I thought my words might act as some salve for their battered egos, but no. Within minutes, they were clustered around me urging me to tell them honestly if it wasn't the best performance of the play I'd seen thus far. When I went back up to Johnny, he asked me how it went. I told him I'd just learnt there was one huge difference between sport and the arts: in sport, everyone knows whether they've won or lost.

As the play rocketed around the country, creating headlines, I was trying to deal with the idea of being publicly *known*. Calling it fame might be at considerable risk of overstating the degree of public awareness I had, but it's useful shorthand.

I'd had a taste of that as a 19-year-old rugby player. It was reasonably localised and short-lived, but being *known* in that sense had been disquieting to someone so young. I'd go to student parties and get one of two reactions from those who knew my name but didn't know me – 'He's a famous rugby player, wow' or, more often, in the North Dunedin student ghetto, 'If he's serious about rugby he must be as thick as pig-shit.'

That reality slippage between the private you and what becomes the public persona seems to be an inevitable by-product of any degree of fame, and mine was pretty minor. Those who can reconcile that difference and live happily with it must be, I suspect, extremely well adjusted with unshakeable self-esteem. If you're somewhat less certain of yourself and your place in the scheme of things, you might be tempted to either shy away from the public persona, and therefore the public arena, or you might try to conflate the two personae by becoming the public you.

I suspect that sort of integration is very difficult, unless the public persona is extremely accurate and profound and/or eternally flattering. I doubt that anyone in history has had that kind of publicity over any length of time. Even John F. Kennedy, Mother Teresa and Jane Campion got bad raps sooner or later. It might even happen to Niki Caro one day. The problem is that if you give credence to what they're saying about you when it's good, presumably you have to believe them when it's bad.

Though fame as a rugby player was, and is more so now, a much 'bigger' fame than that of a playwright, it was also more superficial. The part of me that was in the public arena as a rugby player was little more than a body with a name attached. Television coverage of games was in its infancy and I was never interviewed for radio, television or indeed for the print media that I can recall. Being publicly known as a playwright was a lesser or smaller fame, but deeper, in the sense that the part of me that was exposed was much more fundamental. It's the deal with the devil that the writer's most complete expression of his or her private self, writing, becomes a public act, publication. If you decide to make a career as a writer, you have to have a public 'presence', even if it's a deliberately contrived reputation as a recluse, à la Pynchon. Even if you write under a pseudonym, your pseudonym will need a presence in what is a competitive market.

Yet, people who'd seen the play always assumed I was Foreskin, which was probably unavoidable, but in that sense if I was Foreskin, I was also Moira and Tupper and, particularly in the testosterone zone of my youth, Clean. So in that sense I could, and did, fall back on Shakespeare's defence – 'I speak for all my characters, but none of them speak for me'. But that's not the whole truth, because my discomfort was also about something else.

As I've explained, I wasn't quite the poster boy for the anti-tour protests which I might have seemed. More than most, I had a foot in both camps – rugby and the arts – but I'd had my foot planted in rugby for a hell of a lot longer than my more recent acquaintance with the arts.

Most of rugby accepted the play as being a bit of a piss-take and the sport was big enough to handle it. In fact, crouched in front of the lighting box at Corporate for some performances, it sometimes worried me how easily the rugby players took it – they roared as if the antics were just another laugh in the back seat of the bus.

In '81, when the play seemed almost part of the upheavals and protests, I was still working for Bryan Williams' law firm. BeeGee is the most courteous and measured of men, but the firm's main catchment area was the Ponsonby Rugby Club and BeeGee must have been getting a lot of stick from his diehard rugby clientele about this rugby Judas he was employing. To his credit, he never once told me to back off from my protests or said he was embarrassed by the play. He mentioned it only once, when he suggested to me that if I had come to Auckland and played for the Ponsonby club, under their enlightened player–coach systems, I would not have 'needed' to write the play. However, it wasn't club rugby that burned my dream and I'd also heard stories about the Auckland coach of the time, Bryan Craies, which indicated the Auckland provincial environment wasn't that different from anywhere else.

As I've mentioned, after 1970, Ken Gray had become an admirable man in my eyes. He had more to lose than most for taking a stand way back then, when there was no trendy protest movement and when others like Chris Laidlaw, who was a Rhodes Scholar and should have known better, and Earle Kirton, had both put their hands up to go to South Africa.

Laidlaw and Kirton had caused ructions at Otago University by coming back from overseas in 1970 and using the club to qualify for the All Blacks. Instead, Ken Gray had quietly but firmly made his stand and I saw the effect of that when the As came up to play Petone in the Champion of Champions club tournament. Before his stand, Ken stood next to God at the clubhouse. After his stand, he was a blot on the club's escutcheon; as the club captain said to me in an aside, 'Ken isn't the man we thought he was.'

In '81, Ken and his wife just happened to be sitting right in front of me at the Circa production and when the lights went up at the interval, after Act One in the dressing shed, they didn't move as the rest of the audience filed out, so neither did I. I was petrified that he had hated it and I didn't want to embarrass him by making myself known. After a long silence, I heard Ken's wife say, 'It wasn't really that bad, was it?' It would have been so much easier for Ken to say, as I'd heard many other rugby players do, when asked the same question by their wives and partners, 'No, no, darling, it's nothing like that – this is way over the top.' But Ken, bless him, simply said, 'It was worse.'

Others, however, felt the play was a betrayal of a sacred trust and that what I'd done was akin to breaking the old rule, the omerta rugbyista, that what happens on tour stays on tour.

Kit Fawcett had broken that rule in the '76 tour of South Africa, when he'd got off the plane and told a woman reporter that the All Blacks were going to score more off the field than on the field. That made predictable headlines back home and, just as predictably, many of the tourists started getting anxious calls from wives and sweethearts. Kit was off to a bad start and, after a number of other blunders, was eventually ostracised by the team. The last straw came towards the end of the tour in a game against Orange Free State. The All Blacks were losing narrowly when Kit got the ball deep in defence in the last minute and blasted into a wonderful weaving, stepping run which beat every defender but one. He had team-mates outside him. If he'd drawn that man and passed, the All Backs would have been unbeaten outside the tests. Kit, being Kit, had to try to beat the man. He was castled, ball and all, by the last defender; the try was eaten and the game was lost.

Towards the end of *Foreskin's Lament*, Tupper challenges Foreskin over a similar scenario, and I can understand why Kit once told me he thought he was my model for Foreskin. Models for characters can be combinations of people you have known – coaches Duncan Laing and Eric Watson and my father for Tupper, for instance – or you can spin a character off a snatch of dialogue you've heard, or the way someone speaks. Whatever the genesis, the writer has to make so many decisions about a major character that he will inevitably have to get to know that 'person' far better than he ever knew the model, unless of course the model is a close friend or family, which is dangerous. With Kit, any inspiration he provided came more from the situation he found himself in than from his personality or intellect.

I'd captained Kit at club level and knew how difficult he could be. I've described him elsewhere as an outrageous talent driven by a brain the size of a pea, but that's probably a bit harsh. He wasn't unintelligent so much as disinhibited – he seemed to have no sense of convention or of others' sensibilities. His mouth would start talking before his brain was engaged. At one practice for the As, I had finally had enough and was walking back to bop him one, when I was diverted by the coach. Something had to give. My solution was to make an effort to spend more time with Kit at the Captain Cook, try to get to know him. We drank a few beers and ended up talking about Kit's fantasies, pretty standard ones centring on pneumatic blondes, from what I remember. Even though I didn't have much to contribute to that discussion, I had no further problems with him. The All Blacks, by contrast, seemed to have an inclusive template for dealing with some kinds of outsiders, but no way of dealing with others.

In 1970, for instance, the All Blacks had been worried about how Keith Murdoch, who had a reputation as a bit of an animal, would fit in on that tour, and whether he would stay out of trouble. Their solution was to put Colin Meads on Keith as his shadow and mentor. There was no trouble – Murdoch's worst problem was a rumbling appendix. Kit was no Murdoch. The challenges he posed for the team were of a different order, yet Kit couldn't be successfully mentored or managed through the '76 tour. It intrigued me that the élite of the New Zealand rugby culture, even under one of the most enlightened coaches of the time, J. J. Stewart, had no way of accommodating a personality like Kit. When I heard in Italy about Fawcett's ostracism from the All Blacks over the last couple of weeks of that tour, it struck a chord in me.

As disappointed and frustrated as I was with rugby's social intransigence, and as angry as I was with the game for compromising the good name of this country in its blind dalliance with apartheid South Africa in '70 and '76, I was uncomfortable with the thought that in writing the play I had betrayed some sacred trust. I became quite sensitive about suggestions that in attacking rugby I'd somehow shat on my birthright and damaged it. I'd written the play believing that my birthright had betrayed me.

seven

Sapling

If writing had become one great 'escape' from the superficial world, an expression of my inner self, the other great escape had always been sport, or my relationship with the physical world, because sport was simply an extension of that.

> For nature then
> (The coarser pleasures of my boyish days,
> And their glad animal movements all gone by)
> To me was all in all. – I cannot paint
> What then I was. The sounding cataract
> Haunted me like a passion: the tall rock,
> The mountain, and the deep and gloomy wood,
> Their colours and their forms, were then to me
> An appetite; a feeling and a love,
> That had no need of a remoter charm,
> By thought supplied, nor any interest
> Unborrowed from the eye.

When Wordsworth wrote *Tintern Abbey*, kids had no television, no computers, no spacies. Neither did I, until I was 14, when black and white TV arrived, with one channel, only available in the evening. The contours of the natural world – the ditches, paddocks, swamps, parks, creeks, bush, cliffs and beaches in and around Oamaru – were both console and screen to us. Only we weren't looking *at* them, playing *on* them: as children we were animal elements *in* them: they haunted me like a passion.

To begin with, for me, the physical dynamics of 'sport' were unstructured solo pursuits in the company of others, rather than team games. We ran or biked everywhere. We played cowboys and Indians in the Hut Trees, an empty section at the back of our section, with a 'special' boy who was older than us and who got a real slug gun for Christmas to go with his cowboy hat and chaps. I became a very good Indian, creeping soundlessly through bush and grass, while Billy took pot-shots at whatever moved with his slug gun. Or we'd go 'exploring' – places like the breakwater down by the wharf, and the caves up on Cape Wanbrow and the underground watercourses of Devil's Bridge, and the 'Maori' drains in the pine forest on the hills behind the north end of town, which we'd been told were dangerous. We'd nick fruit from an orchard in a valley near the pines, owned by Old Man Russell, whose Gothic homestead sat on top of the hill, then run back into the pines and hide when he saw us. I recall a foggy morning when he came after us, how close he crept to us through the wet mist as we pressed our faces into the pine needles . . .

There was running to get places, running to get away from someone or something, and running to beat other people, which took the form of races, long and short, and a game called bullrush, where you had to use speed and body swerve and feint and fend to evade tacklers. Despite having long levers which I couldn't control as well as some of the more compact kids, I loved bullrush, and we played it at school and in the park next to our house on Thames Highway. That park now seems so small, so manicured. Then it seemed so vast and wild. Some of the trees have gone and the holly hedge has been replaced by iron railings, no doubt so that parents can keep tabs on their children playing there, and so that paedophiles can't use the vegetation as hides.

Bullrush was easy because there were no rules and you didn't need a ball. But one of the older kids in the neighbourhood got hold of a ball soon enough and it was ovoid, not round, and our every instinct was to pick it up and run with it, and play an extension of bullrush. We picked teams, so that instead of one against all we had team-mates, and we learned that if the pass was timed, you could beat players with the ball without having to run around them. We seldom played touch rugby, because it led to too many fights over whether someone had been touched. Full tackle gave greater certainty, but it did tend to punish the younger players. I can remember being dumped hard by a boy who was several years older, but as tears welled, one of the other older boys told the tackler to back off and order was restored.

We never kicked in our pick-up games. Instead, if we didn't have enough bodies for a pick-up game, we played kicking games, like 'Gainy' or force-back. In 'Gainy', we developed rules, so that you couldn't just use one foot, or just punt, you had to learn to use your weak foot and you had to learn to drop-kick.

As Foreskin said:

I was part of a whole generation that grew up on wintry mornings, running from between Mum's warm coat-ends on to dewy green fields that seemed as vast as the Russian steppes . . .

At school we had formalised rugby games: we wore striped jerseys and, those who could afford them, boots. The matches, held on a Wednesday afternoon at the A & P Showgrounds were, from the very start, the highlight of the school week. One of the teachers refereed, and there were notional concepts of forwards and backs at set-piece and there were goalposts. But, within minutes, the game became a no-position swarm of kids swirling around the ball, usually losing any concept of which way they were playing.

Despite my height and awkwardness, I must have had some talent because I remember being picked for the North Otago under six stone seven pound team. I remember that selection because I don't remember the game at all – I was concussed for the first time and lost a whole day.

Sometime after that, rugby became a huge frustration for me, because it was governed by weight, not age. I was heavier than most of my contemporaries, so I was always playing with older kids, sometimes quite a bit older. I ended up playing down the grades, with the worst players of older age groups. Until the fourth form, I generally played rugby with the overweight, the blind and the hopeless, while my older brother, Richard, who was small but very quick of foot and hand, played with his friends and my friends. It was the same with boxing. While I was getting knocked around by older kids at Ave Luxon's gym down by the shunting yards, Richard was becoming runner-up New Zealand champion in his weight, fighting kids his own age.

I wrote long letters to Kel Tremain and Colin Meads, asking for their autographs and explaining my predicament. They wrote kindly three-page hand-written letters back, encouraging me in my rugby but, no doubt worried about my prospects, urging me not to neglect my schoolwork.

In 1961, when I was 10, Dad took us to see my first really big game, France playing the combined North Otago, South Canterbury and Mid Canterbury side at Fraser Park in Timaru.

Our team was getting a battering and Michel Crauste, known as 'Attila the Hun' because he was huge and bald and had a Zapata moustache (quite unlike Attila, as it turned out), seemed to be at the centre of everything. During a break in play for another of our players down injured, Pie Madsen's mum walked out onto the middle of the field in her hat and coat and brogues, whacked Attila the Hun on his bald nut with her umbrella and told him to leave our boys alone.

Some spectators were afraid for Mrs Madsen, but I was surprised the French got off so lightly. On my first day at Waitaki's Junior High School that year, I'd had to walk past a classroom window from which her son Pie was hanging, telling me in detail what he was going to do to me come lunchtime. From inside, I heard a plummy voice which I later recognised as belonging to Mr Sandecock, the French teacher, calling, 'Madsen, please return your head to the classroom.' Pie didn't even pause for breath, just casually shouted back over his shoulder, 'Get fucked, Gravel-balls.' I knew then that whatever trouble I'd got up to at primary school was small beer. As far as I was concerned, any woman who'd given birth to Pie and his equally dangerous brother Joe was a fair match for 15 Frenchies.

In the midst of my frustration over not being able to play with my own age group, in about 1962 or 1963, I saw Peter Snell run at the Waimate Boxing Day Highland Games. I couldn't believe his power and speed, as he ran down the front markers in the Handicap Half-Mile, like a Sherman tank bowling rabbits. From that moment I wanted to win an Olympic gold medal for the 1500 metres more than I wanted to be an All Black.

Until I saw Snell, I'd regarded 'harriers' with a rugby player's contempt – runners were right down there with soccer players. After seeing Snell, I and a few mates, Bruce Hunter (Blondie), Trevor Sutherland (Suds) and John Laing (Hongi), committed ourselves to a Lydiard training regime and athletics became my principal passion from about 12 or 13 through to the age of 16.

Virtually every day after school, I'd put on the sandshoes – adidas trainers were too expensive – and Suds would come round from Clare Street, and we'd run up to collect Blondie from Raglan Street and Hongi from Fleet Street, run past St Kevin's College and up the fearsome Buckley's Hill. From there, we had two training circuits, a five-miler that went past the reservoir and down Derwent Street and back to the North End, or the eight-miler, which looped further out to the Ardgowan Hall, before coming back to town down Eden Street, past the house that Janet Frame grew up in. At the weekends we'd sometimes run a longer course, a 12-miler that looped even further out to Airedale and back in through Devil's Bridge, past the farm where my father had been brought up. All these roads were surfaced in white shingle, and from most of them you could look out west towards the snow-capped peaks of the Kakanuis and think you were part of a vast country.

We joined the North Otago Athletic Club and raced in Otago championship meets and for Waitaki in the inter-secondary school competitions. Blondie was a sprinter/quarter miler, I was an 880 yards/miler and Suds and Hongi ran mile/three miles, though we crossed over a bit too. When Blondie ran the odd half-mile, I found him difficult to beat because of his finishing sprint and similarly, when I moved up a distance, I could generally beat Suds and Hongi in the final sprint if I could hang onto them. None of us were mugs. Hongi was as talented as any of us but left school early and joined the navy. Blondie went on to become New Zealand champion over the half-mile, eventually getting the title taken off him by a certain John Walker. Suds who, when we started, had a godawful style and a breathing impediment – we could hear him coughing along behind us – became one of our top three-milers and cross country runners and came within a hundredth of a second of breaking the four-minute mile, which was a stunning feat, given his lack of basic speed. To do that time, Suds would have been running each quarter within three or four seconds of his best time. If the top middle distance runners of today could do that, the mile record would be 10 seconds lower than it is.

I got within a second or two of two minutes for the half-mile when I was 16 and was one of the top in my age group in Otago. I also broke the Otago Under 17 three-mile record, but it was disallowed because I was running against older athletes. At Waitaki, I won the Senior Championship half-mile, mile, two miles and set a school record in the high jump, only to be pipped for the Senior Athletics Prize by Blondie, who won the 100, 220,

440 yards and long jump and broke *two* records. That was my last real flourish as a middle distance runner. In the fourth form, weight classifications were dropped for rugby, and I was able to play again with my mates.

That year, 1965, Blondie and my brothers, Richard and Peter, and I biked 80 kilometres up State Highway 1 in the dead of winter to see the Springboks play at Timaru. Dad had told us that, in the desert during the war, they were advised not to drink water while exercising as it only made you thirstier. So, around St Andrews we all hit the wall, becoming light-headed and wobbling around on our bikes. The sensation was terrific and we fell about on the grass verge in fits of giggles. Early winter darkness overtook us just out of Timaru, so we made camp with our pup tent in a stand of pines among the low hills to the south of the town. I can't remember one detail about the game next day, but that second night in the pines remains etched in my memory.

We made it back to our pup tent and settled down for the night with several meat pies, a bottle of milk and a candle. We lit the candle, unwrapped the pies and opened the bottle of milk. We were just getting a bit of oral purchase on the pies when the candle ignited the waterproofing in the tent. We dropped the pies, grabbed the milk and tried unsuccessfully to douse the fire with it. Pete, who was a year younger than me, was trying to undo the ties at the other end of the tent to get out when we decided to abandon ship and charged like panicked water buffalo towards his end of the tent. The squashed pies made for slippery footing and by the time we reached Pete, we were travelling pretty much on the horizontal, hit him amidships and projected him out through the severed ties into the cold darkness beyond, where he landed head-first on a wet gooey mess, followed by the rest of us, forcing him deeper. There was just enough light from the blazing tent to identify the slimy substance that had cushioned Pete's landing and was now dripping ghoulishly from his head and running down his face and shoulders: a lamb's afterbirth. No shelter, food or drink made for a very long night as we waited until first light so we could hop on our bikes and generate some heat.

I'd begun to dream about the All Blacks again, and began to see a pathway I could follow: the Waitaki First XV, then the fabled As at the University of Otago, where heroes like Keith Nelson and Tony Davies and Laidlaw and Kirton played, then, maybe, Otago and . . .

In '67 and '68 I made the Waitaki First XV and played with my mates, some of whom turned out to be exceptional players. Blondie was the star at wing, and went on to have a chequered career as an All Black. Ian Hurst also became an All Black and many others became very good provincial or senior players. But the most talented of us was our first five-eighths and fellow ginge, Geoff McLeod. Geoff was big for his position, had startling acceleration over 15 metres, had a good step and fend, great hands and a huge boot – at punting practice, two of us would have to relay the ball back to him. Just out of school, Geoff was thrown into senior rugby in Dunedin, got a badly broken leg in his first game and never regained his confidence.

Despite the ever-present danger of injury, I always thought rugby less painful than running. You might or might not get hurt in a game of rugby, but in a half-mile race, you *knew* you were going to be in excruciating pain for the last 300 yards. I can remember spectators laughing at our rictus grins as Blondie and I battled each other up the final straight, in the advanced stages of oxygen debt and full of lactic poison.

By comparison, rugby with the First XV had been much easier. Malcolm Kissel, our coach and my English teacher, was definitely not a Tupper. He was a Presbyterian lay preacher, and had tall, square-jawed almost western movie star good looks, but he also had a gammy leg so, being teenagers with a cruel eye for any defect, we called him Plonk.

I'd had a dreadful start as a bullied first former at Waitaki Junior High, but was saved by doing my second form year at the newly opened Oamaru Intermediate, where I was taught by Glen Blackie, the first of a couple of influential teachers who expected excellence both in class and on the sports field. By the time I got back to Waitaki as a third former, I was bigger and better prepared, and Plonk was one of the teachers, like Derek Bolt and another English import called Barrington-Prowse, who made my subsequent years at Waitaki Boys fulfilling.

Plonk, like Glen Blackie before him, quite unselfconsciously modelled a perfectly seamless integration of sport and intellect. In a third form English class Plonk involved us in an exercise that has stayed with me ever since. He asked each pupil in the class to think of a subject, something of personal interest and intrigue. He didn't want to know what the subject was; it would remain entirely confidential. He then asked us to try to think about that one subject – and only that – for 10 minutes, during which there would be absolute silence. He made it clear that there would be no post-percolation tests, no questions, no discussion afterwards about what we had thought about or indeed whether we had thought about anything at all. He then looked at his watch and said, 'Go.'

I can't remember what I thought about, but I do remember staying on whatever subject it was for that 10 minutes, and by the time Plonk looked at his watch again and said, 'Stop', I was gobsmacked at how many highways and byways a mere 10 minutes' thought had taken me down, at how far I'd travelled and where I'd ended up.

Plonk was similarly laissez-faire at First XV practice. He would *ask* us if we felt like running down to the end of the park and back as a warm-up, he would *suggest* that we try such and such. When some of us would be late for the final team talk on a Tuesday night before important secondary school games because we'd rather watch the finish of *The Monkees* on TV, that would draw a frown from Plonk but that was about it. He was Christian in his attitude, thought the world of us and had no idea what his boys got up to – or so we thought at the time.

Six of us had bought a very old Mercury V8 – it still had running boards – and we would range as far and as wide as the pine cones we would sell for petrol would take us. There was a constant tinkle of beer bottles in the boot, and though quite a few people fell off the running boards of that car, Johnny McCombe went one better and managed to fall out the back door in the middle of town on a Friday night. We thought the Mercury looked like an Al Capone sort of car, so we plastered bullet-hole transfers across the back passenger windows. We also had a rifle stashed under the back seat for shooting seagulls. One day out at Bushy Beach, we got bored with the seagulls and decided to go for real bullet holes and turned the rifle on the car, sitting side on to us about 30 metres away. We'd just drilled a few through the back passenger windows when a white face suddenly appeared right in the firing line. We'd forgotten that Blondie was sleeping off a hangover in the back seat. Blondie agreed, though, that the effect of the bullets through the windows beat the hell out of transfers.

The coaching and management of our team was very loose, compared with other First XV regimes we heard about: we were woefully undertrained and had no real tactical plan or strategy. The upside was that our results came from the sheer enthusiasm and talent we brought to every game. By the end of a long and challenging season in '68, we were still having as much fun as when we started – and were unbeaten (the closest match was a draw with Christchurch Boys' High), even though in those days Waitaki played the top echelon schools. The other testimony to Plonk's methods was that so many of his players carried on playing, whereas many First XV players were burnt out by too much intensity too young.

After my final year at school, I tried to keep training for middle distance over the summer, but I'd decided by then I wanted to go to university, which meant getting a summer job.

I became an offsider at Waitaki Holdings. That summer there was a drought in North Otago and we had to bring hay over from Central. Sometimes that meant a 4 a.m. start, to get over the Lindis Pass to Tarras, then a long day in blazing hot paddocks picking up hay bales and loading an articulated tray and trailer, before making the return journey. Sometimes it was 9 or 10 p.m. before I got home. Other times I would be on the 'banana boat' through to Queenstown, dropping off vegetables on the way over the Pigroot, and through the Cromwell and Kawarau Gorges, and picking up stonefruit on the way back. On that one, at least we got to stay overnight in Queenstown, then a cute little country town.

I would do some training when I could, but training on top of that workload simply drove me further down, so I tended to give away the running and just do the high jump, where I got second on a countback in the Junior Nationals at Whangarei. Even better, the wonderfully notorious Auckland lawyer Brian 'BJ' Fox was our liaison officer, and fulfilled his duties by getting us to the right party afterwards, where I got drunkenly bold and seriously kissed by the wife of an Olympic athlete, which turned out to be the closest I ever got to my Olympic dream.

By the time I got down to Dunedin to begin university, I was jaded from the long summer and thought I'd have a year off all sport. I was the first of my family to go to university and knew I had to pass my exams that freshman year, if only to prove to my father that I hadn't enrolled there as another work avoidance strategy.

In Dunedin, I was contacted by a lecturer at the School of Physical Education – I can't remember his name – who was the coach of national high jump champion Bill Spiers. This guy said he'd seen me at Whangarei and he was sure that if I put in the time and effort under his coaching I could succeed Bill as national champion.

Initially, that seemed like an offer that I couldn't or shouldn't refuse. While I was waiting to start with him, a couple of mates at University College, or Unicol, persuaded me to come down to University Oval and play a trial game for the University Under 20 team. I was still feeling stuffed after the summer, but went down and played half a game. I was quite impressed with the standard – all the guys trying out were First XV players from the length and breadth of the country. Because there were so many aspirants for those Under 20 teams, the trials went on for several weeks as players were gradually winnowed down. Every week, the next trial team would be posted on the noticeboard and my name would still be there, even though I hadn't turned up for any of the subsequent matches. Someone – I've never discovered who – really believed in me. When I was named in the final trial, I decided I'd better turn up. By that time, Orientation Week had come and gone, along with a succession of parties, and I'd made a lot of friends in Unicol, some of whom were also still in the Under 20s frame. So I played in the final trial and made the Blues, the top of two teams.

I had a difficult conversation with Bill Spiers' coach, who was a really nice guy. I felt instinctively that it'd be better for me if I played rugby. Rugby players are generally gregarious types. By then I'd been around serious runners and jumpers and though there were always some successful crossovers, I could feel the difference in psychologies. Some years later, as part of my rehab after a serious leg injury, I joined some other rugby players in a novice eight rowing shell and had an enjoyable summer learning that difficult sport, catching crabs up and down Otago Harbour and the Taieri River. Rowers, it seemed to me, were more like runners, more introverted than your average rugby players. Even in an eight, they tended to be working away silently, taking their problems out on the end of their oars. Our coach, a true-blue rower, kept yelling at us through his megaphone to quieten down in the boat, to stop talking and yelling and laughing. It took him half the season to realise that's the way we worked, that it didn't necessarily mean we weren't concentrating.

The high jump was very much a solitary pursuit which always

ended in failure: if you won the competition, you tried for the record; if you got the record, you tried to set a higher record. When you finally failed, you stopped. The training too was solitary. I would have been training with Bill, doing weights and agility stuff, but that would be it. I'd had a taste of that with Warwick Nicol, the Oamaru cop and national hammer-throwing champion. In my last year at school, he had kindly let me use his weights room in the old jail behind the Oamaru cop-shop, and we had travelled to some meets together in Warwick's car, with his boxer dog. My main memory is that when the boxer farted, we had to do an emergency stop, open the doors and throw ourselves out. I'm always on for a fart joke, but that definitely wasn't as much fun as the First XV, and the Under 20s rugby option at Otago seemed to offer more fun.

We were students not schoolboys, and we didn't have to go home and answer to our parents after the parties. My year with the Blues was a blast, under coach Dave Leslie and manager Graham Gosney who, though not quite as laid-back as Plonk, still kept it fun. We ran, we passed, we scored, we partied. Prop Paul Sapsford and I did a revue together at the Unicol concert, a satirical number called 'Pooh & Piglet', where I played a vaguely homosexual Piglet to Paul's oblivious, eternally hungry Pooh. Paul was a devout Christian from Invercargill who loved Bob Dylan. He was the only one out of that Blues team to become an All Black, but by the time he finished with rugby, or rugby finished with him, he was a feared rugby animal called Sapper, and an alcoholic.

There were two other beanpole bloodnuts in the Blues, Peter Hazeldine and Paul Hewitson, both of whom also kicked for goal. I was considerably quicker than either of them, but if you'd

115

watched the team play that year, I doubt if you'd have picked me to go further in rugby than them. Something happened to me over that summer.

When I went home to Oamaru, I worked as a builder's labourer on the new fire station. My fellow labourer was George Frame, Janet's brother, the model for Toby from *Owls Do Cry*, on which I'd just finished sitting finals papers for English I. After so many years of making huge imaginative leaps into very specific English or American settings, it had been exciting to study something that conjured up not just a generalised New Zealand but, very specifically, my own home town. So many things from Frame's childhood also resonated for me, from the women biking to the woollen mills to the dreaded undertow eating away at the foreshore, and it was inspiring to read about something I knew so intimately, rendered so imaginatively yet so accurately.

When I first got to know George and saw how accurately Janet had depicted him as Toby in the book, it seemed cruel. George, like Toby, collected rubbish and once took me home to his place at Willow Glen for lunch, where he had stacks of what looked like useless junk. He bragged to me that he had enough railway lines to run a line right down Chelmer Street. I didn't ask why anyone would want to do that and, gradually, I came to realise that Janet hadn't been cruel, because George would never have got past the first page of *Owls Do Cry*. These days there's a Janet Frame Trail around Oamaru, but back then she was pretty much unacknowledged by the town, apart from belonging to the crazy Frame clan. Janet's uncle used to race us kids home from the matinée session at the Majestic on his bike and was rumoured to water his garden in the rain.

Leading up to Christmas, I couldn't settle at home. The work at the fire station was boring, apart from when George and I got to collapse the concrete shutters, where George proved he was almost as appalling as I was in the arts of manual labour.

At Unicol I was used to dining with 300 people, but at home I couldn't stand the noise that seven of us made around the table. My year-older brother Richard had left school and was working as an architectural draughtsman, my year-younger brother Peter had just left school and was due to start with NZI, while the youngest two, Derek and Judy, were still at school. They were all just carrying on as we always had, talking across one another, no standing on ceremony, five- or six-way conversations, admonitions, arguments, jokes.

Parents must look askance at their progeny sometimes, no matter how much they love them, and wonder how they got lumbered with that particular mix of genetic material. Dad, a strong man but not tall, one of 13 children from a very Irish family subsisting on a small farm at Devil's Bridge, watched with rising alarm as I grew and devoured and grew some more. He would shake his head in disbelief at the amounts of food I was shovelling into my gob and worry aloud to Mum that 'that little bugger'll eat us out of house and home'. My mother's saintly instinct was just to make sure I got what I needed – a huge cooked meal with pudding in the middle of the day (we'd ride home from school for lunch); a packet of Chocolate Wheaten and a bottle of milk after school; and she'd always sit beside me at the dinner table in the evening so that she could surreptitiously slip me some food off her plate to make sure I got through the night. Mum came from a quieter, English family in Dunedin and must have wondered sometimes how she'd ended up in the middle of such a rowdy bunch.

It wasn't really the noise of my boisterous family that upset me. I didn't tell anyone, but I was lovesick for a girl I'd met at university, who loved someone else. It was unrequited puppy love, the sort of thing that happens to most people at about 12, which says a lot about my emotional development at the time. Before Christmas, miserable and making everyone else miserable, I took myself off to a job at the Conical Hills sawmill, down in south-west Otago, near Tapanui. I'd never been south of Dunedin before, and the train out of Dunedin's grand station seemed to be heading towards the end of the earth.

I was a disaster in the sawmill, awkward and unhappy. Within the first couple of days I brought the mill to a stop by mismanaging the waste-wood belt and creating a blockage. But at the workers' camp – 50 or 60 huts nestled in against a forest about a mile away – I noticed there was a group of guys who didn't work at the sawmill. We played pick-up rugby in the evenings and they had some weights which we macho'd about with. These guys told me they worked in the forest and why didn't I come work with them? I thought that had to be more fun than being trapped inside a sawmill with screaming trees, so I finished up there. The sawmill bosses didn't seem too upset to see me go, and next morning I hopped into a four-wheel-drive forestry van with Carthy and Pita and Api and some others.

We were driven up into the Rankleburn Forest in the Blue Mountains, given our lunches and long-handled slashers and told to be back at the van at five. Our job was to release-cut young pines with the slashers – clear scrub and gorse from around the young saplings so they could get light and water. We were paid by how many chain we cut, and if we did over a certain number, we'd get a bonus. The guys, always after extra money, called themselves The Bonus Gang. I discovered they were mostly recent releases from the Invercargill Prison Farm, Maori from up north, trying to get money together to get home. They were great. We'd go like cut cats up steep hills and down ravines, ploughing through bracken and gorse, swinging those slashers. We'd have lunch in some clearing out in the middle of nowhere, in boots and shorts and sweat bandanas. They all looked like Mexican bandits, and I must have looked like Worzel Gummidge, but they didn't seem to mind my lowering the tone.

To begin with, I found it difficult to stay with them, and my hands blistered – we rubbed meths on them – but they always slowed to accommodate me, even though it cost them money. It might not have been all altruism on their part: the country was rough and we covered many miles each day and maybe they feared they'd lose me. Soon enough, my blisters callused over and my fitness improved and I could go as hard as any of them. At night, back at the camp, we'd eat dinner and play pick-up rugby, always tackle. It was a tough game. The Tongans and Samoans at the sawmill versus the Maori from the forestry, both teams sprinkled with the odd whitey who didn't know better. I didn't know better and loved it.

When I got back to university for my second year, I was still only 19 and was eligible for another year with the Under 20s, but I thought I'd give the senior trials a go, for experience as much as anything. I'd had a taste of senior rugby the year before when I played one game for the Bs and felt like a boy among men. I was playing number eight and when the scrum packed down I found myself confronted by two huge arses, belonging to future eminent surgeon Jock Carnachan and Mark Oram, Jacob the cricketer's father. I stuck my head between the two of them and tried to push, but as soon as the weight went on the scrum, these two massive arses would heave and billow and pitch, and I found it took all my strength to cling on, thrown about like an empty dinghy on stormy seas.

When I got back from summer in the forest, the first senior trial game was against Maheno, a club from Oamaru, and that worried me. At school, the First XV had played in the Senior Reserve competition and the tough country boys, and men, had taken a lot of pleasure in roughing up the schoolboys. In some ways, the inter-secondary school games were easier because we were playing kids our own age. Maheno had a number of grizzled farmers, like Doug Grant who had propped for North Otago for years and was legendarily tough. Worse than that, they knew I was an Oamaru boy and would doubtless take a proprietorial interest in my 'education'.

We kicked off and I charged up on the receiver and forced him to spill the ball. I grabbed it and ran through, round or over a number of players and scored under the posts. Just like that. I walked back to halfway as stunned as everybody else. I had no idea I could do that. The rest of the game went a lot like that, though not quite as spectacularly. Suddenly, I felt like a man among boys: I was bigger and stronger than any of them, Doug Grant included. I wrestled with some of the Maheno farmers and threw them around like bags of chaff and almost felt sorry for the old men. The long levers I'd always had a bit of trouble controlling were now at my command. Over that summer the Rankleburn Forest, the Bonus Gang and a bit of age had grown the muscle to match my bones and I knew I was ready for something more than another year in the Under 20s. How much more, I could never have guessed.

eight

The Doodle & the Bugle

Playing for the celebrated Otago University As was exactly as I'd imagined it. My first game of senior rugby was alongside Chris Laidlaw and Earle – Ernie – Kirton, who'd both returned to play a bit of club rugby so they could qualify for the All Black tour of South Africa later that year. My first lineout take, I palmed the ball down to Laidlaw and was very proud of myself until, as I went past him to the next ruck, he said gruffly, 'Get two hands to it next time.' I decided to hold my tongue and that paid off. He broke round the side of a ruck shortly after, did all the donkey work, then flipped the ball into my hands so that all I had to do was fall over the line to score my first try in senior rugby.

Laidlaw seemed aloof most of the time. I thought it was just me, but BeeGee told me years later that on that tour in 1970, before the first test, management decided that the new caps should room with old hands, to help settle the pre-match nerves. Bryan was paired with Laidlaw and over the course of three days and nights rooming together, Laidlaw hardly said a word to the nervous young 19-year-old. Perhaps Laidlaw was shy and lacked the common touch. Certainly, when I met him later, he was friendly enough and his Sunday morning radio programme shows how intelligent and erudite he can be.

Kirton was an entirely different proposition. After the game, he loved having a beer in the Provincial Hotel, owned by our manager, Bill Mercer. With a glass of beer in one hand and a cigar in the other, Ernie would wax lyrical about the pleasures of the game he loved, and give us the benefit of his many and varied insights. Sometimes I almost felt I was sitting at the knee of a favourite uncle when Ernie was in liquid voice. I'd stagger home through the centre of town, loading up at the pie cart at the top of Dowling Street with fish, chips, dim sims and Scotch eggs, enough to last me all the way down Princes Street to the flat, using the takeaways as body heaters in various pockets until I was ready to devour them.

I had another, strange encounter with Ernie in London years later, when he had a dental practice at Windsor. Mac, the jazz pianist and singer from Pembroke Street, and I were wandering the streets at about three in the morning after some do or other and were keen to keep partying, when we spotted one of those basement marquees signalling the existence of a club. We got in there just as they closed the bar and turned the lights off. Absolutely blind, I was blundering down a carpeted hallway when I tripped over a small round immoveable object smoking a cigar. The lights came on just as I picked myself up to confront the person I'd fallen over – Ernie, cigar and glass intact. What were the chances?

Our coach that first year in the As, and the year after, was Duncan Laing. He was the perfect coach, bluff, hearty, full of Taranaki lore. Nothing happened in the years of rugby I spent with

Duncan that hadn't already happened back in Taranaki. We called him Doodle, because he was fond of telling us, whatever we were doing, that he could do better with his doodle. Ernie had the odd difficulty with the Doodle's straightforward approach. We were doing ruck and runs, and Ernie was supposed to go one way but went the other, because, explained Ernie to Doodle, 'the numbers told me to go that way'.

'Bugger the numbers, son,' said Duncan, 'you go the way *I* tell you, or the only numbers you'll be seeing are the ones on the end of my doodle!'

Training with Duncan was fun. He seemed to realise he was coaching a team with a tradition of free spirits and he backed off his Taranaki instincts just enough to let us do our thing, but still put together a pack that outplayed everyone that year – some achievement, given that almost everyone in our pack wanted to be a loose forward, including our loosehead prop, Bede Bloodnut McElwee, and our hooker, Doug Lingard, when he played. Even our tight-head prop, Pete Smith, was very atypical – he was a showboat, who'd been a champion swimmer and he liked to remove his shirt and show off his superb pecs at every opportunity.

Marty Ewen and I drew the short straws and ended up as locks. Marty was not happy and that had consequences: he was the Pavarotti of flatulence and could break up scrum practice at will. During matches, he took his frustrations out on my shorts, which he'd try to rip every game, so that I had to change my shorts in front of the grandstand. When he was sick of that he'd rip Pete's jersey so that Pete could show his pecs and scare the opposition.

Duncan was endearingly forgetful. When he became Olympic swimming coach, it was no surprise to any of us who knew him that he was refused entry to one of the venues because he'd forgotten his ID. He forgot times, appointments, air tickets, names – nothing, it seemed, was immune to the huge holes in the Doodle's memory bank.

Once, I bet the squad that if I disappeared from practice, Duncan would forget I'd ever been there. I was equally certain that if I reappeared after the showers, Duncan would have forgotten I *hadn't* been there. So when the ruck 'n' runs went way over into the shadows of the poplars down at University Oval one night, I slipped into the gloom, made my way back around to the old grandstand, had a shower and went back to the flat for a beer. An hour or so later, I reappeared in the dressing room, tied a shoe as Duncan came out of the shower, drew attention to myself by telling him he'd forgotten his doodle in the shower and collected my winnings.

Duncan's biggest difficulty was remembering our names. The last practice of the week, when he named the team for Saturday's game, was a painful exercise. Duncan would say, 'Hooker . . .' then search the faces in front of him for Paddy Finnigan or Doug Lingard, whichever he'd chosen for that week, then increasingly desperately ransack his brain for either of their names. Paddy and Doug did have a passing similarity to one another in the shade, which is probably why the girl they were keen on turned them both down. Most of the time Duncan would settle on 'You, son, you're on'. I was more straightforward, because he'd known a Jock McGee back in Taranaki, so I was always Jock. On one occasion before the naming of the team, Duncan took me aside and asked me for the hookers' names again, so that he didn't embarrass himself this time. I told him they were Daggy Linnegan and Pug Finnegard. Duncan looked at me like thunder for several seconds, then said, 'Thanks for your help, Jock. I'll remember that.' He didn't, thankfully.

Duncan's day job was, of course, national swimming coach. Given his approach to rugby, it was difficult to see how he could be so successful at swimming, a highly technical sport which would, on the face of it, seem to require a very different approach from that of the blood and guts rugby coach. Once I went up to Moana Pool to see him about something and he was coaching some tiny tots, who were swimming two widths of the pool. Duncan was standing at the side of the pool as the little ones flailed up, touched and set off again. One wee guy was way behind the others and when he finally touched, he gasped to Duncan that he didn't think he could make it back across. 'Son,' boomed Duncan in his best foghorn voice, 'you'd better get going back across, otherwise I'll go downstairs, pull the plug, and you'll be washed out to sea!' I left none the wiser.

For all his bluster, Duncan was a benevolent presence, someone you could joke with, and he had a wonderfully colourful turn of phrase. It was Duncan's line to Marty that I pinched for Tupper in *Foreskin's Lament*. Marty was constantly moaning about having to play lock when he was, in his own mind, a 'blindingly fast' loose forward. Duncan finally had enough and told Marty he was so slow he couldn't pull a sailor off his sister. Marty's mouth was quicker than his legs: he replied that if he ever saw a sailor with Duncan's sister, and she looked anything like him, she'd have to be grateful. Duncan challenged Marty to a race, over 15 yards. It was a big occasion and the team lined up to barrack. When the flag went up, Duncan made a bee-line for Marty and the 15 yards turned into a sumo stagger. By the time they fell over the line, everyone, including Marty and Duncan, had completely cracked up and Duncan had us in the palm of his hand.

Duncan was one of the models for Tupper – obviously so to those who knew him – but when he saw the play at the Fortune Theatre in Dunedin, someone asked him afterwards quite pointedly if he'd seen anyone in the play he recognised, and he said yes, that 'bloody smart-arse, Jock'.

We won the senior championship that year, and I was happy to have come through my first season of senior rugby relatively unscathed, missing only one game through injury. 'You'll win so much lineout ball they'll carry you off, son!' boomed Duncan at training before that game. I was never quite sure what the causal connection was, but, sure enough, we won and the zambuks carried me off.

Even so, I was surprised when I was picked for a trial match at Balclutha for the Otago team, because I'd been warned that I'd have to get my hair cut before I was selected for Otago.

I had auburn locks curling down to my shoulders and this seemed to upset some people. Duncan had taken me aside after one practice and said he'd been told that if I got my hair cut, I'd be a good chance for Otago. I told Duncan to tell whoever it was who'd passed on the information to get fucked.

I'm sure Duncan didn't pass on my message, but the hair thing was a constant refrain over the next few years. After the Otago vs Lions game in '71, I happened to end up in the urinal beside Charlie Saxton, who at that time was a powerful councillor on the NZRFU. It was late at night and I was a bit pissed and so was Charlie, so when he told me I should get my hair cut if I wanted to be an All Black, I patted him on his completely bald dome with my free hand and told him he was just jealous. I doubt if it helped my cause.

This de facto 'bad hair rule' seems ridiculous in retrospect. The Swinging Sixties didn't make it to middle New Zealand until about '68, so it's probably not surprising that they were at least a full decade late in penetrating New Zealand rugby. In 1970, I was still one of very few rugby players at senior level with long hair – the others I can think of were Bob Burgess and Grant Batty, when he still had some.

Even at the As, it was mostly short back and sides and blazers to the team talk and game on Saturday. I remember being asked pointedly by management, after wearing a denim jacket and then a ski jacket to games and after-match functions, whether I had anything else in the wardrobe. I did – Mum and Dad had bought me an expensive three-quarter length coat and Mum had carefully sown my name-tag onto it (and every other item of clothing I possessed, including my undies, so that 'nothing would get lost in the wash'). That coat was the most beautiful thing I'd ever owned and there was no way I was going to wear it to the rugby, leave it hanging in the heady dressing room sweat and liniment aromatic, cure it in cigarette smoke at The Provincial house bar, then stuff it full of pie cart takeaways for the early-morning trek back to North Dunedin.

Within two years, everything had changed, at least in the As. I was captain while Bugs Taylor was injured for much of that season and I suddenly looked reasonably conservative among the shaggy locks, beards and beads sported by the likes of Kit Fawcett, Ross Gard and Willy Isaacs, quite apart from Johnny Matenga's incomparable afro.

When I was picked for the first Otago trial match, hair and all, I was in two minds as to whether to play, because it was another big step up and I felt it might be too early for me. Before I could pull out, someone at the *Otago Daily Times* wrote that, despite my promise, I'd not really earnt a trial and wasn't up to rep rugby. That was a red rag to a bull so I went and played that trial, then another one at Alexandra. I should have known I was going to be picked when Eric Watson, the Otago coach, came and sat beside me on the bus on the way back to Dunedin. Eric told me every dirty, foul story he could think of about the goings-on in provincial rugby, to see if I flinched. I must have passed the test, but only because I was acting; I was actually scared shitless by some of the stuff he told me.

In my first few games for Otago, against the likes of North Otago and South Canterbury, I did quite well. Against South Canterbury I'd scored the first try and kicked a penalty from halfway, but I was still the new-boy hippy and most of the team didn't know quite what to make of me. There were a few fellow students in the team, but none as young as me. I was still 19 and most of the forwards, particularly, were tough old buggers from the hinterland, the likes of Tony Kreft and Warren Townsend.

My father was very proud – he'd been waiting for 19 years for some sign of normal New Zealand manhood from me. He had built his painting business on a relentless work ethic. I'd lie in bed on winter mornings listening to his footsteps on the concrete floor of the garage, *running* as he loaded the van and trailer with tins of paint, bottles of turps, sandpaper rolls and ladders and brushes in the pre-dawn darkness. He was mostly bewildered to have bred a son who seemed to have such an aversion to manual labour of any kind, so when I made the Otago rugby team, it was a rare sign of normality which needed to be savoured, and he came down from Oamaru to stand on the terrace at Carisbrook to watch me in my second or third game.

He was about to tell all and sundry on the terrace that he was my father – he didn't like saying anything too approving to our faces, but would skite about us behind our backs – when Otago were awarded a long-range penalty. It was outside Laurie Mains' range, and because I'd fluked that long-range penalty against South Canterbury, some elements in the Carisbrook terraces started chanting, 'Give it to the girl! Give the girl a go!' Meaning the one with the long hair and ringlets. Once Dad realised it was his son they were referring to, he never said another word for the rest of the game.

The next game was the annual derby against Southland, where I'd be marking the fearsome Bob Barber. Some of the tough old buggers in the team must have shared the concerns of the Carisbrook terraces, because on the bus trip down to Invercargill, one of the props, Lindsay 'Wank' Clark, decided to run an uglies contest, with the assistance of his hooker, Dave 'Brick' Pescini. Wank had a wide smile and engaging personality, but two uglier bastards you wouldn't want to meet – both had scar tissue instead of eyebrows, flattened noses and ears like Brussels sprouts. The rest of the team was hardly a picture of pulchritude either, but when Wank and Brick handed out the prizes – just the honour of the title really – I didn't just win the award for being the ugliest bastard on that bus of extremely ugly bastards, but according to Wank and Brick I was also the second ugliest bastard. I was only 19 and none too secure about the way I looked, but I tried to take it as a compliment and wondered whether it was sign of acceptance in the Otago team 'culture', though in those days that word best described the contents of the oven and fridge in the average student flat.

It was during the Southland game that I came of age in rep rugby by proving I wasn't only ugly but also pretty stupid. Bob Barber was at that stage a Maori All Black and later an All Black, and was the Sione Lauaki figure of the time. He was originally an Oamaru boy and I knew his mother, and when I saw him warming up, his size and power, I was tempted to go over and introduce myself and threaten to tell his mother on him if he was mean to me.

At the first lineout, I rose high above Barber, stretched to the max and palmed the ball down to the half-back. A split second after that, Barber's elbow rammed into my exposed solar plexus and I collapsed to the ground like a burst balloon. Play went on through the backline, someone dropped the ball and the ref whistled for a scrum.

When they set the scrum, they realised I was missing and expectant faces turned back towards me on the other side of the field. I couldn't get my crushed diaphragm to expand so that I could catch a breath and felt like I was suffocating. I pushed away the zambuk, struggled to my feet and did a kind of a run-crouch across the field, rasping for breath and turning puce. As I approached the waiting scrum I saw Barber standing there with a shit-eating grin on his face, and the red mist descended. I took a huge swing at Barber right in front of the ref. I missed him by plenty, and the force of the unconsummated punch swung me round in a pirouette and I fell backwards into the arms of our big prop and skipper, Tony Kreft, who caught me.

132

'It's all right, ref,' said Kreft, setting me upright with a big wink at the referee who had the whistle in his mouth, about to blow and maybe send me off. 'He's a student.'

Everyone except me seemed to understand that code, which seemed explanation enough for what had happened. The ref ignored my transgression, the scrum was set, I took my place and off we went. I had no further trouble with Barber and as far as the team was concerned, anyone stupid enough to take a swing at Bob Barber couldn't be all bad and I was accepted into the fold as slightly eccentric but potentially useful.

The rest of that season was a blur of rugby. Each step up in class was a worry, initially, but after a couple of minutes, the strength and stamina from the Rankleburn Forest would kick in and I'd start to feel bulletproof. Quite a few of the players I opposed were stronger than me when the game started, but I was so fit that the longer the game went on, the stronger I became. I've never seen those guys from the Bonus Gang again, never had an opportunity to thank them for making my rugby career.

I began reading about myself in the newspaper, described as 'pure gold' and 'All Black material' and even 'Earmarked for Greatness'. I was even being compared with my boyhood idol, Kel Tremain, whom I marked in an early season charity game the following year, by which time I was even stronger, after a summer in the freezing chambers stacking frozen carcasses. In a tussle for the ball at the end of the lineout, I accidentally caught him with an elbow and he turned on me, rubbing his head and calling me a big clumsy bastard. Mortified, I said, 'I'm terribly sorry, Mr Tremain.' He ran on, thank God, otherwise I would have got down on my knees and begged forgiveness and told him what a great man he was for having hand-written a three-page letter to a 10-year-old. In retrospect, that may not have made him feel any better.

Even the girl I'd been smitten by over the previous summer, whose attitude to rugby was studied indifference, was moved to irony by the publicity I was getting and told me it was good to see I'd become such an important 'commodity' of the rugby union. Commodity? Not only were we not paid, we had to pay a sub to the club to be allowed to play, then on top of that buy our own jerseys, shorts, socks and boots. If we ever did get given anything, we had to give it back. In fact I may have compromised my chances of becoming an All Black by trying to keep my South Island jersey after an inter-island game at Trafalgar Park in 1970.

The inter-island match was one of the showpieces of the year back then and though I only made it because the top 30 players were in South Africa with the All Blacks, I was one of the youngest forwards ever selected for that team, and regarded it as a huge honour. I thought if I kept the jersey, I'd have both a keepsake and a practice jersey, but Bob Duff, who coached that team and was an All Black selector, went back to the laundry bag, counted the numbers on the dirty jerseys, tracked me down and made me give it back.

My elevation as a rugby player happened very quickly, and I was struggling to keep up with the sudden acceleration of my prospects of realising my All Black dream – and the personal cost of doing that. Though senior rugby for the University As was like an extension and development of First XV and University Blues rugby, similar in spirit and kind, playing for Otago was not.

Eric Watson, known as Bugle owing to a nose that was even more spectacular in size and hue than mine, was a decent man, a signwriter who smelt comfortingly of paint, like my father. Off the field, Eric cared about his players and had a good sense of humour, as well as Duncan's endearing habit of being a terrible traveller who could arrive at an international airport with no tickets or passport. On the training pitch, however, he was a martinet who would quite often make the training harder than the matches. Jung's collective unconscious had an entirely different meaning under Eric.

Eric's training seemed designed to reduce the forwards, at least, to mindless automatons. He'd tell me over and over again not to think, that he didn't want anything clever. There was fuck all chance of that, after Eric had driven us into severe oxygen debt with a brand of repetitious semi-opposed ruck 'n' runs which someone told me dated back to the legendary Otago coach, Vic Cavanagh. He would drive us to the point where we lost all sense of self-preservation, where we'd run, bind and hit, run, bind and hit, over and over again, until we lost all sense of individuality and became a mindless eight-bodied rucking machine. As the oxygen debt deepened and we became individually almost unconscious, the pack as a whole acquired a kind of collective consciousness, where nothing mattered but hitting that next ruck and shifting the bodies obstructing you.

I'd have to concede that it worked, up to a point. Against the '71 Lions, the Otago pack drove collectively and won a ton of ball. However, there was little effort or imagination applied to what happened *after* we won the ball, and we booted the hard-won possession to J. P. R. Williams, who said thanks very much and ran it back at us. We lost by a substantial margin.

It was anti-personality rugby: the thought that any of us played the game to express ourselves would have been greeted not with laughter but fear. I was percolating away on this stuff, but I was very young in an environment where virtually everyone was a lot older and more experienced than me – the difference in psychological maturity between 19 and 26 or 27 is vast – and I was aware that it would be precipitate of me to offer too many opinions or complaints. Petulance on top of golden ringlets wouldn't be a good look. I was also the archetypal student, the subject of a lot of mostly good-natured banter by Eric and the players from the local clubs and the farming hinterland.

I tried to keep my head down, but in the back of my mind, as much as I had thought about it, I'd always seen sport as an expression of character, sometimes even a determinant of character. I didn't admire the Muhammad Alis, Peter Snells and Ken Grays of this world simply because they were athletically gifted, but for the character, courage and content they displayed, both in the heat of battle and in their lives. I always wanted to see, in their performance, what they were, see inside their hearts and minds. Then I wanted to know more about what they were outside the sports arena. I suppose you could see sport as the ultimate escape from self, but I never did; I always saw it as the expression of a deeper self, the sporting equivalent of the dramatic *sine qua non* – to show, not tell. What a privilege to see that kind of truth of character revealed, whether in sport or drama, rather than having to make do with the level of self revealed by small talk when, say, acquaintances meet at the supermarket. A necessary social skill, sure, but if that's all there is . . .

While my mind pondered on matters such as these, Bugle was trying to deprive it of oxygen, both for the Otago teams of '70 and

'71 and the Junior All Blacks in '72. Iain Gallaway described Eric in his autobiography, *Not a Cloud in the Sky*:

> His particular sense of humour and his simple directness did not always endear him to those who had not been brought up in his ways to know and understand him, and he sometimes found difficulty in communicating with the student community. His continuing contests of one-upmanship with the academic quartet of Davies, Laidlaw, Kirton and McGee are now part of Otago rugby folklore.

Fair enough, and most of it was good-natured, but matters came to a head in the tropical heat of northern Queensland. In Rockhampton, at the fag end of a tough tour where the Juniors had played and beaten New South Wales and Queensland, Eric gave us a session of his special ruck 'n' runs on the morning of a night match. I knew a little about physiology and recovery from my years in middle distance training and at some point I asked Eric, 'What about the pH factor?' I was referring to our bodies' chances of recovering if we were worked too hard too close to the game. Eric thought I was being a disloyal smart-arse, making an in-joke about some science fiction movie or book, and told me to shut up or I'd be sent home on the next plane. His patience might have been stretched by the likes of Grant Batty, Joe Karam and Andy Haden, who gave the Juniors a higher smart-arse quotient than any Otago team I'd been part of. We only had a couple of games left, so I made it onto the plane with the rest of them, after a very successful tour.

Eric wasn't stupid; he was simply a man of his time and place. The episode in Queensland did highlight the lack of any scientific basis for the training we did, but in other areas Eric was psychologically quite astute and had a gift for bringing a collection of bods together and making them feel like a team. He had generally been very supportive after selecting me so young, but by the end of that first season, it was clear that I also exasperated him. In retrospect, I'd have to concede that Eric made quite a few allowances, in attempting to accommodate me within the team culture.

In his team talks before the game, he would go round the players, discussing their role, what he expected, geeing them up, asking each about his opponent that day, 'Is he better than you? Is he?' In many cases, given an Otago team that was not overly blessed with individual talent, particularly in the backs, the honest answer would have been a resounding, 'Yes, Eric, he's much better than me!' I remember a winger from Taieri, Sid Brown, who got a three-man overlap and a 15-yard start and was still chased down from behind by a 17-stone Fijian lock with a bristling moustache. There was more fast-twitch fibre in that Fijian's moustache than in Sid's entire body. But everyone understood that Eric meant his question to be rhetorical so no one spoke. I noticed, as that first season went on, Eric was leaving me to the end of his team talks, then obviously struggling to find something to say to me about my role and about his expectations. By the end of the season, he had washed his hands of me in front of the team. He told me I might as well just go out there and do whatever I bloody well liked, because I would anyway, no matter what he told me.

Some of the other players were concerned for me, but I thought that was an extremely enlightened attitude and admired Eric for it. I also earned his ire for jumping in the air after I scored the winning try against Waikato. I think he was more pissed off about the try than the celebratory jump, because it meant he couldn't drop me for another week, even though for most of the game I'd gone walkabout and been outplayed by Paul Anderson who, like me, was chosen by the *Rugby Almanac* as one of the five most promising players of 1970, but who, unlike me, really ought to have been an All Black.

Certainly, Eric's successor at Otago, a character called Sammy Simpson, was worse. Sam had all of Eric's 'philosophies' but none of his warmth and humour – or if he did, I never got the benefit of any of it. I remember once asking him if he wanted me, as number eight, to practise any moves off the back of the scrum, which Brian Lochore had shown 10 years earlier could be very effective. 'One half-back is enough, McGee,' said Sammy. 'You just stick your head in there where it's dark and keep it there.' The trouble was, by then, after two or three seasons with Otago, my head was already in a dark place trying to figure out why I was playing a game in which there was no expression of individuality, and, for me anyway, no joy.

Then, as now, I found it was important sometimes to stop and try to remember why I started doing something, why it seemed important, and test that against the present reality. Memories of bullrush and pick-up games in the park, the spontaneity and sheer physical exultation of sport, seemed long gone. That feeling was exacerbated by the Canterbury factor.

nine

Canterbury Tales

The Bob Barber foul play incident, and my response, was part and parcel of provincial rugby back then. I felt able to live with it at that level – an opponent would try to intimidate you and as long as you gave a clear indication that it wasn't on, everyone got on with the game. But what the Canterbury team of that era was doing was of a completely different order.

That first season, 1970, I missed the game against Canterbury at Carisbrook, but played in the return match in Christchurch, which was a Ranfurly Shield challenge. Playing this team was not an experience I, or any sane person, looked forward to. During the game, I wondered whether I'd ever live through it. I'd never played in front of a crowd of that size and found it a revelation – you could tell when the ball had left the scrum or ruck by the roar of the spectators. The game seemed to go so much faster and because I was fast, I liked that. But, though I'd been warned, I was absolutely stonkered by the attitude of the Canterbury team.

Before the game, the wise heads at Otago were trying desperately to get Keith Murdoch back from South Africa in time to play for us. They said that if we had Keith in the side, Canterbury would play football, but if he wasn't there, there'd be mayhem. Keith made it back to Christchurch after the rest of the All Blacks – he'd been delayed in South Africa by a grumbling appendix – but not in time to play for us. And the wise heads were so right. We were systematically dismembered.

I lost my first locking partner – our lineout supremo, Tony Banks – to a gashed head from a boot. That left me as the only forward with any real height. I was eye-gouged as I stared heavenwards for an up-and-under. I'd barely got my vision back when, in a loose mêlée at the back of the lineout, I saw Grizz Wylie line me up for a haymaker that was coming all the way from Glenmark. I stepped back, grabbed the shoulders of the referee, a little guy from Southland, and said, 'Look at this, ref!' At that moment Wylie let fly and dear old Warren Townsend, salt of the earth from Central Otago, with a jaw the size of a front-end loader, wandered right into it. Towner, whose main claim to fame was that he could recite every verse of *Eskimo Nell* –

> When a man grows old and his balls grow cold,
> And the tip of his prick turns blue;
> When it bends in the middle like a one-string fiddle,
> He can tell you a tale or two.

– went down in a heap. He was tough, got up and played the rest of the game, concussed. The Canterbury half-back had a field day thereafter, breaking round the blind-side of our scrum past

Towner, who was probably trying to remember who the fuck Dead-Eye Dick and Mexican Pete were.

Our hooker was concussed, our half-back was concussed. We lost, narrowly. I wouldn't shake Wylie's hand when we left the field. I didn't want anything to do with any of that pack. What had happened wasn't rugby as I knew it. I was sick with the effort I'd put in and by the time we got through the after-match drear and got back to the hotel I had to hit the sack. It was four or five to a room in those days, and by the time I woke up the party was clearly in full swing because a couple of my room-mates were rooting away in the beds alongside me.

This wasn't that unusual. On the Juniors tour, the guys who hadn't been selected for the next game were invited out to one of those notorious bachelors and spinsters parties, while the rest of us had to get an early night. I woke up about two in the morning to unmistakeable sounds from the single bed next to mine. I lay there for a while, getting more and more pissed off at missing out, then finally decided to take action. I crawled across to the next bed. The big beefy forward was on top and she had both hands clawing his back. I leaned over and carefully added my fingers to a previously unscratched part of his back. He didn't notice at first, then I could see him making the calculation – 'One, two . . .? If she's got both hands round me, who the fuck?' When he turned his head and saw me on the floor making a face at him, he lost his composure – and his erection – and I finally got some sleep.

After the Canterbury shield game in 1970, I began to feel better about 9.30 or 10 p.m., got out of bed and went downstairs to the house bar. It wasn't pretty if you were still sober. The cloud of cigarette smoke had settled up against the ceiling and was gradually working its way downwards as the evening progressed, enveloping everyone. The faces were flushed with booze and sweat. The women's make-up had congealed and retracted into their pores, a grotesquery that wasn't helped by the garish lighting. The best you could do was drink as fast as you could – alcohol seemed to soften the lighting.

I'd missed all the food and decided to get a burger takeaway from across the street. Keith Murdoch came with me. We put in our orders and had to stand around waiting, while drunken revellers spilled down the street from closing pubs. Keith was a magnet. They were Canterbury fans and immediately started abusing him, even though he was still wearing his All Black blazer. One little guy who looked like an overweight jockey tried to pick a fight with Keith. He had to stand on tiptoes and reach up to jab Keith in the chest. His mates were lining up. They wanted to be able to tell their children, presumably, that they'd been maimed fighting Keith Murdoch. Keith just laughed in his surprisingly high-pitched giggle and shrugged them off.

Keith seemed at least human, compared with Canterbury. The year after our first shield challenge, Canterbury played the '71 Lions, a game that was recently listed as number six in a history of '50 Moments of Sporting Infamy' put together by London's *Daily Telegraph* sports correspondent, Brendan Gallagher, who described Canterbury's part in that game as 'one of the bloodiest, most premeditated assaults in rugby history . . . which resulted in Scottish prop Sandy Carmichael, Irish prop Ray McLoughlin and Irish No. 8 Mick Hipwell being invalided off the tour, as well as leaving Irish flanker Fergus Slattery with concussion and without two teeth'. These were the last days before saturation television coverage and before touch judges could intervene for foul play. Canterbury took full advantage of these constraints.

I'd had further contact with the likes of Grizz Wylie in '72, when the Juniors played the All Blacks. If we'd played the All Blacks at the end of that tour, rather than at the start, we'd have beaten them. As it was, we nearly stuffed them in Wellington, where we were beaten 13–9. That game was an encounter with the old guard of All Black forwards. There was no way guys like Frank Oliver or Hamish Macdonald or Alan Sutherland were going to outjump Andy Haden, John Callesen, Paul Anderson or me, so the game was full of blatant fouls. At least I got out of it unscathed, but my luck ran out when I got back from that Australian tour.

In my first club game back, I captained the As against the Californian Grizzlies, and had been toeing the ball through when one of their props went down on the ball and rolled back up my leg. This meant I was running full speed one way, while my leg was being rolled back the other way, trapped between my sprigs in the grass and the weight of this prop. It was a lot like the Michael Jones injury against Argentina, and others since, which are replayed in slo-mo and which I can't watch. I was diagnosed with a torn medial ligament. At hospital they debated whether to operate and, foolishly, listened to me while I was still feeling great on the morphine, and decided instead to immobilise it.

Years later, when I had cartilage problems from the loose knee, the surgeon told me that I'd torn my anterior cruciate ligament as well and should have had a knee reconstruction. Back then, diagnostic techniques and X-rays weren't as sophisticated, so they sent me 'home' with a full leg plaster. Home was a dingy student flat where the Saturday night party was in full swing. I was propped on a sofa and everyone signed my fresh plaster and I had a few beers and felt no pain, until I woke up on the floor at four in the morning in a deserted flat. In agony, I dragged myself down the hall to the phone and croaked out the words every mother secretly wants to hear from her recently departed student son, 'Come and get me!' My mother had no idea I'd been injured, because after I was carried off in a club game a couple of years before, she'd refused to listen to any more of my games on the radio.

I was in the plaster for a couple of months. By the time I got it off, my leg had wasted and I had a hell of a battle at the Physiotherapy School getting full movement and strength back into it. When I managed that, my knee seemed to have more movement than it had before, particularly if I bent it inwards. I was anxious to get back on the field, but by the time I did, the club season was over and the provincial season had begun. I made it back into the Otago team. Unfortunately for me, the first or second game I played was against Canterbury in the mud of Carisbrook.

I was silly enough to take an up-and-under in front of our posts with the Canterbury pack bearing down on me. Either I forgot to call 'mark' or the ref didn't hear me, and I was splattered face down in the mud like a piece of cartoon roadkill. While I was thus engrossed, the Canterbury pack tap-danced up my legs and over my back. Someone, with surgical precision, used their sprigs to slice open my knee along the exact line of the recently healed medial ligament. When I extricated myself from the mud and hobbled to the next lineout, my knee felt stiff, but I couldn't see anything initially through the slimy mess. By the time I got to the lineout the knee had locked up and I could see the blood welling through the mud. I went off and someone claiming to be a doctor washed the wound out with water, then scrubbed the wound with a scrubbing brush, stitched me up and gave me a couple of painkillers.

You'd have to say the standard of medical back-up in those days wasn't great. The year before, again playing for Otago, I'd been concussed making a tackle. I must have known I was in trouble and asked Laurie Mains where the gate was. Laurie, showing the single-mindedness that later characterised his coaching, pointed me back towards the scrum. I stuck my head in a peculiar place, but no one remarked on it. Luckily, the ref blew for the end of the game shortly after. I followed the teams off, into the dressing rooms under the main stand, asked someone where my clothes peg was, undressed, followed everyone in to the showers, followed them out, asked where my clothes peg was, got dressed and wandered out the door. Derek, my young brother, was outside the door of the main stand, waiting to take me home to Oamaru for my older brother's 21st. He had to stop me as I walked past and tell me who he was, then who I was. We had to pick up a couple of my mates and a girlfriend from their flats in North Dunedin. I didn't know their names or where they lived. I might still have been wandering round South Dunedin if Derek hadn't been waiting for me.

Things weren't so bad after the '72 Canterbury game at Carisbrook, when those sprigs sliced open my knee. Cuts aren't that painful, and with the analgesic and the after-match alcohol, and a party that night, I was fine. Until the proverbial four o'clock in the morning, when I woke to a raging infection in my leg, red and swollen to twice its usual size. Cuts may not be painful but infections are. I made a lot of noise until I woke someone in the flat who rang dear old Les Winslade, the As manager, who once again took me to A & E, and waited around while they cut open the stitches to let the shit out. The wound developed into an ulcer that finally healed up some weeks later, on the Wednesday before my first All Black trial.

I must have been a real chance for selection, judging by this exchange in Iain Gallaway's book. By 1972, the world had moved on and hair everywhere had grown, except at the NZRFU, where nothing much had changed it seemed, not least the bad hair rule. I'd started a job as staff solicitor at Gallaway Son & Chettleburgh, where Eric was a client. Iain writes about Eric complaining bitterly about my wearing a suit and a tie to the office: 'Why can't he dress like that when he comes on tour with me – he always wears a scruffy teeshirt, and jeans with holes and jandals'. This was a prelude to Eric asking Iain to ask me to get my hair cut:

> Greg was playing at number eight the following Saturday, in the final trial to select the 1972–73 All Blacks to tour the United Kingdom. Eric said: 'I can't see him at Twickenham with hair of that length. Can you persuade him to have it cut?' I said that it was extremely unlikely but I would give it a go. After putting it off for some time, as Saturday approached I finally plucked up my courage and suggested to Greg that his selection for the All Blacks might be enhanced by a visit to the barber. He stood up and, towering above me, he leaned over, looked me fairly and squarely in the eye and said very quietly, 'Mr Gallaway, a New Zealand jersey doesn't mean as much as that to me.' I felt duly humiliated, turned and slunk out of his office.

On the Thursday, I flew to Wellington and checked into the Grand Hotel, then went downstairs to the dining room for something to eat. I was one of the last players to fly in and by the time I got down to the dining room, it was full, apart from one seat, at a table shared by Grizz Wylie, Sid Going and Alan Sutherland. My heart sank.

All Blacks trials were far more important than they are now, and the triallists were ranked before they got there by whether they were in the late trial – the main trial – or the early trial, the curtain-raiser. I was in the early trial, which meant I had an outside chance of being chosen as one of the 30 players who would be going to Britain. The NZRFU seemed to use two hotels in Wellington, the Grand and the Midland, and put the Possibles from both trials in one hotel and the Probables from both trials in the other, so that there was some separation between the teams that had to face each other.

This was an artificial concept, because the 'teams' only had one or two practices together and, despite the standard PR blurbs from the coaches that a team that plays as a team wins, and a winning team gets its players noticed, everyone knew it was every man for himself. That was taken too far when Pole Whiting was sabotaged by his own All Black 'team-mates' in a final trial before the '71 Lions tour, because the old guard on both sides of the trial divide decided his face wouldn't fit the All Blacks. Despite that, I liked the trial dynamic. It gave me a free hand as a loose forward to react to situations, go where I wanted to, rather than be stultified by some system imposed by the coach, as I was used to in Otago.

By the end of '72, I'd played Canterbury several times and the experience had not improved and I'd still not been able to bring

149

myself to shake hands at the end of the game and pretend that what had happened out there was forgiven and forgotten. I'd marked Grizz Wylie a couple of times and we'd never exchanged words other than the foulest of curses on the field. Once I'd upset him by taking the ball off him at the back of the lineout and I could hear him coming after me, cursing and swearing and punching, for the next 10 minutes.

When I saw the empty seat at Grizz's table in the dining room of the Grand, I desperately looked round for others but there were none, so I had no choice but to walk over and sit down. He and Sutherland and Going had been talking animatedly. From the moment I sat down until we finished the three course meal, not a word was spoken. Except once when Grizz told the waitress, 'Fucken soup's cold.' It was gazpacho.

I put my reservations aside and gave guts in the early trial on Saturday and despite the fact that I wasn't match fit and blew up a bit in the second half, I probably performed the best of the four number eights on the day. After the game, Brian Lochore congratulated me and said I must be in. I thought I was, and it was a strange feeling. I didn't feel elated at the prospect; I was hard pressed to work out how I felt. The boyhood dream was almost realised. I kept thinking that I ought to feel different, that I ought not to be so unsettled about the reality of being trapped in close proximity, for a couple of months on the other side of the world, with the kinds of men I'd had dinner with at the Grand.

The Junior All Black tour to Australia earlier that year had opened my eyes to the realities of spending time in that utterly artificial but very intimate environment, where you had a number that you called out every time you got on the bus and where you were forever waiting for the next organised activity – breakfast, the bus, practice, the bus, lunch, checkout at the hotel, the bus, check-in at the airport, the plane, the bus, check-in at the hotel, and always, overarching everything you do, The Next Game. I once asked my father what he remembered most about the war, and he said, 'The queues. Queuing for everything from food to taking a shit.' It reminded me of touring.

After the trial, I avoided the after-match gathering in the bowels of the stand at Athletic Park, drinking warm beer and eating cold pies, waiting for the announcement of the team. Instead, I had a drink with my brother Peter, who was working in Wellington, at a quiet bar. He delivered me back to Athletic Park in time for the team to be read out. When my name was missing from the 30 All Blacks for the tour, whatever my previous reservations, I was stunned that I hadn't been selected. It might have been the first team I'd ever missed out on.

I was later told by someone who'd spoken to a journalist who'd spoken to the Bugle who'd spoken to the All Black selectors, that I'd hadn't been selected because I couldn't be 'controlled'. Whatever the reliability of that second-hand hearsay, in retrospect I'd have to concede that my old nemesis Bob Duff and his selection panel made the right decision: I might have played well enough on the day to be selected, but I would have made a poor All Black, and not just because my face and hair didn't fit. I wasn't good enough. I could do some spectacular things very well, because of my speed and athleticism, but I couldn't or wouldn't do the bread and butter tasks with any consistency. I could run down most wingers if I got the angle on them, then miss a couple of sitters around the ruck.

I didn't have the physical or psychological avoirdupois to be an All Black.

I went back to Dunedin and to my job with Iain Gallaway, and tried to work out what I was feeling as I watched the All Black tour of Britain turn to shit for Keith Murdoch, when he beat up a poor wee 17 stone 6 foot 3 inch security guard at the Angel Hotel in Cardiff. The English media, led by John Reason of the *Daily Telegraph*, had been waiting since '71 to get Keith, though by rights they should have gone after worthier targets, like almost any forward from the Canterbury team that played the Lions. Reason, a poisonous bastard whose name was a complete misnomer, had come to an Otago practice before the game against the '71 Lions for an interview and had hung around scrum practice until Keith told him to bugger off. That was the sum total of Keith's sin. Keith withdrew from that Otago team just before the game, and also from the All Black team later that year. He told me he liked to travel, the implication being that because there was no tour in the offing that year, he couldn't be bothered playing.

After the Angel Hotel incident, the NZRFU showed the kind of cringe-inducing lack of backbone, independence and fortitude they were to demonstrate later in '81 and '85 and bowed to pressure from the Poms. Keith was thrown out of the tour. I knew he wouldn't come home and face the media. He was shy and inarticulate, which is not the same thing as being dumb, but most in the media didn't make a distinction. I knew where he'd go because we'd talked about some of the places in Western Australia we'd both worked, like Paraburdoo and Mount Tom Price. Sure enough, he disappeared off the plane at Darwin and was tracked down some time later by T. P. McLean at another of the places we'd talked about, Mount Newman. Predictably, Keith had only two words to say when T. P. finally bailed him up in the Western Australian desert: 'Fuck off'.

As the '72–'73 All Black tour staggered on, with captain Ian Kirkpatrick feeling shamed that he hadn't stood up for Keith against Ernie Todd, the terminally ill manager, I became increasingly certain that the selectors had saved my sanity by leaving me out. I read about the black hat mafia who controlled the back seat of the bus, and it was no surprise to see that among them were my loquacious dining companions from the Grand Hotel, Wylie, Sutherland and Going, who had grown Zapata moustaches to go with the black hats, just in case the message wasn't clear.

For the next two years, I kept trying to play as if the dream was still alive in me, but I wasn't the same player. I had excuses: I was working full time as a lawyer and completing my professionals for entry to the bar, which meant I had lectures before and after a demanding job. I couldn't train with the same intensity and lost fitness, strength and speed, beginning in '72 after I'd spent the summer in Australia, working in very hot conditions. In retrospect, I doubt any of that would have happened if my focus hadn't changed; there would have been ways of managing the workload, particularly with an employer as benevolent as Iain.

In '73 I was selected for a New Zealand Universities tour to Australia, which was notable for one of the greatest speeches I'd ever heard. One of our short managerial retinue stood on a chair when we assembled in Wellington and told us that we'd be billeted in Oz with other students, because there was no money for hotels, and that he'd heard about 'you student bastards', he'd heard what we got up to, sinking huge amounts of piss and rooting women and he just wanted to say one thing to us . . . As we groaned inwardly, expecting the usual punch-line, dire warnings about what would happen if we let down the honour of the team, etc, he told us that with a bit of luck he wouldn't be far behind us! He was true to his word, at least in the booze stakes. We couldn't talk to him in the morning because he was hung over and, in the afternoon, chances were he was pissed.

The coach was pretty laissez-faire too, which was okay with us. We were running lineout drills before the first 'test' against Australian Universities at Canberra, when the speechmaker made a rare pre-lunch appearance. He wandered up and down with a long face for a minute, then declared himself to be an extremely worried man. I told him to bugger off and let us get on with it.

We won the first test, but I was involved in an incident where Rupert Rosenblum, their kingpin international five-eighths got a neck injury that put him out of the series. He'd got very slow service from his half-back after a lineout and I'd got to him at about the same time as the ball. I hit him on the up in a hard, fair tackle and came down on top of him, but as he hit the ground, our lock, Groper Grant, collected him with a boot, accidentally I'm sure. Dave Brockhoff, the boorish Aussie coach, made it clear that he blamed me and that I'd deliberately targeted their star and put him out of the series.

When we reached Sydney, we got off the bus and were assigned our billets. Groper and I were put with a guy in a neck-brace – Rupert Rosenblum. I suspected that we were in for a very nasty stay, but just the reverse. Instead of being fed bananas and alcohol for days on end in some grotty flat, as had happened in Melbourne and Canberra, with students who wanted to prove they were the biggest pissheads in Australia, Groper and I were fêted in Rupert's Vaucluse mansion, with its own thermatically controlled wine cellar, and we got to meet Rupert's father, Myer, a very impressive, leonine lawyer. Turned out Groper was related to Rupert by marriage and Rupert, unlike his coach, was happy to accept his injury as an accident.

Apart from the stay with Rupert, the rest of the tour was a bit of a nightmare for me. Brockhoff got fixated on me and before we played in Sydney, I could hear him raving about those 'dirty black bastards' in his pre-game team talk. During the match, he roamed the white picket fence around the picturesque ground at Sydney University, calling his forwards in on me. I could hear him screaming whenever I got the ball. I don't know why he bothered. I wasn't playing well and had other worries, like my girlfriend back in Dunedin, who had missed her period. I felt the heat all the same as fists and boots sought me out anytime I was within cooee of the ball. That was scary, and after a few beers I bailed Brockhoff up at the end of the after-match drinks in Sydney, and was in the process of telling him he was a psychotic maniac, when someone stepped between us.

For my sins, I was given the captaincy of the team for the game against Queensland Country up at Armidale. We were beaten – from memory the only time on tour, so that didn't sit well – but I also collected a perforated ear drum from a swinging arm by 'the white Russian', Jules Guerassimoff, who was as hard as his name. The doctor, proving that post-game medical misadventure was not confined to New Zealand, peered down my ear after the game and gave me the all-clear, so I went for a swim when we got to the Gold

Coast. By that evening I indeed had a perforated ear drum, which was now infected from the pool.

The ear was extremely painful and very messy, spewing seemingly endless reserves of what looked like waxy excrement over whatever was in close proximity to that side of my head. I missed the second test at Brisbane, but was beginning to come right when we flew back to Auckland for a last and totally meaningless game at Eden Park. The changes in cabin pressure upset my ear and it erupted again. We arrived in Auckland at midnight and got to bed at our various billets by about two in the morning of the day of the game. For some reason, management was pressuring me to play and I foolishly agreed. Perhaps I needed to make up for leading the team to a loss at Armidale; perhaps I felt obliged to cover for the guys who'd played the second test. My only game at Eden Park was played in a torrential downpour which ensured that my ear got a further dousing of liquid muck.

Getting back to Dunedin meant a resumption of my punishing daily schedule of law lectures, study, rugby practice and work. Despite the relief that my girlfriend's period had arrived, I was physically and emotionally buggered and when I was selected for the '73 Juniors, I didn't feel I could do that commitment justice and withdrew . . . Then I watched with mixed feelings as the nucleus of the '72 side demolished the All Blacks at Carisbrook.

That match and the unprecedented internal tour which followed it might have been the last gasp of the old guard All Blacks, the leftovers from the 1960s. That decade had been a great era for All Black rugby, but most of the quality and nous went when the likes of Lochore, Gray, Tremain and Meads left the international stage. Some of their replacements had the physical grunt but

156

lacked the talent, rugby IQ and mana to go with it.

I played out the rest of '73 for the As and later in the year I played for South Island Universities against the North, a trial match for a New Zealand Universities game. I was pretty desultory by then about rugby, but not about what happened in that match. As I cleared the ball from a lineout, a fist smashed into my face and broke my nose. Before the explosion of blood obscured my vision, I got a clear view of the colour of the sleeve supporting the fist. White. One of my team-mates. I can't know for sure, but the way it happened didn't feel like accidental friendly fire. Nor can I know for sure whose fist it was, but I have a strong suspicion as to who owned it – one of my supports who was supposed to be protecting me.

Later, when people told me that they thought the inciting incident of *Foreskin's Lament*, Clean kicking his own captain in the head, was far-fetched and unrealistic, I usually mumbled something like, 'Well, it's fiction, y'know' or 'Call it artistic licence', though I suspected through personal experience it wasn't. Then someone, after they'd seen the play, told me a story about two brothers who'd been competing for one spot in a senior club team in Wellington: one had deliberately maimed the other in order to make the team.

Up until my 'mate's' fist took it out, my nose had had a charmed run, given its size. I had it straightened with what looked like an iron shoe-horn and novocaine needles, but shouldn't have bothered. Once broken, noses break more easily next time. Instead of a semi-permanent scab on the bridge of my nose for the season – it'd heal for a week then get knocked off the following Saturday, then heal up again just in time to get scraped raw again next Saturday

– I now seemed to get my nose broken about every fourth game.

All was not lost. By the beginning of '74, even the NZRFU finally realised that major changes were needed, that the All Blacks needed a new broom. I was clearly going to be part of that new age – I was picked for the final All Black trial in May 1974, opposing Andy Leslie, who was to be appointed the new All Black captain. Andy was a radical departure from what had gone before and the scene was set for me too. All I had to do was play halfway well and I would have been in.

The trials were held in May on a beautiful Indian summer's day at Athletic Park in Wellington. It was so hot that Kit Fawcett, sitting in the stand after the early game, took his shirt off and sunbathed bare-chested in the main stand. That probably put his All Black selection back a couple of years.

Out on the field, waiting for the kick-off, I felt strangely unexcited about the 80 minutes ahead of me. If I couldn't get excited about the opportunity presented by a final All Black trial . . . I closed my eyes and tried to work up some focus and enthusiasm, but instead felt the sun on my face and found myself wishing I was somewhere else – the beach, the bush, the bar, anywhere.

I sleepwalked through the game. Andy Leslie was chosen. Bob Barber, who went off after 20 minutes, was chosen. Laurie Knight, who came on to replace Bob Barber, was chosen. I was chastened. In that moment before kick-off, I realised what I'd been denying since that evening in the Grand Hotel: my dream of being an All Black had evaporated, and I was left going through the motions, playing without passion or joy.

I was still captain of the As and thought I'd see out the season. My attitude had also been modified by the injuries I'd suffered.

Serious injury has to have an effect. After the first one, I was okay, but after the second one, instead of doing what a loose forward must – throw myself with reckless disregard precisely where angels would fear to tread – I was a split second slower to the ball, as my desire to do the right thing fought with my memory of the pain. Split seconds make a difference and I was less effective. However, there were things I wanted to accomplish for the club – win the Cavanagh Shield and put in place a squad system incorporating a rotation policy to stop the acrimony that came from the As regularly pilfering players from the Bs and the Bs from the Cs, destroying any chance of building any team unity in the Bs and Cs.

However, my charity towards the Bs didn't extend to the rugby field and, to my shame, I betrayed my own rugby ideals before my season was ended. The Bs number eight was playing very well and, had I not been captain of the As, might well have taken my place. I wanted to end on my own terms and was anxious to assert myself when the As played the Bs. He carried the ball up and I hit him in a legitimate tackle. What happened after that is difficult to be clear about. The player ended up with a pulped nose as a result of coming into contact with my knee. As we landed together after the tackle, I remember seeing his face a split second before my knee hit it. Could I have stopped it? I'm not sure. Going into the tackle, I intended to hurt him. Had that intent made me, at best, reckless in the ensuing mêlée, at worst, the sort of player I'd come to loathe? Whaddarya? I was no longer sure.

I didn't have much of the season left to agonise. In a club game against Green Island, I was triple-teamed in a lineout. As I came down from quite high, I was trying to slip the ball to my half-back.

I couldn't see him because the guy I'd jumped against had his arm around my throat and was forcing my head up. Another guy was trying to grab the ball off me and a third, one of the props, was pushing my hips outwards, towards the half-back. I managed to get the ball away, but I'd lost any sense of where the ground was or what angle my left foot was at when it came into contact with the field. There was a hell of a crack and I found myself sitting on the grass with my leg straight, looking at the sole of my left foot, twisted unnaturally back towards me. Play stopped: I wasn't the only one with a white face. The sound of the bone breaking and the disfigured leg made most players a bit queasy and apparently there was some reluctance to continue once I was stretchered off. They did continue and we lost, putting us out of the final.

There was a doctor in the crowd, but he wouldn't pull the foot out. I understood that dislocations should be pulled back into place as soon as possible so when this guy refused to touch mine, I thought I must have shattered every bone in the ankle. I was thinking amputation, never walking again, let alone running. The match was being played at the far end of Tahuna Park and I had to be stretchered all the way across to the entrance, where the ambulance was waiting. I grabbed the laughing gas and kept the pain at bay until we got to the hospital, by which time I was shaking so hard with shock they had to hold me down on the stretcher. I was given morphine and, just before I blissed out, someone pulled the ankle out and it plopped roughly back into place.

Later, they were supporting my leg just under the knee to X-ray the ankle, which had undergone one of the worst dislocations the orthopaedic surgeon had seen. When they asked me where it hurt,

I told them it hurt most where they were holding me. They X-rayed further up and discovered that the force of the ankle turning under had broken my leg up under the knee.

Back in plaster. I was at least accustomed to the sensation of that sudden change from athlete to cripple and the fretting that goes on for the physical movement that had always been an oxygenater, stress relief and sleep inducer. I read somewhere that Maurice Duggan, badly crippled by polio, always ran in his dreams, and so did I, and will forever, no matter how bent and crippled.

Some old players are stopped in the street by people who remember a moment of magic, a moment of sublime skill that has stayed etched in their memory, burnished by the passage of time and a declining grip on reality. Instead, I get stopped in the street by late middle-aged men who fix me with gnarled hands and gimlet eyes and tell me 'I was there at Tahuna Park when your leg snapped'. Great. Thanks for the memory.

That accident was proof, if I needed it, that rugby is too demanding to play out of imagined obligation. Italy was to teach me that it was too tough to play just for money. If you can't revel in the fierce joy of the game, it will bite you. But fierce joy is one thing; the kind of rugby epitomised by the Canterbury team of the early 1970s was quite another – brutal, joyless and boring.

There were a couple of sequels to those years, quite apart from Clean and *Foreskin's Lament*.

In the 1990s, I agreed to give a speech at my old high school, Waitaki, at a dinner after an annual quadrangular tournament. I decided to talk about how brutal and foul top-level New Zealand rugby had been when I played, and how lucky these kids were to be playing the game now, where they could look forward to provincial and representative rugby that was clean, fast and exciting. I wanted to tell them that they had an obligation to carry forward the spirit of First XV rugby, the joy and exultation they had shown that day when playing the game. I had intended to illustrate my point by recounting a couple of unsavoury incidents from my career, the kinds of things that they should ensure did not come back into the game. Both anecdotes, inevitably, involved that brutal Canterbury team of the early 1970s. As we sat down to the top table with the coaches of the four schools involved, I recognised, just along from me, Tane Norton, the hooker from that Canterbury pack.

I was discombobulated. Should I change my speech? I didn't want to attack him personally – though Tane wasn't mentioned, he and everyone there would know he was implicated – in front of his boys. On the other hand, I felt it was a cautionary tale that needed to be told. In the end, I went ahead with the speech, trying to keep my references to the Canterbury team I was talking about as unspecific as possible. There were two people there, however, who knew exactly who I was talking about. Afterwards, Tane made a point of seeking me out to tell me that, whatever happened in the past, there was no way he would encourage his boys to go out and play like that. Too late for me, but I'm glad for those kids.

I also finally exchanged words with Grizz Wylie, in 1990, when he was one of the 'real' veteran players who supported the actors in a film I wrote with Dean Parker, called *Old Scores*. Grizz was a mellowed beast by then, gruff but friendly enough, but up close, I've got to admit, the eyebrows still worried me.

While the success of *Foreskin's Lament* meant I had to relive that period of my life to some extent, I became increasingly impatient to move on. I was unabashedly careerist and wanted to find out whether the play's success would give me a shot at something larger, something which at that time in New Zealand was even more exacting and rigorous and ambitious than being an All Black, or even than writing one successful play: I wanted to see whether I could earn a living from writing.

ten

Tooth & Claw

At the Playwrights' Workshop in 1980, where *Foreskin's Lament* debuted, there was a panel with various luminaries from theatre and radio and television drama. I was sitting on a burning question for one of the panellists, Roger Hall.

My inquiry betrayed not just my naiveté, but my desire to get out of law and forge a career in writing. I wanted to know how playwrights actually earned money, how they were paid. I had no idea about royalties. Paddy Chayefsky, the great American who wrote *Network* and *Marty*, had said about writers, 'Money is all we talk about. The fact is, you can trust a writer who talks about money all the time. I'd be very careful of a writer who starts talking about his art.' But as I listened to all the earnest, literate questions being put to the panel, it was clear they hadn't heard of Chayefsky's dictum, so I chickened out and thought I'd better not lower the tone.

I was to find out about money soon enough, as *Foreskin's Lament* was produced up and down the country during the first half of the 1980s. The first burst of royalties, coupled with the security of a six-month literary fellowship at the University of Auckland, gave me the courage to put a deposit down on a small cottage out west on the Manukau Harbour at Parau. The fellowship also precipitated the farewell to my legal career, which was no great hardship by then, since I may as well have been digging ditches for all the interest I had in it.

My reasons for doing law had been threefold and none altruistic. I had a mate at Waitaki Boys' whose uncle was a prominent Oamaru lawyer and had a house up the South Hill with a full-sized pool table and a wine cellar and I thought that was pretty cool; I had to find something to do at university or I was heading for a job my father had jacked up with the Oamaru branch of NZI; and I needed a 'meal ticket' degree, something that would lead to a job – doing a BA would tend to confirm my father's suspicions that university was just another way of indulging myself and avoiding real work.

Once I'd made it through the first year and got into law proper, however, I'd really enjoyed it. We had to read a lot of law reports and I became fascinated by the story-telling talents of some judges – Britain's Lord Denning and New Zealand's Peter Mahon and Woodhouse, for instance – as they recounted the facts of the case before them, and then by the rationales they conjured up to justify the application of the law to those facts. The structure of an outstanding decision or legal opinion appealed to me as having a beautifully wrought elegance, rather like the perfect symmetry of a DNA cluster must appear to a geneticist. I also became interested in the jurisprudential bases for law itself, the philosophical justification for laws, the reasons why a collection of individuals reaches and maintains a consensus to abandon many of their individual rights in order to live together collaboratively in society.

When I left university and was given a job by Iain Gallaway, he warned me that the realities of the practice of law were somewhat different, and in fact I can't remember ever discussing with any of my 'learned friends' in either Dunedin or Auckland the finer jurisprudential underpinnings of society. I can remember doing squillions of memoranda of transfers and mortgages and a scheme of arrangement for a company and drafting a private member's bill and sending out several thousand default summons, in my name, to debtors of companies we acted for (before the days of debt collection agencies). One of the poor bastards 'I' was suing rang me and threatened to track me down and rearrange my face. Pretending a great deal more equanimity than I felt, I told him my face was already closed for alterations – the broken nose phase – but the scaffolding should be off soon. In the meantime, why didn't he just pay his debt and get the court system off his back?

I gravitated into conveyancing and commercial law because that was what my mentor needed me to do. My court appearances were infrequent, despite my solitary A+ in evidence, and I had to make time for court work over and above my other responsibilities. The realities of court work, too, were not exactly high-minded. It seemed to me the best defence lawyers were the ones who didn't get too passionately involved with the guilt or innocence of their clients but were able to respond phlegmatically to evidential challenges and the foibles and prejudices of a jury full of everymen and women: in other words, manipulate and test the rules of the adversarial game rather like an openside flanker at the breakdown.

When I left Dunedin in '75 to do the locum tenens at Henderson, I found that being a sole practitioner didn't exactly lend itself to the consideration of finely wrought legal argument either. Milan had a huge client base for a sole practitioner – most of the Dallies in West Auckland, it seemed – and controlled a substantial nominee investment company which committed funds for mortgages. The size of the practice had worn him down so that, by the time he and Shirley went overseas, there were some unexploded grenades lying in wait for me. After six months of 6 a.m. starts, I had a better appreciation of why Milan got tired.

By the time I'd done my OE and got a job at Williams McDonald & Co. in 1979, I was content to be the back-up backroom boy out the back, only very occasionally having to take any real responsibility when either BeeGee or Kevin McDonald were away. On one of these occasions, when they were both away playing a Golden Oldies tournament in the States, I made a rare appearance in court on behalf of a client who should have known better.

I was working late and both secretaries had gone home. From my office, I heard the reception bell sound and went through to greet a couple of characters who were obviously detectives. I recognised one of them and asked him if he was here about one of Kevin's files I was handling. Morrie the D looked straight through me with that bloodless stare which every self-respecting D seems obliged to cultivate and asked, 'Is your name Gregory William McGee?'

They charged me with disorderly behaviour. The summary of facts said that I'd set alight an 'effigy' – my Junior All Black jersey stuffed with straw – during the final All Black–Springbok test and had then thrown it at police. Struggling to take it seriously, I told them I'd set it alight but I wasn't the one who picked it up and threw it at police lines. I expected them to take me at my word and drop the charge, but they didn't do either, whereupon I decided the whole thing was a waste of time and decided to act for myself. I was aware of the adage that the lawyer who defends himself has a fool for a client, but was buggered if I was going to waste someone else's time and my money.

The defended case lasted the best part of a day, and I had some fun cross-examining the police witnesses on what they understood an effigy to mean. Did it have hands or legs? Did it have a head? Did it have a face? Did it look like anyone you know? One police witness was just out of Trentham Police College and I was having trouble reconciling his point of view of the chaos at that intersection with the location of police lines. He finally admitted, sheepishly, cheepishly even, that he'd got separated from his colleagues, became frightened and had taken refuge in a Cheep Rubbish Bin at the far side of the intersection. By the afternoon, the hearing was no longer fun, just tiring, and when it came to make final submissions, I was ready to concede that my actions, particularly given what else was going on at that intersection, were within the broad compass of the Crimes Act definition – 'behaves, or incites . . . any person to behave . . . in a . . . threatening . . . or disorderly manner that is likely in the circumstances to cause violence against persons or property to start or continue'.

However, proving that I wasn't the one who threw the burning jersey at the cops was worthwhile because the judge offered me a Section 22. This part of the Criminal Justice Act is much beloved of first offenders and students and I'd used it a few times myself – for Anton Oliver's naked uncle, for instance – in circumstances where, though technically guilty, the consequences of a conviction far outweighed the seriousness of the offence. The judge expressed some concern about the effect of a conviction on my career as lawyer. I thought for a fleeting moment of letting him know I was about to abandon the law for a much worthier profession, telling lies for money, where a conviction for this offence might be regarded as a badge of honour, then pragmatism reasserted itself and I applied for a Section 22.

With my last dodgy client released into an unsuspecting society, I farewelled the grubby preoccupations of law and climbed the hill to the lofty environs of academia. I had the use of an office in the English Department of the University of Auckland for six months and the people there, like Terry Sturm and Bill Pearson, were most welcoming, and not just because I was literary flavour of the month.

To begin with, I revelled in the time and freedom the fellowship provided, and beavered away on my second play, *Tooth & Claw*. I'd thought being paid to be at a university without having to study anything or pass any exams would be close to heaven, but as the weeks and months went by I found it increasingly difficult to drag myself to that office. The Auckland campus seemed to lack Otago's ambience, perhaps because it was a commuter campus, where the students clocked in and out for the day, then went home to Mum and Dad in Remuera or wherever, whereas at Otago the campus was the focal point of the surrounding student ghetto, where we all lived and had some commonality of age and purpose and where even the Richie Riches pretended they were as poor as the rest of us. Whatever the cause, I found the whole academic environment at Auckland quite unsettling and by the end of my tenure I was coming in only on Fridays, to collect my mail and wolf down a subsidised lunch at the senior staff room in the old Government House.

Despite losing my interest in the practice of law, I'd never lost my interest in jurisprudence; the irony was that I'd had to leave the law in order to advance my thoughts on it. My second play was set in a lawyer's office above a burning city. It had been inspired by the Brixton riots of 1980, and Lord Scarman's 1981 report on them, which he called 'the worst outbreak of disorder in the UK'. Scarman pointed to 'racial disadvantage that is a fact of British life'.

By the end of the '81 tour, which had become a 'law and order' issue, I was convinced the essential premise for the Brixton riots existed here – a substantial racially disadvantaged, disenfranchised underclass, with no stake in society and no prospects. I was also intrigued by the basis for the so-called 'rule of law', which is no rule at all, but rather a delicate societal consensus that unbridled individual rights – the law of the jungle, Tennyson's 'Nature, red in tooth and claw' – will be waived in favour of certain nebulous but essential values, such as peace, harmony and justice.

I'd seen in Italy how essential it was that these societal values be embodied in the state, and what happens when the citizenry becomes cynical that the state can deliver them – justice in particular. By the time I left, I was convinced that it was easy to live in Italy as a stranger as long as you didn't understand what was really going on. The Mafia wasn't just a southern phenomenon in 1977, because the cynicism about lo stato, which gave rise to it, was pervasive right across Italy. Very few people had any confidence that the state could help them in matters of any substance: they accepted that corruption was endemic and would always be so. This acceptance of lo stato's corruption and impotence informed and poisoned the nation at every level.

I knew of someone who had lost his father. He and his aged mother decided to invest the only money they had from the father's estate in buying a business that could provide for them both. In Italy at that time, there were routinely two bank accounts – the official one, upon which taxes were paid and which, of course, had not much money in it – and a secret one where the real money went. The son paid a purchase price based on the turnover of the secret account, about which the vendor gave him verbal assurances, but which of course he couldn't put in writing and the purchaser wasn't allowed to see until he'd paid the substantial non-refundable deposit. When the son took over the business, he found the turnover figures were complete bullshit and he'd blown his and his mother's inheritance on a lemon.

In New Zealand the son might have tried to sue, though there was nothing in writing and his reliance on potential turnover that he knew was defrauding the IRD might not have helped in court. In Italy, the son had no option but to go and see the local godfather, a very rich and influential businessman who may or may not have helped set up the original rort. The godfather took the son's new business under his wing, fed him enough clients to keep him solvent and, of course, also wrapped him in a web of fealty. The clients who came to the son's business would have been others equally beholden to the godfather, bound to go where directed.

Towards the end of my sojourn in Italy, I was given an audience with this man in his marble mansion. I understood he might offer me a job, but I never got an opportunity to apply, once he saw the length of my hair. Instead, he delivered a long monologue about Italy's problems – pinkos, in a word – and his part in its salvation. When my time was up and the audience was terminated, I was clear in my own mind that it was time to move on to London.

This system of grace and favour from powerful individuals was potent only because people believed that these individuals had more direct power than the state to 'help' and 'protect' them. That protection might extend to leisure activities, such as ownership of a sports club, where right-thinking fathers could send their sons and daughters, secure that they would meet only like-minded children and not be exposed to any leftists with long hair and beards.

Italy was thus, more than most nations, a collection of societies within the larger society and many of its citizens owed fealty not to the larger society but to their own infra-society. When and if the godfather ever wanted a favour in return from these people, a favour that might contravene the laws of the state, where would their loyalties lie? Italy reinforced for me how dangerous it is to allow a populace to grow cynical about the state, to have any substantial group of citizens who feel so disenfranchised and unprotected by the state that they give their loyalty, support and aspiration to some infra-societal group – or gang – which may sooner or later make demands on them that are at odds with the state's laws.

I took no comfort from what I'd seen in New Zealand during '81, and in particular the way Muldoon had manipulated that tour to advantage himself and his party, at huge cost to the country as a whole. The frustration and anger I'd seen on the streets – and the way the tour had become a focal point for disadvantaged Maori in particular – sent clear signals that the delicate consensus of goodwill any state needs to retain confidence in its laws and various agencies was being rapidly eroded.

The other lesson was Australia. I'd spent the 1971–72 summer university break trying to make some money over there, first as a premium wheat-tester at Narrabri in north-west New South Wales. The weather didn't oblige and while we waited for the wheat to ripen, I ended up chipping cotton in Wee Waa, along with the other desperates of Oz society, immigrants from Yugoslavia or Italy or Greece who were trying to earn their fares home after the Aussie dream had turned to nightmare. There were no 'old' Australians working on the cotton, only these poor 'new' Australian immigrants with their blistered faces alongside the original inhabitants, Aborigines. Seeing first hand how Aborigines were treated was genuinely shocking.

Someone at Wee Waa must have known the words to the song 'Sixteen Tons' – 'I owe my soul to the company store' – and turned them into a business plan. It was like something out of the American South. The underpaid workers had to buy from the company store and were encouraged to purchase booze and stuff they didn't need, as well as the necessaries, at exorbitant prices so that they never got out of hock, and therefore had to keep working for the company for peanuts.

The rains came and the Namoi flooded and that was the end of the wheat, but it didn't matter where Ferg, Keith Ferguson, and I went in Oz looking for work, we found that unique Australian three-tiered class system. At the top were the 'old' Australians, the diggers, the bosses, descended from convicts and the flotsam and jetsam of British society. Underneath them, a distant second, came the 'new' Australians, the immigrants. And way beyond them, scarcely registering on the scale as fellow humans, were the Aboriginals. There's a speech in *Foreskin's Lament* – 'dings dallies dutchies dagoes, boongs chinks gooks wogs commies coconuts pommies polys woollys gollys spics spades spastics' – which owed a lot to the racism of that summer in Oz.

After we were washed out of the wheat, and couldn't get a job in Sydney, Ferg and I hitchhiked to Perth. That was Ferg's idea; I would have given up and gone home. Ferg was short, portly, knock-kneed, weak-wristed with a fey, plummy voice, but proved himself to be a tough little bastard. We slept on beaches or wherever, and found ourselves standing for hours on the side of the road at the end of small towns waiting for a ride west, where we watched these other people who lived at the margins, shabbily dressed Dickensian shadows who seemed to float at the very edge of Australian society, like dark scum on a pond.

At Ceduna we caught a ride across the Nullabor with a couple of Sydneysiders who were so paranoid about the few Aborigines we saw on the side of the road that the guy in the passenger seat would keep them covered with a .303 out the window as we accelerated past. The one night we spent on the Nullabor, they slept in the back of the stationwagon with the windows jammed up and the rifle between them, while Ferg and I slept in the scrub as an early warning system 'in case the boongas come for us'.

After giving blood for tea and biscuits in Perth, our money gone, Ferg and I got a job at a farm near a small town between Perth and the southern coast, shooting kangaroos. As we got off the train, looking like shit after having slept rough for over a week, we were still hit on by drunk Aboriginal women – 'gins' – offering a fuck for a coin. They and their families lived in humpies in the long grass of an abandoned section beside the church in the centre of town. The locals didn't seem to see them. It was as if they were completely invisible.

When we crapped out there – Ferg couldn't shoot a rabbit at 10 paces, let alone a leaping kangaroo – we got back to Perth, saw an ad and bullshitted an earthmoving contractor called Caratti that we were farm boys who knew how to operate tractors and harvesters, and that dozers and scrapers would be a cinch for us. We were believed, we thought, and were flown north to Paraburdoo by a red-headed South African maniac who kept us from dozing off over the interminable desert by doing loops and swoops so that our guts ended up in our mouths.

Paraburdoo was part of the Hamersley Iron complex in from Port Hedland, just a collection of refrigerated huts at the edge of the Gibson Desert, populated by 1200 men and three elderly fat whores in a caravan who could no longer turn a trick in Perth. Carattis had a contract to build a runway for jet aircraft and were way behind, which is why they were desperate enough to employ Ferg and me. When we were given our jobs, it became clear that they hadn't believed a word of our bullshit. I was given a tractor with a huge vibrator on the back, which I drove up and down the graded airstrip at a pace that only just kept the swarms of flies off my face. Ferg wasn't so lucky: he was a spotter for the huge dump trucks and would stand with his flag out on the margins of the airstrip, dark with flies. A dump truck would approach through the heat waves, Ferg would hold up his flag to give it a target, the truck would dump its load, the flies would lift off Ferg like a cloud as the dust from the truck descended on him. The dust would settle and the swarm of flies would return to their perch. Ferg's wit eventually got him a cushy number in an air-conditioned office as the foreman's general factotum.

We were told that the temperature was over 120 degrees Fahrenheit the first three days we were there. It was so hot that I got nose-bleeds just from climbing onto the tractor in the morning. The heat and red dust engendered huge thirst and there was only one pub to slake it: a partitioned off piece of desert with no roof apart from a bit of a lean-to over the bar. It was like the Wild West and it paid to keep your head down, drink your beer and not venture opinions on anything of note. Again, the three classes of Australian were all present and correct, but the only true diggers there were bad bastards on the run from the law. The lone policeman in 'town' had a hut across from the bar and, understandably, didn't seem terribly interested in putting himself about.

There were quite a few Maori working there. They had a great reputation in Western Australia as 'blade men', gun operators of the huge bulldozers that pushed the scrapers when they were loading. One evening we were in the beer queue at the pub when a new arrival, one of these diggers who would have been on the run interstate from maintenance orders or worse, was right behind us and mistook the Maori we were standing with for a 'boonga'. He saw the curly black hair, leapt to what he thought was a logical conclusion, grabbed this guy by the shoulder and told him to fuck off to the back of the queue and wait till everyone else had a drink. He didn't realise his mistake until he came round on the gravel floor. He picked himself up and wobbled bloody-faced across the street to the cop shop to lodge a complaint, but our man in blue saw him coming and locked the door.

There was only one Aborigine on the workforce, a guy called, with deliberate irony, Lord Ted, who was mercilessly ripped off by some digger when he sold his car. When we tried to intervene on Lord Ted's behalf, this digger was utterly gobsmacked that anyone would bother taking a boonga's side. He refunded the money like a lamb, shaking his head in wonderment at our stupidity. One of the bosses told us that culls were still happening every few years on the big stations north of Paraburdoo. We didn't understand at first what he was talking about. We assumed it was kangaroos. He was talking about Aborigines, probably apocryphally, but we'd seen enough of the lucky country by then not to be too sure.

Out of this plethora of high ideas and low experiences, I produced a very dull play.

Tooth & Claw was premiered by Downstage in 1983. Phil Mann, drama lecturer at Vic, science fiction author and practical – and passionate – man of the theatre, directed the play with huge enthusiasm and understanding. Phil was married to Nonnita Rees, who succeeded Judy Russell as the Executive Director of Playmarket and the Association of Community Theatres. New Zealand Theatre and playwrights in particular were indebted to both Phil and Nonnita. Phil's intellectual energy was gargantuan: he would direct rehearsals all day, then in the evening after dinner, over some beers, we would go through all the notes that had arisen during the day and discuss rewrites. By 11, I'd be fading rapidly, while Phil would just be taking off, getting ready to fly into dissections of drama, literature, politics, the world and indeed the universe. My piking around midnight must have been a disappointment to him. Phil would be one of only a couple of genuine intellectuals I've ever met; people whose range and depth of both knowledge and curiosity confirmed my own paltry limits.

We had a fine cast, with Gary Day carrying the main burden, on stage throughout, but the production was undermined by the limited technology of the day. The screen/window of the lawyer's office set high in a tower block was supposed to project various things, from devastated riot-stricken street scenes to police line-ups, but primarily it needed to convey the sense of a burning city, a society descending into chaos, with the fire edging closer. The designer, Tolis Papazoglou, a bearded bear of a man, tried to will the back projections for the screen/window into focus during the technical rehearsal (Ruth Harley, now CEO of the New Zealand Film Commission, at that stage Chief Advisory Officer for Drama at the Arts Council, was getting her hands dirty helping rig the lights) but as soon as the stage lights were brought up, the projections were completely washed out. There was no solution to be found in the time available, so the burning city, supposed to be such a strong element of the play, was represented by red and pink and yellow lights washed across a 'Manhattan' silhouette of black tape. The realities of rough theatre.

I'd been hoping the lawyer's office set so high above the burning streets would be a metaphor for dislocation, alienation and dysfunction, but what was left was a bleak, wordy, very static play in which much of the real action seemed to be happening somewhere off-stage.

You could say that today's technology would better enhance the ideas underpinning the drama, but, on the other hand, you could also say, as some critics did, too many ideas, not enough drama, which is probably more accurate. You could also say that the play was prescient in the sense that Thatcherism, which had become ensconced in Britain in 1979, was about to be delivered to New Zealand the following year, albeit courtesy of a Labour Government. My social antennae may have been working, but my creative imagination failed me. I could have done something much more interesting and dramatic with the ending and with the character of the secretary at the very least and exploited the incipient love triangle. I could have done something a hell of a lot more interesting with the whole thing, really. As a vehicle for such high ideas, *Tooth & Claw* was a clanky old jalopy.

Some people liked it. Ray Henwood called it 'Shavian', which didn't necessarily mean he enjoyed it. My Uncle Gordon, who had been in advertising, spluttered that at least it was a play, unlike my last one (*Foreskin's Lament*) which was – what's that other word beginning with P, he asked? Polemic, I offered. Polemic! *Tooth & Claw* was joint winner of the *Dominion* play of the year for '83, along with my third play, *Out in the Cold*, but probably got the audience it deserved and did moderate business around the main centres during 1983 and 1984, shadowed by *Out in the Cold*.

If *Tooth & Claw* was about high ideas, *Out in the Cold* was about low cunning – a solo mum's attempt to infiltrate the high wage male bastion of the freezing chambers, the setting for my short story by the same name. The characters from the short story, Strawberry and Porridge, jumped very comfortably from prose to play.

In every way, *Out in the Cold* was a contrast to *Tooth & Claw*. Where the latter had taken nearly two years to write, *Out in the Cold* had been written very quickly over the course of a month immediately after the inspiring 1982 Playwrights' Workshop, which had given rise to several plays – *Outside In* by Hilary Beaton, *Objection Overrruled* by Carolyn Burns, *A Street Called Straight* by Seamus

Quinn and Renée's *Wednesday to Come* – which made the mid-1980s a watermark for indigenous drama. Where *Tooth & Claw* was static, *Out in the Cold* was full of movement; where *Tooth & Claw* was bleak, *Out in the Cold* was funny; where *Tooth & Claw* was long and turgid, *Out in the Cold* was over in an hour; and, most importantly, where *Tooth & Claw* was high in ambition but low in execution, *Out in the Cold* was just the opposite. I know which I preferred.

Danny Vendramini directed the premiere of *Out in the Cold* brilliantly in traverse at Theatre Corporate, with Harry Sinclair playing Jimmy, the disembodied voice up on the chilling floor, whose main task was to hurl the plaster cast lamb carcasses down the chutes with split-second timing to Paul Gittins, Geoff Snell and Judy Gibson below.

That production of *Out in the Cold* remains the only one of any of my plays I've been able to sit through without getting a severe headache. Maybe that was because it was only an hour, but I think it's more likely because that production perfectly realised the play. It might also be because I think there are fewer moments in that play where I cringe in anticipation. Plays are a succession of moments, some better written than others. In *Foreskin's Lament* and *Tooth & Claw*, there were moments where I seldom saw the actors do complete justice to my writing, but many more where they saved my arse. That production of *Out in the Cold* was, for the first and only time in my experience, cringe-free.

My response to *Foreskin's Lament* had by then become problematic. I was proud of it and grateful for what it had given me, but found it increasingly difficult to sit through it and listen to those words hammering around my head yet again. At one stage in the mid-1980s, I reckoned I could have recited the whole thing almost word for word from beginning to end, and I came to hate going anywhere near it. Even by '99, when the Auckland Theatre Company revived it at Sky City, I barely managed to stay in my seat through the opening night performance, despite Roy Billing reprising Tupper when he was at last the right age to play him, and a beautifully balanced Seymour from Karl Urban. Worse, when I went backstage to thank the cast, they insisted that I come back the following Wednesday night because they would have bedded things in by then and I could expect to see a much better performance. There was no way out, so I agreed to return.

The ticket was waiting for me at Sky City. I had a glass of wine in the vestibule, but when the bells rang to call the audience to their seats, I couldn't force myself through the door and fled into the casino, where I haunted the blackjack tables for two hours until the play finished, then went backstage and managed to convince the cast, by agreeing with everything they said, that I had seen a much improved run.

My allergy eventually spread to opening nights of any play. In the late 1980s Dean Parker had kindly given me a ticket to the opening night of his adaptation of *Great Expectations*. It was at the town hall and I made it right to the double glass doors opening into the vestibule, wherein the usual opening night theateratti of the time were gathered in anticipation, braying and cackling, spraying 'Darlings' and 'Dear hearts' at one another. The sound hit me like a force field and I couldn't bring myself to push through the doors. I went on another night, which is usually a better way to appreciate a play anyway – opening nights are full of false one-off dynamics produced by a completely unrepresentative audience, most of whom have not paid for their seats.

Back in '83, *Out in the Cold* was well received and those plaster cast lambs made their way around New Zealand over the next couple of years to most of the studio (smaller) auditoria of the professional theatres. By the end of that year, with the literary fellowship long gone, along with my part-time job in law, the realties of being a professional playwright began to strike home. I was feather-bedded to some extent, as I was right through the mid-1980s – by continuing productions of *Foreskin's Lament*, but they were diminishing as the play completed its first run round the small circuit of professional theatres. It was no comfort that if *Foreskin's Lament* had been that kind of phenomenon in a country the size of Britain, I could have done a John Osborne – bought an estate in Surrey, become a member of the Garrick Club and developed a persona, visage and political views which were all dead ringers for Colonel Sanders'.

The lesson from *Tooth & Claw* and *Out in the Cold*, which were both reasonably well received, was that gross royalties for an average New Zealand play were paltry on the face of it, and on a dollar-per-hour analysis, unconscionably poorly paid. It was clear that theatre royalties alone would provide an eking rather than a living and while that might have been okay, cool and contrarian even, for someone in his 20s with nary a pot plant of a dependant, it wasn't so cool if you were in your 30s and married with children.

eleven

From the Covered Stand to the Terraces

I'd met someone special at one of the many parties at Bayfield Road in 1980. My attempts to chat her up didn't so much fall on deaf ears as bemused brown eyes. She did tell me her name, Mary, but other than that I didn't make a lot of progress. Her witty rebuttals of my best attempts to impress her and her instant understanding of my baser motives didn't put me off. If anything I was impressed by her perspicacity.

When I first met her, Mary was still living, rather shakily, with the father of her second son and could see, she told me later, that I was potential trouble and complication. Some months later, I met her at another party and we talked for hours as if no one else was there, while her partner slept in the car. After she'd extricated herself from him, we spent more time together, making romantic rendezvous at Cornwall Park during lunchtime breaks from her part-time job as a counsellor at the Auckland Medical Aid Trust. She was a year younger than me, a brown-haired brown-eyed beauty with a strong sense of social justice. Like me, she'd done her thousand Ponsonby parties, but was originally from a small town, Gisborne, and was as happy in the country as in the city. She loved reading, cooking, could create a garden, back a trailer, double declutch and was sexy as hell. She'd survived an earthquake in Guatemala and prison visits for the Ponsonby People's Union and seemed to have such a womanly confidence in who she was.

She was also fiercely protective of her children. While I tried to kiss her brown shoulder, she tried to warn me that she had two children and did I understand what that meant? Of course I did, I blustered. She told me that if her 18-month-old son was here with us now, he'd be pulling at her breast for milk. Did I understand that? Of course I didn't, I had no idea, but what I said was that I was living at Bayfield Road with a little boy, Sue's son Andrew, and that I was accustomed to children being in the house. Which was true enough in so far as it went, but being a flatmate of a mother with a child, and having no responsibility other than enjoying the child's company, is not the same as being the partner of a woman with two young children.

Mary was trying to tell me that if there was any conflict of interest between her children and me, I had no chance: the children always came first. I couldn't fully understand what that meant until I was actually in that situation; it's not something you can really appreciate in the abstract. In my rapid movement from pot plants = 0 to little boys = 2, I didn't always, or often, cover myself with glory. But in time, I came to see that Mary's way was the only way, that if the adults aren't capable of acting like adults, the children don't get a childhood.

In some ways, Mary's oldest son, Oliver, seemed at the age of seven more socially adept and worldly than I was at 30 plus. That wouldn't be news to those who know Oli – he's a benign force of nature. I never had any trouble knowing what Oli wanted or needed, whereas Mary's second son, Guy, was a quiet wee chap, athletically very gifted, which was a lovely connection for me.

Step-parents mostly get a bad rap and I can understand why. The couple don't have that honeymoon period when they get to know each other as individuals, rather than as parent and de facto parent. There's an immediate need to nurture and sustain three relationships, not just one. Not always easy. I've seen many standard couples, who have had the benefit of that childless time together, still get ground down under the stress and pressure of a young family. I hate to think how I would have coped had I not liked the kids, but Oli and Guy were easy to like, and eventually love.

In June of '83, Mary and I got married, a registry office job with a party afterwards at her grandmother's. Once married, and with Mary pregnant, I found that my aspirations for us as a family were pretty standard. In my 20s I'd cut my cloth to suit aspirations that weren't at all material, but even then I'd never wanted to live in a garret and sacrifice life for Art, and certainly wouldn't wish such an existence on a wife and children – even if Mary had been struck mute, opinionless and helpless, which she most certainly wasn't. I wanted to be able to help provide for our family and have all the usual things: a house, a mortgage and at least one car between us that didn't have to be push-started and didn't cause a cold sweat at warrant of fitness time and palpitations every time we ventured onto the motorway.

At that stage, we both had small cottages out west, Mary in Laingholm, me over the hill at Parau. We hadn't particularly wanted to be that far out, and had both started looking in Ponsonby, but properties seemed to be going up by the week and we found our respective deposits didn't meet any of the rising inner-city purchase prices. Our house searches took us further and further out from the centre in concentric circles until we found ourselves in the bush way beyond Titirangi. By the time Caitlin was born, however, in November of '83, we'd sold both cottages and scraped up a deposit and a substantial mortgage for a run-down two-storey house at 8 John Street, Ponsonby.

I recently read a review of a memoir where the reviewer was absolutely scathing about the memoirist's reference to the birth of his child as a defining moment in his life. Apparently it's the standard stuff of memoirs, and boring and predictable, so I won't go there, other than to say it was true for me. I didn't distinguish myself at Caitlin's birth because I was so overcome. When Mary's waters broke in the delivery suite, meconium was present and I heard the doctor say to the midwife that the baby must be distressed and let's get her into the theatre. But there was no time for that: Caitlin was already crowning. What photos I'd seen of crowning babies showed a membranous cranium, almost transparent, through which you could almost see the throbbing brain. When Caitlin crowned, her cranium looked uniformly opaque and white and I thought, Dear Jesus, Mary's going to give birth to a huge bone. I offer this in my own defence to explain why, when Caitlin finally slipped out into the world, I was so discombobulated that I mistook her umbilical cord for a penis and told Mary it was a boy with a whopper.

I think I got better at being a father after that, and having a child of my own may have made me a more understanding stepfather to Oliver and Guy. Having a child was also my first experience of unconditional love and my first experience of true fear, that is, fear for someone other than myself, or perhaps fear for myself if anything happened to her.

American parental advice used to wax lyrical about quality time, partly I think as a salve for all those fathers – or parents – who were out the door in the morning before their children were awake and back after bedtime at night. I don't blame those parents for trying to comfort themselves with such aphorisms – and better quality time than no time, after all – but caring for children is as much about quantity time, being there in all moods in all seasons, and if being a freelance writer gave me nothing else, it at least gave me the huge privilege of playing a full part in Caitlin's life from very early on.

The nature of my employment also allowed me lots of time to develop a full appreciation of the fact that theatre royalties alone were not going to cut the mustard. In '83, I developed my first case of what I came in time to recognise as Freelancer's Frenzy, a panic that the work and money are going to disappear – or have already disappeared – and that your present project, if you have one, is your last.

Freelancer's Frenzy is a kind of St Vitus' dance which can hook you up with some very strange partners. While still living out west, I got involved with a buccaneering German naval hero from the early 20th century and a wildly eccentric theatre director. Jonathan Hardy had been approached by a small group of Auckland businessmen, one of whom was in advertising, to adapt the two

189

Lowell Thomas books, *The Sea Devil* and *The Sea Devil's Fo'c'sle*, about the hearty German mariner, Felix von Luckner. Jonathan invited me along to a meeting with the businessmen – I wasn't sure in exactly what capacity, but I assumed I was to be co-writer.

Jonathan at that stage was wonderfully mad. He was also Artistic Director of the Mercury Theatre. I came into his office there one morning to find him standing on his desk, swinging a samurai sword and screaming, 'Where is he? I'll kill the cunt!' The cunt in question turned out to be Mervyn Thompson, who'd given the current Mercury production a bad review. Mervyn, of course, before he turned critic, had himself turned up at a Christchurch critic's house after a similarly bad review of one of his plays, pushed his way inside and started throwing the critic's collection of antique china at him.

Jonathan had had a quadruple bypass and had adopted various strategies to prevent further stress to his heart. Reichian therapy worked as some sort of emotional valve, while duende techniques relaxed him before performance. These efforts were somewhat undermined by his clandestine desire for fatty steaks, which he would hide from his partner David in a cupboard in his Glen Eden house, then, after David had departed for work, invite me round for a slap-up feed of grease.

Jonathan and I had got on well together when he directed the Mercury's '82 production of *Foreskin's Lament*. I thought it was a tribute to the cast that the play opened at all, because Jonathon was a great proselytiser and whenever I attended rehearsals, the cast were either lying on their backs screaming like banshees (your Reichian therapy) or wandering around with slack jaws making noises like brain-dead morons (your duende technique).

The businessmen were in awe of Jonathan's Oscar nomination for his co-writer's credit on the hit Aussie film *Breaker Morant*, and offered us a writing contract to adapt the Luckner story for film. I was still unsure about my role because Jonathan was hard to pin down. After we got the contract, and the actual work began, it became clear: I would do all the actual writing; Jonathon would give me half the money and as much encouragement as I needed.

The Sea Devil's adventures on the high seas led to ennui on terra firma for me: long hours sitting in Mary's car outside her small cottage at Laingholm (because there was no room inside to write and my car had no windows) as I dutifully attempted to reduce the exciting but interminable adventures of old Felix to a screenplay that could be shot for a budget of next to nothing.

It petered out, as many of those projects did, in a gradual realisation by both parties that they were wasting their money and I was wasting my time.

As I went on I became better at saying no to these sorts of projects, of steeling myself to believe that something else would come along. This was helped by slowly developing the necessary equanimity to make financial commitments and plans as if I was a regular person, and being able to ignore the fact that I could seldom see more than three months into the future. Occasionally, that would still grate.

In the mid-1980s I gave one of a series of lunch-time talks by 'artists' at the art gallery in Auckland. I chose to talk about the romantic myth of impoverished artists dying young and proclaimed that true Artists should assert their 'God-given right to poverty, disease and early death'. The mainly blue rinsers in the audience probably thought I was a quite peculiar young man and deserved exactly that. They probably also thought, had they been asked, that such a fate would have been preferable to the other obvious option – writing for television.

In '81, on the back of the success of *Foreskin's Lament*, television came calling in the person of Chris Hampson. I'd first seen Chris on the panel of luminaries at the Playwrights' Workshop in 1980, when he'd been the Commissioning Editor of Drama at Radio New Zealand and looked the part – long ringleted hair and rimless glasses saved by an aggressive jaw – but I wasn't at all attracted to the idea of radio drama and can't remember a thing he said. A year later, he'd become one of the first script editors at the TVNZ Drama Department. There were no independent production houses back then – all television drama was done in house and the house concerned was a concrete citadel called Avalon, out in the Hutt Valley. Hampo told me TVNZ wanted to do a series of one-off plays called *Loose Enz*, a mixture of hours and half-hours. I was offered one of the half-hour spots.

Some of the one-off plays were marvellous – I particularly remember *The Pumice Land* by Stephen G. Walker. Mine wasn't. *Free Enterprise* was a bit of a wasted opportunity, because instead of writing something original for the medium, I took refuge in what I knew and simply adapted *The Terminal Café*, a short melodrama I'd written for stage. *Free Enterprise* was set in a greasy spoon café at a bus terminal, where a dero puts one over the woman behind the counter with the aid of a mouse – the mouse, at least, wasn't in the stage version – and gets a free sandwich. At a stretch, you could say it was ahead of its time, being an attempt to satirise the market economy, still a couple years away from being let loose by the Labour government in 1984.

The mouse provided one of the key actions and I remember watching on the sound stage monitor at Avalon as they tried to get the creature to run the right way for the camera. I was suitably embarrassed. If a writer turned up today with a script where a mouse was involved in a major plot point, the only shooting that'd take place would be a .303 through the author's forehead. But I was a famous young playwright and in those days in television, the writer was still king, sort of, and I was indulged, even by Hampo.

By '83 I was readier for the challenge of television. That was the year I met Trevor Griffiths, the English playwright who'd initially found fame in the 1970s with plays like *Occupations*, *The Party* and *Comedians* but had latterly written searing television plays like *Country: A Tory Story*, *Oi for England!* and *Reds*, a movie starring Warren Beatty. Ironically, given his effect on my attitude to theatre, I'd met Trevor in Canberra, at the annual Australian Playwrights' Conference where I'd gone for a reading of *Tooth & Claw*.

Trevor was the visiting Eminent Playwright, and it was hoped he would repair the damage done the year before by the previous Eminent Playwright, a drunken and dissolute John Osborne, who'd apparently sobered up during one panel towards the end of his two-week visit and asked where the fuck he was. On being told he was in Australia, he pronounced himself absolutely appalled to find himself in the arsehole of the world and demanded to know how this had happened.

Trevor was a much nicer chap, a northern Englishman who was happy to tell me how he'd almost taken his name off *Reds* after Beatty 'reamed' his script. He'd finally walked out shortly after Beatty had fallen in love with Diane Keaton and come to the conclusion that *Reds* wasn't really about John Reed and the Russians after all, but was essentially a love story, with a major part for someone who looked just like Diane Keaton. Trevor had decided not to take his name off the script, because there were deeply embedded structures there that 'Beatty was too incompetent to fuck up'.

Trevor had a screening of his latest television play. That was in itself a sign of the times – that showing a piece of television was allowed at a Playwrights' Conference in 1983, because writing for television was still a worthy endeavour and alive with possibility. *Oi for England!*, about a gang of skinheads, had power, authenticity and immediacy – and a kind of street cred that was often missing from theatre. *Tooth & Claw* had been inspired by some of the same things as *Oi for England!*, but in comparison my play seemed abstract, wordy and sterile.

Over a couple of pints one evening, Trevor told me that, this workshop not withstanding, theatre was no longer where it was at. Theatre was the covered stand and real writers needed to get down on the terraces – television. That was a seminal moment for me. There was another waiting for me, after *Tooth & Claw* was read, late in the conference.

John Romeril was my dramaturg, which worried me. He'd written *The Floating World*, the best Australian play I'd ever read, so I admired him enormously in the abstract. But in the flesh he came across as one of those ascetic, severe socialists, who, in another time, might have been a soldier of the Inquisition. My opinion of him was coloured by an incident early in the conference, where I'd seen him in dramaturgical action and he'd frightened the shit out of me.

The principal function of a dramaturg at these workshops is to be the playwright's friend during rehearsals, as the director and actors inevitably zero in on the weaknesses of the play, and particularly during the evaluation sessions that follow every reading. This is a direct and potentially lethal exchange between the playwright and up to 100 or so people, mostly experienced theatre practitioners of one variety or another, who have attended the reading. Although it hadn't been true of my own session after the reading of *Foreskin's Lament*, where Ralph McAllister's initial comment had been quickly and eloquently countered by Professor Don McKenzie, I knew that quite often whoever stood up first and expressed a strong opinion inevitably coloured everything that followed. If the first strong opinion was negative, the whole session was likely to be toxic. In that event, the dramaturg was supposed to be up there at the playwright's elbow, to prevent his or her blood ending up on the floor.

Not Romeril. At the evaluation session where I'd seen him in action, Romeril had led the attack on the playwright. I think he saw something flabby and materialistic in both the play and the playwright and clearly detested both. An attack from that quarter was unexpected, savage and bloody. The playwright, whom I'd had a beer with earlier, a pleasant man who was an admired painter, had taken the next plane back to Sydney and, as far as I know, has never written since.

Romeril was much kinder to me during the evaluation session, perhaps because I was a guest. But afterwards, privately, he told me my dialogue was crap and needed to be taken to with a heavy blue pencil or, failing that, an axe. I had a day or two before I flew out and couldn't afford to change flights and, besides, I couldn't paint. So I tried a different approach. I asked him to put his blue pencil where his mouth was. To Romeril's credit, he took my script away for the night and next day handed it back to me.

There was blue pencil everywhere, but when I went through it, I started to see recurring patterns in what he was attacking – prolixity, qualifiers, unwitting or witless repetition, literary inversions that might look good on the page but dragged on stage, as well as all those old deadeners, the 'wells' and 'looks' and 'buts'. Romeril said the cumulative effect of all of these might in reality be only a couple of minutes over the course of the play, but the psychological effect on the audience was to make the play seem interminable. He told me I was trying to reproduce speech as it was spoken in reality and that was wrong. If you taped some random speech on the street, then reproduced it word for word on stage or screen, the audience would die of boredom. Every word in a script had to be *chosen* and *specific*, not random and generalised. Did I think great painters reproduced exactly what they were looking at? That was probably an unfortunate analogy, given what he'd done to the last painter he'd met.

'You're the writer,' Romeril said. 'You're the artist. Make your choices, show *your* reality and the meaning you take from it, don't just repeat, unmediated, some generalised reality, even in dialogue.'

I've never seen Romeril since. I hope I thanked him. More probably I said, 'I knew that.'

Which I did, but sometimes you need an outsider to confirm stuff that's swirling around in your head. My other plays, *Foreskin's Lament* and *Out in the Cold*, had been largely full of characters who spoke colloquially, which made the dialogue direct and colourful.

In *Tooth & Claw*, particularly with the central character, a lawyer, I'd got carried away with the idea of characters who were erudite and in trying to make their dialogue articulate and literate, I'd clogged the action between the characters. It's worth remembering that Henry James was a disaster on stage.

Romeril's advice was too late for *Tooth & Claw*, which had already premiered, but was at least of some benefit to the published version. But I began feeling that giving the writer too much respect might not always be helpful: I felt in retrospect that *Free Enterprise* and *Tooth & Claw* could have benefited from more rigorous appraisals of some elements of the scripts. Maybe, given some of the experiences I've subsequently endured, I should have been careful what I wished for, but Romeril's blue pencil did me a particular service, given what was ahead of me in the immediate future.

Trevor Griffiths had recommended a collection of essays on writing for television called *Ah Mischief!* to which he and other British playwrights, such as David Edgar, David Hare and Hugh Whitemore had contributed. It was full of aspiration for the possibilities of television as a dramatic medium (many of which make pretty sad reading nearly a quarter of a century later), balanced by cautionary tales. Among the latter was this warning from David Hare, which I might have done well to commit to memory: 'This strange botched-up medium is too good for a writer to resist, but too unreal for him to risk giving his entire loyalty to.'

twelve

Reality TV

While I was ready to be released from the confines of the theatrical covered stand and leap down into the mud, blood and beer of the television terraces, I can't pretend this fascination with television was all Griffiths-inspired altrusim. About the same time at another conference, Australia's foremost playwright, David Williamson (*Don's Party*, *Emerald City*, *Gallipoli*) was asked what he was most proud of. 'My tax problem,' he said. Of course it was tongue in cheek and probably calculated to be deliberately inflammatory to an audience of literati, but it impressed me enormously – as did his height. David and I could talk to each other in a crowded room without bending almost double to pick up what was being said at lower altitudes.

Towards the end of '83, I got a commission to write an episode of *Mortimer's Patch*, a country cop show. I was stoked. I'd seen some brilliant episodes, including one written by Maurice Gee, set among the spring blossoms of an orchard. I wanted to tell a story, called 'Nothing Changed', about a Maori Battalion veteran who was despondent about how little had altered for him and his people, despite the sacrifices he and his mates had made for this country. He was particularly soured with the younger generation in his own hapu, some of whom had become street kids.

Where was the cop show? Good question. In fact, I'd made the classic mistake of new writers to a series: I'd written the episode about the guest characters, because they were mine, and made the core cast peripheral because I didn't really know them. In those days, you could get away with that kind of thing.

'Nothing Changed' was a good experience for me in television, after the staginess of *Free Enterprise*. The story was inspired by a wananga for youth at risk I'd done at a marae on the shores of the Manukau while I was a consultant with the Neighbourhood Law Office in Grey Lynn, and I was able to use my contacts to enable us to shoot the episode there. It was also notable for the debut of Temuera Morrison in his first 'adult' role, as one of the street kids. He teased me for years about the huge dialogue demands I placed on him. He had two words and one of them was 'Honky'. I can't remember the other one, but I bet he still does.

But it was the *Roche* series which gave me a real introduction to the realties of television – the need for story (one commercial hour of television, now shrunk to about 43 minutes, usually devours more story than two hours of stage), the need for visual rather than verbal moments and resolutions, and the need for economy of dialogue, where Romeril's dicta helped.

In early '84, Chris Hampson and a producer called Peter Muxlow asked me and Dean Parker if we had any ideas for a drama series. Peter Muxlow had just produced a series written by Grant Morris and Keith Aberdein about a taxi firm in Wellington. *Inside Straight* was slick and professional and had been well received by the audience. Why was there no second series? Because Peter was a bit bored by it; he'd rather do something different. Those were the days!

Grant and Keith were understandably pissed off by this cavalier attitude but Dean and I weren't about to look a gift horse in the mouth and we came up with an idea for a series about two brothers running a trucking firm. *Roche* was mainly Dean's idea, inspired by the Bower brothers, who ran a trucking firm out of a depot in Dickens Street in Grey Lynn. They were colourful fellas, socialists running a highly competitive capitalist enterprise, who had been involved in protests and all kinds of scrapes with the law. We talked to them, went to truck stops for research purposes and put together some story ideas, which eventually became scripts. Along the way, Simon O'Connor came on board, and we agreed that we'd divide the nine episodes up equally.

The result was some reasonably good drama for the time – I particularly remember Dean's 'Fathers and Sons' episode – but there was bugger all continuity or commonality between one week and the next. *Roche* looked like nine one-off plays using the same characters, locations and props (the trucks). But I learned a lot about series drama.

After I delivered the first draft of my first episode, I was summoned to Avalon for notes from Tony Isaacs and Hampo. I was more than a bit apprehensive – Tony was a very experienced director and, by reputation, didn't suffer fools. As soon as I was seated in front of his desk, ready for my first serious notes in television, Tony picked up my script, weighed it in his hands and said it felt a bit heavy to him, which meant it was too long. Seemingly at random, he then ripped four or five pages out, screwed them up and threw them into the wastepaper basket, then looked with twinkling eyes at my ashen face and said, 'That feels better.' I was ready for a little more editorial rigour, but theatre was rife with stories about the shallow and mercenary nature of television, and in that instant I thought they must all be true. Hampo, sitting to one side, took pity on me, while Tony pissed himself, and explained that the photocopier had spewed out five repeats of the same page.

Roche meant staying overnight at Wellington, and Hampo asked me to stay at his place. He and his wife Ruth Jeffery were living in a huge old wooden villa up the back of Kilbirnie. The driveway was a dust road that wound through the pines for a couple of kilometres from its entrance near the zoo in Newtown. Hampo had an Alfa Sud and hurtled along the dust road like a bat out of hell. Once home, he'd cook something superb and open bottle after bottle of wine, extolling their virtues, then when we were good and drunk, take me on hair-raising rides up through the trackless pine forest in his little Suzuki Samurai four-wheel-drive.

I felt immediately at home. His driving was a lot like mine and even more like my older brother Richard's. When Hampo got a certain glint in his eye, and a certain set of his jaw, his boundless enthusiasm reminded me of a contemporary Mr Toad, with rimless glasses instead of monocle.

A year or two later, he was co-producing *Illustrious Energy* down at Clyde when I visited him on the shoot. He insisted on taking me over the bridge and down the old orchard track on the other side of the Clutha, which was in flood. We came to a bluff, where the track disappeared under the swirling waters of the biggest river by volume in the country. Mr Toad was all for driving on. We'd had a few drinks, but not that many. Hampo wouldn't be dissuaded until I'd stripped off my jeans and waded into the river, trying to follow the track. Ten metres in, I was up to my thighs and waving one foot into the current, looking back at mad Mr Toad with that glint still in his eye – Look, no track! – who was finally persuaded to turn back.

Hampo had enormous curiosity about almost everything, except sport. He had a literary background. He had started as an editor at Longman Paul, after a year teaching English; he had a BA Hons, after beginning a law degree. Years later at ScreenWorks, a judge saw him credited at the end of *Street Legal* and tracked him down to thank him for redirecting her life and inspiring her as a pupil all those years ago. I'd never met anyone quite like him. His curiosity and enthusiasm were infectious. For books, cars, clothes, theatre (he was a founding member of Circa Theatre, which had premiered *Foreskin's Lament* in Wellington, and acted and directed there), music (he played guitar), wine, food, technology and, always, jokes. A script editing meeting never started without a joke, or three. He couldn't remember the name of someone he met five minutes ago but he never ever forgot a joke.

The best jokes, the ones that demand you accept a fantastical, bizarre premise, then deliver a punch-line from left field, are finely wrought works of story-telling art, and we developed favourites which have stood the test of time, like the Irish zookeeper and the orang-utan, or the digger who walks into an outback pub with a crocodile around his neck, or the guy who babysat the gorilla, or the British explorer and the nine-foot Watusi. They were always unattributed, but wherever they came from, Hampo and Tom Scott seemed to own the customs clearance house for new jokes entering the country, and they'd race around their mates, trying to be the first to spread them.

Hampo would pick me up at Wellington airport when I came down for script meetings and drive me out to Avalon. He'd always have a new joke, and failing that, an old one. Often we'd be in tears, unable to see and have to pull over and stop. When Hampo wasn't telling jokes he'd burst into a verse of Denis Glover –

> I'm an Odd Fish
> A No-Hoper:
> Among Men a Snapper,
> Among Women
> A Groper.

– or James K. Baxter. Or he would declaim in doggerel, extempore, usually scatological, which he'd launch into on a wing and a prayer and almost always get home on a perfectly rhymed punch-line.

We had enormous fun on *Roche*, despite Peter Muxlow's eccentricities as a producer. For example, we all thought John Bach and Andy Anderson were perfect for the Roche brothers, Mick and Tony. Bach was ideal for Mick because he was older, physically imposing and had a bit of big brother authority about him. Andy would be ideal as the younger brother, an impish free spirit who was constantly testing the limits of his brother's patience. Peter listened to all this, then said he had a wonderful idea. We could almost see the light bulb above his head.

'Let's change them around!' exclaimed Peter. 'Let's have Andy play the older brother and John Bach the younger!'

We looked at him, stunned, as Peter developed his theory that because they were so perfect the other way round, we shouldn't do that but cast against type! We won that one, though I don't remember how.

There was no winning on the titles music. Peter boarded a lift at Avalon with Dean and me and said he'd just got the titles music for the show from the composer and it was fantastic. He just happened to have a tape cassette with him and he could play it for us right there in the lift as we travelled up. It was plonkingly soporific. We couldn't be polite. I told Peter it wasn't music, it was muzak. Dean said it was appropriate that we'd heard it in a lift. Peter was wounded to the quick.

Perhaps unsurprisingly, when TVNZ said they wanted to renew the show for a second series, Peter said he wasn't interested in producing it. The new Auckland-based Head of Drama, John McRae, offered Hampo and John Laing, who directed *Beyond Reasonable Doubt*, and these days is producing *Outrageous Fortune*, the job of joint producers of the second series – possibly as a means of loosening the Avalon shackles. John Laing and his wife Robyn, producer of *Mr Wrong* and *Ruby and Rata*, had a company called Meridian Productions with offices and studio space in Wellington city, and Hampo and John saw an opportunity to move the production from the dead hand of Avalon into the city, where most of the show was shot.

Meanwhile, negotiations were going on with John Bach and Andy Anderson, who were both being difficult about coming back. It was a case of what I learned to recognise later in *Street Legal* – Second Series-itis: if a show gets a second series, it is by definition a success and the actors involved will take credit for that success.

They may not have been stars before this vehicle came along, with the scripts and characters and production values to showcase their talents, but they are now, and will need to be paid a lot more than they were on the first series if they are to return. Andy wanted quite a lot more money. John didn't necessarily want as much as Andy, but if Andy got that much, he certainly wasn't prepared to take less, on principle.

Hampo and John had to explain that under the New Zealand system of funding, the budget for the second series is invariably the same or less than the budget for the first series. Having said that, Hampo and John had some sympathy for the actors' points of view. They thought they could find savings in the budget to resolve the actors' demands by shifting the show into town and by using a then innovative production technique called block shooting. In those days, filmed series drama like *Mortimer's Patch*, *Inside Straight* and *Roche* were all shot on an episode by episode basis, with a new director and a two- to three-week shoot for each episode. Block shooting, used everywhere now, saved costs by combining a number of episodes into one shooting block, so that, for instance, you could shoot out a location for all episodes in one visit, rather than go back several times, with attendant costs of time losses and location fees.

Only a few years earlier, Avalon had been the national production centre for television drama, but now head office had shifted to Auckland. Hampo and Laing were proffering these changes as a means of ensuring that Avalon, and Wellington, would be able to retain at least some hold on filmed television drama production. But the mandarins of Avalon were adamant that innovations like block shooting would come to Avalon over their dead bodies. They couldn't or wouldn't see that their corpses weren't the point – and within a couple of years, drama production had effectively shifted to Auckland and Avalon became a dead husk.

On one occasion at the Meridian loft, I walked in on Hampo and John dealing with one of the TVNZ production assistants, who was asking, 'What about my petty cash box? I don't think they'll let me bring it with me, will they?' Hampo and John were reassuring – a petty problem, surely. But the production assistant knew better. It became clear that some people actually liked working within the concrete fortress at Avalon. While we freelancers were welcome to come and go and provide the odd bit of energy and light relief, those stolid denizens regarded us as cowboys and, unlike the ad, none of them wanted to take their sinuses anywhere near Arizona.

Then, early in '85, we had a meeting with Andy Anderson and asked him where he saw his character going in the second series. 'Back to Oz,' said Andy. Eh? 'The punters have all gone home,' he elaborated, though the first series hadn't even gone to screen by then. Andy was reacting to cuts of the episodes he'd seen and as far as he was concerned the audience wouldn't be watching because he wasn't on screen enough. Right . . .

That evening at Armadillo, after quite a few drinks, I asked Dean and Simon if there was any other actor we'd like to write in, to replace Andy. 'Billy T. James,' said Dean, who had written the role of the Tainuia Kid for Billy in the movie *Came a Hot Friday*. So we invented a character called Winston McAtamney for Billy and hoped he might be interested.

We were still beavering away on the scripts for the second series, when the first went to air. The audience seemed appreciative, and most reviewers, in the main, liked it. Ratings were fairly primitive in those days, and there were only two channels, but the results were promising. We had good reason to hope that a second series could build on that groundswell so that *Roche* could become an iconic piece of New Zealand television.

But now we were finding it difficult to get commitment out of other actors, like Denise O'Connell, who played Mick and Tony's sister, Kate, and TVNZ, being the monopolist in the marketplace, wouldn't budge on the budget. Then John Bach got an offer from Oz for a series about a famous Melbourne bank robbery and said he had to take it, despite the contract he'd signed with us. Then Hampo, who might have had a touch of Freelancer's Frenzy himself and was up to his ears in other projects, got tired of fighting the Avalon Monster and resigned. Wayne Tourell, the director of the *Mortimer's Patch* episode 'Nothing Changed', came on as producer.

'Work on,' we writers were told by Wayne, 'Nothing's changed.'

I was naïve and worked on; Dean, the experienced cynic, saw the dead writing on the wall at Avalon and decided graffiti in Ponsonby was a better bet. Then Wayne Tourell was gone and, bugger me dead, there was Peter Muxlow in his place. Where would it end? Right there, as it happened, when the second series of *Roche* fell over. That was 1985.

Through '84 and '85 I'd also been working on a screenplay called 'The Bonus Gang' for Cinepro, Don Reynolds' production company, which had just finished a thriller called *Trial Run*, starring Annie Whittle. The ubiquitous Hampo was involved as script editor/co-producer. 'The Bonus Gang', based on my experiences working in the Rankleburn Forest, was an update of the Robin Hood story, where the gang hit targets in towns, then retreated to the fastness of the forest.

I enjoyed writing the screenplay and it was my first experience of working with – for – Don Reynolds. The Don was big, rumpled and mostly cheerful. He told appalling jokes with huge relish but, more importantly, he paid out when he said he would. However, the project stumbled at the Film Commission fence and 'The Bonus Gang' became a foundation file on the shelf which becomes the longest in most scriptwriters' offices – the one labelled 'Unproduced'.

In the meantime, I hadn't exactly abandoned theatre. In fact, I'd been sucked further in.

thirteen

Guru Voodoo

By 1984, the fruits of the 1982 Playwrights' Workshop were in production around the country – Renée's *Wednesday to Come*, Hilary Beaton's *Outside In*, Carolyn Burns' *Objection Overruled* and Seamus Quinn's *A Street Called Straight*. They were joined by established writers in other genres, like Maurice Shadbolt with *Chunuk Bair* and Vincent O'Sullivan with *Shuriken*, while Roger Hall was as fecund as ever. It was a golden age for New Zealand theatre and should have been a cause for enormous celebration, but, instead, there was bitterness and disillusionment as firefights exploded between playwrights and theatres right across the country. Even Roger Hall was in dispute with the Mercury over their production of *Multiple Choice*.

Part of the problem was that the theatres were accustomed to performing plays written by people who were overseas or dead; they were not used to having extant playwrights turn up at rehearsal to express opinions about matters like direction and casting. On the other hand, Roger aside, most of the playwrights weren't accustomed to the realities of production: the terrible choices and compromises that needed to be made, the way the play never looked and sounded exactly as it had in your head, and the feeling of exposure and fear of failure.

I remember Maurice Shadbolt seething in a wine bar on K Road just before the opening of *Chunuk Bair* at the Mercury. Maurice had been attending rehearsals up until the last week, when he'd been asked to stay away. He'd worked himself up into a lather about the lack of respect and the way they were 'fucking up' his play and wanted to pull the production, or injunct the Merc. I'd heard the other side of the story from Ian Mune, the director. Maurice had turned up at rehearsals every morning and taken nearly an hour of valuable rehearsal time delivering his notes directly to the actors – a no-no, but he was a famous novelist, so he was indulged. Ian said Maurice was utterly pedantic, telling one actor that the pause after line such and such was actually three dots, not two, and he should therefore hold the pause an instant longer. In the end, Maurice just kept drinking, did nothing and opening night went well, with Mune putting together a production that served the play brilliantly.

Many of the disputes, however, were substantial: plays being cut, appalling direction and casting over which the playwright had no consultation, and, on one occasion, a play being presented literally as a two-ring circus (it would have been three if they could have afforded the extra ring).

In response to these problematic playwrights who had opinions about how their plays should be staged and directed, certain artistic directors were advocating that henceforth new plays should be developed in house, that the only way forward was for playwrights to be nurtured within the bosom of professional theatre, so that new plays could be collaborations by theatre savvy people, rather than works by some playwright appearing 'out of the bush' with a play under his arm. No prizes for guessing who Elric Hooper thought was Exhibit A when it came to bushy appearances.

In April 1984, the New Zealand Writers' Guild hosted the international writers' guilds in Wellington. In a keynote speech, I told the international delegates that I didn't think it was enough any more to simply congratulate ourselves that professional theatre was surviving in New Zealand, at whatever cost. I drew attention to the huge gulf between the public stances of some theatres and their private practices, giving the example of Raymond Hawthorne (I didn't name him) who, in the same year that Theatre Corporate's theme was 'The Rights of the Individual', had refused his actors and production workers the right to march in support of a general strike, declaring 'theatre was above that sort of thing'. On another occasion, at a theatre where the production workers were striking to bring their minimum wage up to subsistence level, one of them came along to see the show and was refused a ticket by the outraged artistic director who screamed at him, 'You are the enemy – get out!' The show the production worker wanted to see – and buy a ticket for – was Dario Fo's *Can't Pay, Won't Pay*, which perfectly underlined the schism between the theatres' public or artistic stance and their private practices.

In my speech, I said that some of our artistic directors were guilty of too much incipient guruism. They were in a powerful position to push their employees to embrace whatever pet religious or psychological whim they were in thrall to at the time, from Gurdjieff to Subud. Our professional theatre, I said, often projected ethereal themes of individual dignity while crushing the dignity of their own workers, putting on socialist or liberal plays while their own internal structures were fascistic. Accordingly, I urged the Arts Council to keep funding playwrights to write plays, rather than funding theatres to 'develop' plays. And I urged local playwrights to stay in the bush and keep these theatres at arm's length, so they wouldn't be subjected to the mad whims and psychological brinksmanship of these would-be gurus.

Having publicly declared myself, I felt compelled to do what I could to help my fellow playwrights keep the gurus at bay. My direct action took shape in two initiatives, one of which has endured for the benefit of local playwrights, and the other of which ended up as the biggest home-made bomb in New Zealand theatrical history.

For me, the key to any improvement in the relationship between theatre and playwright was the commissioning and production contract, which was so outdated that it caused many of the problems and misunderstandings. I felt it was too vague, and loaded in favour of the producer, the theatre. I wanted a document that forced both parties to work through some of the difficult issues, so that at least playwrights and theatres were better informed about what was going to happen by the time the production contract was signed. Small matters like nominating the actual venue to be used (most theatres had a main theatre and a studio theatre and the difference in seating numbers – and therefore potential royalties – was huge), a guaranteed minimum running time (so that, as in one case, huge cuts didn't have to be made to the play to comply with fire regulations about ingress and egress), the playwright's right to attend rehearsal and airfares and per diems if he or she had to travel from out of town to do so. But the real advances, and sticking points, concerned the clauses that gave the playwright the right to be consulted over the theatre's choice of director and cast.

Tony Taylor, then artistic director at the Fortune in Dunedin, said that the new agreement was 'restrictive and not conducive to creative theatre'. Elric Hooper, artistic director at the Court in Christchurch, was more direct about the possibility of his theatre implementing the new agreement: 'Over my dead body,' he said.

Lovely man, Elric, but notorious for proclaiming a resolute stance on shifting sand. After advising me, in 1980, to change the name of *Foreskin's Lament*, he'd arrived late at the '82 Playwrights' Workshop and proclaimed publicly that the whole thing was 'an exercise in onanism'. Then he saw the plays and proceeded to buy a couple of them to premiere at the Court. If nothing else, you had to admire the man for his flexibility.

To some extent the disputes were a coming of age. Professional theatre in New Zealand had largely been established and nurtured by a group of people who had chosen to become cultural exiles. The Raymond Hawthornes and Elric Hoopers had fled the cultural desert of philistine New Zealand in the 1960s for England, where they'd had to develop RADA accents and reinvent themselves as Englishmen in order to develop their acting and directing crafts. This personal history of powerlessness and alienation probably wasn't the best training for the positions of power they now found themselves in. They had done the hard yards, they had taken the big risks and they had given birth to professional theatre in this country and now these Johnny-come-lately indigenous playwrights were trying to tell them what they could and couldn't do within their own fiefdoms.

I knew that if the new agreement was going to happen, I'd need some muscle behind me. The Writers' Guild had never been much involved in theatre and was keen to extend itself from television and film, so I got the green light for its support. The guild also called in entertainment lawyer Malcolm Black, formerly lead singer for The Netherworld Dancing Toys and these days a record company executive, and we launched into the negotiation process.

As a precursor to that negotiation, I believed that the Association of Community Theatres (ACT), which represented the various professional theatres throughout the country, had to be separated from Playmarket, which represented most of the playwrights. Both organisations had been run by the same people from the same premises in order to amortise costs, but also because the interests of professional theatres and playwrights had thus far always been congruent. Clearly, now that the battle lines had been drawn between theatre producers and writers, there was a manifest conflict of interest.

Ruth Harley, Drama Adviser at the Arts Council and my one-time lighting assistant on *Tooth & Claw*, threw her support behind us and that seemed to help everyone turn a corner, particularly Nonnita Rees, who had worked long and hard for both ACT and Playmarket.

It was a difficult time for many people like Nonnita, who'd done so much to nurture professional theatre in New Zealand, and then to get indigenous plays performed in those theatres. Finally, in the first half of the 1980s, it was happening but no one seemed to be very terribly grateful. Instead, she watched scrub fires between playwrights and theatres burst into flame around the country. As soon as one was put out, another would flare up. They were difficult to anticipate and control.

During this time, Nonnita and others organised a panel of playwrights to talk about the New Zealand theatrical renaissance at the town hall as part of Wellington's arts festival. John McGrath, the famous Scottish playwright, was invited and looked askance as, far from celebrating New Zealand theatre, the playwrights, including Roger Hall, Carolyn Burns, Renée and me, turned it into a total bitch session about the shortcomings of New Zealand theatrical administration. Nonnita, enraged, stormed out of the auditorium, and off down the street. I heard later that poor old Peter Hawes, novelist and writer of intelligent, whimsical plays like *Alf's General Theory of Relativity*, happened to be wandering down the other side of the street, heading to the next session, when he was spotted by Nonnita, who crossed the street, whacked him on the arm, yelled 'Fucking writers!', then carried on down the footpath, leaving Peter wondering what the hell he'd done.

Fortunately, Elric's prediction about the implementation of the new Theatre Production Agreement was just as accurate as his other predictions: last time I heard, that basic agreement was still being used and Elric hasn't yet fallen over.

My other plank against the influence of the gurus was a theatre co-operative called (because, ominously, we couldn't agree on another name) Working Title Theatre, which was begun by a group of us in Auckland who had become disenchanted with the Mercury and Theatre Corporate, during the course of these disputes. Working Title Theatre seemed to me to fit in with Trevor Griffiths' dictum. We were turning our backs on the established theatres up on the hill, the covered stands, and moving theatre down to the terraces.

Like my involvement in the new commissioning and production agreement, and despite my best intentions to be venal, this initiative was going to cost me, and many others, a huge amount of time and effort for little or no remuneration.

Working Title's objective was to produce new New Zealand plays, and we did. We either produced, co-produced or work-shopped's Renée's *Groundwork*, Rosie Scott's *Say Thank You to the Lady*, Stephanie Johnson's *Accidental Phantasies* and Wanjiku's *Black Women*. All of the above were members of the co-op, along with people like Roy Billing, Elizabeth McRae, Martyn Sanderson, Heather Lindsay, Paul Gittins, Andrea Kelland, Judy McIntosh, Aileen O'Sullivan, Donogh Rees, Norelle Scott, Andrew Sharpe, Danny Vendramini, Frank Whitten, Heather Joyce and even Sebastian Black, to begin with.

Working Title was time-consuming and exhausting. There were endless meetings and getting any kind of consensus was difficult. Our meetings were rife with this sort of exchange:

'We must decide on our attitude to Brecht and Artaud,' says Martyn.

'Who are they?' asks Renée.

I think that was when Sebastian, wise man, pulled out.

The feminists thought Heather Lindsay was a bit middle class, with her clothes and hair and make-up, but Heather sweet-talked someone at the United Building Society to sponsor us. Then Martyn Sanderson didn't want United's capitalist logo on our posters for *Black Women*, and the designer of *Groundwork*, John Verryt, supposedly pitching to United, freaked them by telling them Renée's play was a radical work about Maori sovereignty.

There were endless rounds of applications for funding and/ or sponsorship and, as we got closer to production, endless fights about how the percentages of the takings were to be divided up. Suddenly, we felt our co-op, begun altruistically by unpaid enthusiasts to get new New Zealand works on stage, was being regarded as an employer. Which we were, technically. The co-operative model asked actors to subsidise these new works by working for a percentage of the gate takings, after production costs were deducted. That often meant little or nothing for the actors, who worked their guts out for four weeks' rehearsal and two- or three-week run. Not to mention the rest of us, the unpaid producers, legal advisers, accountants, typists, scene painters, light riggers . . . I began to feel a sneaking admiration for the gurus.

It was a funny old time, as they say. The longed-for Labour government had finally unseated Muldoon in '84, and immediately unleashed the dogs of capitalism. Then, in '85, Mervyn Thompson, who'd long been an advocate for workers and women, was tied to a tree by six women, who then blindfolded him, beat him and sprayed 'rapist' on his car.

Proc took shelter in our house at John Street for three nights. He wouldn't go home to his flat because he was terrified the treepists would come back for him, as they'd promised. The change in him was dramatic: the confident socialist man of the theatre with the working class biceps I'd met five years earlier was gone, replaced by a wizened, cowed husk of nerves. He allowed Genevieve Westcott to persuade him to 'give his side of the story' on television. It was a mistake: they lit him like a criminal and he simply gave a face and a name to another piece of meat for the scandalmongers. Flyers plastered around the university accused him of being a rapist and some of the fems told me that whether or not he'd raped anyone, he'd certainly abused his position of power as a university drama lecturer over vulnerable women students.

Mervyn was a socialist who tried to portray the plight of workers and women through his work. He was also, undoubtedly, a flirt and would-be Romeo, and a powerful man in a profession which, for some unfathomable reason, certainly not the money or the dignity, attracted – and still does – more wannabes than were ever going to get a job. But it was hard to believe he had any real leverage with his students when everyone who took his course automatically passed by simply attending.

In the end, I couldn't know whether or not Proc was a rapist: at parties I'd been to, he'd always looked like a bit of a pathetic tryhard. What I did know is that I owed him for his constant support since 1980. I also believed, as a result of my tenure as literary fellow up at Auckland University, that there were worthier targets than Proc up there.

Proc's play, *Coaltown Blues*, was about to open at the Maidment Theatre, which was controlled by the university. When the Student Council tried to close it down, Dean Parker and I went up there on behalf of the Writers' Guild, with the backing of the entertainment unions, and met with a group of wet-behind-the-ears wankers who knew nothing of Mervyn Thompson or his work, but who clearly hated him sight unseen We told them if they blacked Proc's play, the unions would black the Maidment Theatre. They backed down and Proc's play went on, unlike The Depot in Wellington, which caved in and replaced it with a piece of politically correct agitprop written by Simon Wilson.

If the treepist wimmin were trying to replicate the effect of a rape, they succeeded. Proc, in my observation, never recovered his equilibrium, physical or mental, and died of cancer in 1992.

It was all getting very bloody messy. I'd worked my arse off unpaid to help get Renée's *Groundwork* up at the New Independent, and watched at opening night as the fems packed the theatre. I'd have bet more money than the play ever took in box office – the fems all said they absolutely loved it, but if word of mouth sells plays they were lying through their smiles, because no one came after opening night – that among that audience were the women who subsequently tortured Proc. Some of the women in our group, I heard, knew exactly who was responsible.

Other issues soured the Working Title experience. Some of our meetings were held in the garage at the back of the house at John Street, or even in our kitchen. Mary would bring cups of tea and be completely ignored by some of the women, who saw motherhood as some sort of collaboration with the enemy, until some years later some of them began having children themselves. Mary was working part time at the Auckland Medical Aid Centre (AMAC) Trust as a counsellor for women considering abortions, but for certain women in our group, nothing she did could possibly be of any moment or interest.

To offset all the money we were losing on our other productions and to try to get some cash in the kitty, Working Title put on *Foreskin's Lament* at His Majesty's Theatre in April 1986, directed by Danny Vendramini. Rather than just recycle what was now a period piece set in '76 I thought it would be worthwhile updating the play and incorporating some of the experience of '81. Most of what I did was fine-tuning, like shortening the lament, but I also made Clean, the villain, a Maori. This appeared to offend some critics, who seemed to have a proprietorial interest in the original text. Michael Neill, who'd written the foreword to the published version of *Foreskin's Lament* and at whose house I'd dined as literary flavour of the month, wrote a review for the ACT's newsletter. 'Unsatisfactorily revamped,' he decided, and also seemed piqued at its 'vast financial success'.

Vast? I suppose it was, in comparison with anything else Working Title put on. Roy Billing, playing Tupper, as he had at the premiere production at Theatre Corporate and again in '82 at the Mercury, devised a publicity campaign using his expertise from what used to be his day job – advertising and marketing – and garnered huge coverage, much of it free, from a minuscule spend. He galvanised the cast, all of whom had a share in the profits, to put themselves about. Tupper appeared on Radio Hauraki with Phil Gifford and John Kirwan; the whole cast packed down against the Auckland team and got free coverage on the TV news and mentions in the sports magazines; clips from rehearsals appeared on the arts programmes; the cast ran up and down Queen Street at lunchtime dressed in footy gear and handed out flyers; early on the morning of the Round the Bays Race they put posters on every power pole between the city and St Heliers. By opening night, we had less than a dollar left in the bank account we had set up with a loan from the Arts Council, but the cast who had worked so hard inside and outside rehearsals had the satisfaction of standing on the mezzanine by the dressing rooms at His Majesty's and looking down on queues that stretched from the box office out into Queen Street.

Two weeks of pretty full houses at His Majesty's certainly beat the hell out of the customary Working Title dividend: a few dollars and a free copy of the programme. I'm not sure why that success should have been such a problem for the likes of Michael Neill. We hadn't taken patrons away from the covered stands up the hill – both the Mercury and Theatre Corporate had successful productions at the same time.

Notwithstanding that success, it was becoming clear that anything Working Title did was by definition rough theatre because we had no regular funding, unlike the covered stands up on the hill, which were funded on an annual basis and could plan their year. Every Working Title production involved an intense, time-devouring round of ad hoc one-off applications and scrabbling for resources, not to mention actors, directors and crew who were willing to risk their livelihoods to subsidise our ideals for an indigenous theatre.

In '85, I started working on a new play, and in '86 I resolved to try to produce it with private investment. Bugger the Arts Council and the actors' subsidies, I thought: if theatre is truly sustainable, let's set it up on a business footing. It seemed a logical progression of what Working Title had been doing, but it imploded, hugely, and nearly finished my nascent writing career.

The inspiration for *Whitemen* grew indirectly out of the judicial challenge against the Rugby Union to stop the proposed '85 tour of New Zealand by the Springboks. Ted Thomas, later a judge of the High Court, Sian Elias, later Chief Justice, and others reckoned they could use the Rugby Union's own constitution to challenge the validity of the tour, and they needed someone as plaintiff who was a member of a rugby club and therefore had the necessary standing.

I knew Sian from my earlier involvement with the Neighbourhood Law Office in Grey Lynn. She was a leading light among a group of young lawyers who were committed to racial equality in the legal system. I was very peripheral, but people like Lowell Goddard and Rhys Harrison, both now High Court judges, got stuck in on various political and racial ca(u)ses, like the burning of a police bus at Moerewa, where they successfully argued for a change of venue for the trial, on the grounds that the defendants, all Maori, would not get a fair trial in Whangarei. They were preparing to argue innovative 'cultural' defences at the Auckland Supreme Court when the defendants undermined them somewhat by changing their pleas to guilty.

We lawyers did courses with groups like Accord in order to increase our understanding of how racism worked, and on one occasion Titewhai Harawira was invited along to speak to us. Titewhai knew a captive audience of white guilt when she saw one and harangued us mercilessly. We were all sitting there with heads bowed like penitent churchgoers while Titewhai gave us chapter and verse on our shortcomings. It was fascinating to see those very powerful and articulate young lawyers rendered mute with assumed guilt. After a while, I indicated I'd had enough. We wouldn't have taken such a barrage from anyone else, and probably shouldn't have taken it from Titewhai. I came away with the impression that she might have respected us more if we'd argued the point.

In '85, Sian rang me and asked me to be the plaintiff in this case they were considering against the NZRFU. I had to tell her that I wasn't a member of any rugby club and therefore had no standing, but I recommended my mate, barrister Paddy Finnigan, who still belonged to the University of Auckland club. Paddy had had an interesting political trajectory. In our arguments through the years, he had always been willing to give Muldoon the benefit of the doubt, but his actions in '81 precipitated a metamorphosis in Paddy and he found himself marching in the streets and occupying motorways. Paddy and Phil Recordon, now a District Court judge, became the plaintiffs in an action that successfully forced the Rugby Union to abandon the tour, and in that capacity they were far better value to the Ted Thomas-led legal team than I would have been.

At the celebration party in Paddy's chambers, I was struck by the passion for rugby exhibited by Ted Thomas, the hero of the hour, Phil Recordon and Paddy, who all seemed able to remember every second of every game they played. Maybe that's where the case was won and lost – the lawyers for the Rugby Union, Douglas White and Kit Toogood, seemed to have, ironically, no real background in the game.

However, the principal factor in the plaintiffs' success was the obfuscation, evasion, manipulation and stupidity of the NZRFU. Chairman Ces Blazey, while pretending to be neutral, clearly manipulated the council of the NZRFU for a predetermined result on the critical vote to accept the South African's invitation to tour, a result that would give maximum embarrassment to Lange's government. Ces had damned himself with a 'Summary of Position' memo which he circularised to every councillor before the vote. In this he dealt with every objection raised against the tour in a very superficial manner and gave the councillors clear hints on how to dismiss these objections in order to arrive at the 'right' decision.

Days later, in early August of '85, I began writing a play called *Ballboys*, set in the Rugby Union council chamber. There was a meeting of the councillors, 'the boys', a broadly drawn cross-section of male conservative Kiwis, under the chairmanship of one Cyril Embers, who were trying to decide whether to accept the invitation to tour South Africa. I enjoyed it immensely, writing scenes I'd almost nicked from Ces Blazey's memo, in which Cyril coached the boys on how to respond to the media – 'All together now, I abhor apartheid, *but* . . .' It was a farcical satire, or a satirical farce, and was, I thought, sharp and funny. It used many of the techniques I'd become more confident with from television – lots of jumps in location – and was a big move away from naturalism.

By the end of the year, *Ballboys* had been renamed *Whitemen*, and was expanding in several directions, acquiring a large cast and some challenging production demands, such as flying in an All Black angel – the ghost of All Blacks past – for the climax. It went through a workshop process, and my good friend Danny Vendramini agreed to direct it, despite misgivings about the earlier draft he'd seen. We workshopped it, then I put together a 'consortium' of investors – in reality some professional friends and acquaintances and, on a minor scale, Mary and me – and booked the cavernous His Majesty's Theatre.

There were many interesting lessons from *Whitemen*, some extremely painful. One was how things worked if you wanted to get private investment into theatre. It would have made sense to open the play in a small venue, reasonably quietly, and then transfer it to somewhere like His Majesty's if it took off. But it couldn't work like that for the Inland Revenue Department. To get the investors on board, we had to show the IRD that the production had the *potential* to make money, rather than being just a loss-making tax dodge, and to make the figures work for the IRD's potential profit, we needed a lot of seats. So, in a sense, to make the play look like a potential success for IRD, we had to put it on in a venue so huge that the production was almost guaranteed to fail.

On opening night in September '86, I found myself sitting alone up in the third tier of His Majesty's, watching my play die in front of an audience of several hundred (many of them 'paper', i.e. gratis tickets) so far below me I couldn't see them. The cast were magnificent. The production was ambitious and had enormous teething problems that were far from being resolved by opening night. It was one of the worst evenings of my life.

Probably deservedly, the reviews were vicious, but unnecessary, in the sense that they were kicking a carcass. By the third night we had 120 people in that cavern – a full house at Corporate – and we closed the play. Dean Parker brought a bottle of Johnnie Walker round to John Street, but I was so low I couldn't drink it. I'd never make an alcoholic in times of stress: I feel bad enough, without a hangover to contend with.

'There is some demon of perversity abroad in New Zealand theatre at the moment' thundered Michael Neill in the ACT magazine. 'First it persuaded Roger Hall that he was Chekov; now it seems to have tempted Greg McGee with the illusion that he is Dario Fo.' Beating one writer over the head with another is standard critical fare, so fair enough.

Neill went on:

'The trouble with *Whitemen* is there is virtually no plot: it's written as a series of interlinked revue sketches of intermittent hilarity; and Danny Vendramini's fatally even-paced and rather leaden direction only emphasises this weakness . . . Farce can accommodate a lot of bad jokes (it can even thrive on them) provided it fires them hard and fast enough to keep the audience more or less permanently winded; here there's so much breathing space that everyone has time to side-step. The result is that gags that aim at wicked tastelessness become either embarrassing or stupidly offensive, pandering to the racial, sexual and political prejudices they aim to subvert.

All good stuff, because even if he did dismember my play, Neill was giving cogent reasons for doing so by attempting to articulate what he thought I was trying to do with it, then measuring it against a template of its own kind and finding it lacking.

But then Neill revealed the academic naïf. 'Regrettably, the only lesson learnt from that profitable adventure [Working Title's production of *Foreskin*] appears to have been that marketing and money could sell the Auckland public anything. The product of such unthinking condescension now stands exposed.' And on and on he went about 'pre-production hype of raising $150,000 from private investors' and the difficulty of 'seeing where it has all gone . . . not surely into this under-workshopped and under-rehearsed production; nor, one hopes into Guy Richard's hopelessly cumbersome design.'

This impugning of my motives in putting the thing on at all, implying that I was driven by greed, I still find hard to forgive, written as it was by a man who has spent his working life sitting safely up at the university drawing an academic's stipend. The investors lost money they said, perhaps out of kindness, they didn't really need. Mary and I lost money we didn't have. At least the actors were paid.

If Neill had been a practical man of the theatre, he might have reinterpreted the signs he so clearly saw: the play was indeed 'under-rehearsed'. The money we raised was patently not enough. *Whitemen* was a hugely challenging undertaking – huge cast, many sets, complex technical demands like flying an actor in for the climax – and despite the best efforts of everyone involved, the enterprise was obviously underfunded. It needed another two weeks' rehearsal, for instance, and it needed more time in the theatre for tech rehearsal, but when *every* cost is a one-off budget item – from rehearsal space to stationery – rather than being amortised across a year's productions, as for the subsidised theatres up the hill, there was simply not enough money to do the production justice, whatever that 'justice' might have been.

A couple of days before *Whitemen* opened, I saw Danny being interviewed on television saying that, thank goodness, farce was easy. I wondered at the time whether he was being ironically disingenuous, or trying to project bravado in the face of imminent catastrophe, or simply had no idea that the production was so lacking in pace.

Whitemen was, and probably still is, the biggest home-made bomb in New Zealand's short theatrical history. It was, like a lot of the stuff Working Title put on, overtly political, a response to overtly political times. Perhaps *Whitemen* was too much like

Renée's *Groundwork*, which I'd felt at the time was more agitprop than drama, though *Whitemen* had a hell of a lot more humour and, notwithstanding Michael Neill, narrative drive. In any event, its demise was so painful that I've always felt too ashamed to open the script since, until I had to write about it here.

Reading *Whitemen* again has been an interesting exercise. Characters like Cyril Embers and Fergus Boy and Mrs Scrabble and Jeremy Slate and Ack Ack Slement still raise a smile and the energy and vivacity and sheer outrageousness of the thing still pleases me. Writers, much like the critics who routinely use this aphorism, are notoriously poor judges of their own work, but even with that codicil I think the sharpness of the dialogue and the sheer variety of voices was a step up from anything I'd done before. I even began thinking, ironically, that had it been produced by the gurus up the hill, an ensemble theatre like Corporate for instance, with all their resources and an intimate auditorium, it might have been a 'success'.

Instead, the gurus must have been laughing, as *Whitemen* imploded. I should have renamed it *The Gurus' Revenge*. Certainly, some of the speeches I wrote, like this one by Slate, the cynical English journalist and apartheid apologist, seem to prefigure a major disappointment:

> They live at the end of the world, this strange transplanted
> species of Anglo-Saxon, wanting desperately to belong,
> yearning to feel at home in this alien sub-tropical wilderness,
> yet emotionally attached to an Anglo-Saxon culture which
> is light years away and receding. No Venetian contemplates
> his sinking city with more gloom than pervades this place,

this smidgeon of paradise, this God's own. Perhaps its
people know something.

Every writer and director and actor – every creative person probably – has done work which mysteriously disappears from his or
her curriculum vitae. I've noticed that other people have from time
to time decided, with no help from me, that *Whitemen* shouldn't be
part of mine. After rereading it, I've come away feeling that, whatever the magnitude and variety of its faults, it was an adventurous
and courageous failure and deserves an honourable place on my
CV. I much prefer it to, say, *Tooth & Claw*, and a lot of my other
writing, which may or may not be saying much.

However, that's a very recent ex post facto rationalisation: at
the time, both Danny Vendramini and I were very publicly held
accountable and had to deal with the fallout. When I tell aspiring
writers that being a writer is not like being a plumber or an
accountant or a businessman, that they should make it a private
hobby unless they're prepared for reviews so excoriating they
won't want to leave the house for a week, I'm thinking mainly, but
not exclusively, of the response to *Whitemen*. There's some comfort
in not being alone. In 2007, after the All Blacks' ignominious failure
at the Rugby World Cup, Jim Hopkins wrote in his *New Zealand
Herald* column that 'Public failure is a death of sorts . . . Anyone
who's ever experienced the horror of publicly failing to live up
to their own expectations – and those of others – will tell you
there is no mortification more acute or unbearable.' Joe Eszterhas,
in his sometimes hateful, sometimes stunning autobiography
Hollywood Animal, talks about developing the film *F.I.S.T* with
director Norman Jewison. Eszterhas found Jewison to be wise

and funny and very ethical in his dealings. Over the years as the development became a script and then a movie, Joe and Norman became friends. When *F.I.S.T.* tanked, a critical and commercial failure, they never spoke again. Not because either blamed the other or liked each other any the less, but because the failure sat between them thereafter like some icy, accusing ghost.

Danny found it hard to overcome the mauling and resurrect himself here professionally, and shifted back to Australia with his partner, Rosie Scott, and their children. Rosie has become a well-known novelist – *Glory Days, Nights with Grace, Movie Dreams* – and they adapted Rosie's play, *Say Thank You to the Lady*, which Working Title had debuted, into a movie called *Redheads*. Danny eventually gave his movie dreams away and has reinvented himself as a theoretical biologist, taking the core of Darwinian biology and adding some extraordinary new ideas about the genetic transmission of emotions and the origins of instincts. Clearly, *Whitemen* simply wasn't a big enough challenge.

Even though it was not a Working Title production, *Whitemen* had evolved from that endeavour and for me it confirmed utterly, if confirmation were needed, the futility of that enterprise. Tired and dispirited, I was happy enough to abandon the theatrical field to the gurus, who found it hard going too: within a few short years both Theatre Corporate and then the Mercury fell into debt and lack of interest and were gone.

My more immediate concern was entirely selfish: with the canning of the second series of *Roche* and the bombing of *Whitemen*, the only thing I could say with any certainty was that, after taking off solo as a freelancer four years earlier, my writing stocks had gone into free-fall. Fortunately, before the opening night at His

Majesty's, which effectively doubled as closing night, I'd signed a contract that led to perhaps the most controversial piece of television ever made in New Zealand.

fourteen

Dancing on the Coffins of the Dead

One evening in '85 after a Writers' Guild Committee meeting, Ken Catran told me I was about to be commissioned by TVNZ to adapt Peter Mahon's book, *Verdict on Erebus*. When I asked Ken how he knew, he was noncommittal, but I could guess.

Ken boasted that he'd never paid for typing paper in his life. Rumour had it that he had a key to the TVNZ Drama Department in Centrecourt, Queen Street. Because it was a government bureaucracy, no one worked weekends, leaving Ken free to work his way through the empty building, picking up a supply of Xerox paper and any intelligence he could glean.

I had my doubts as to whether his heads up about Mahon's book was the good oil, but Ken was so pissed off when he told me, that I thought there must be some substance to it. He had a right to be pissed off, I suppose. He was the front-runner for the job: he'd just written *Hanlon*, a successful series about the eponymous Dunedin QC who been involved in several celebrity trials in the late 1800s and early 1900s.

In those days, TVNZ writers' contracts had generous residuals, so that when *Hanlon* sold to PBS in the United States, Ken was farting through silk. Unfortunately, he made the mistake of skiting to a journalist about how much money he'd made that year – an unheard of six-figure sum. I can understand the urge, after so many years of being so poor, but among the readership must have been a mandarin from the Inland Revenue Department. Shortly after, Ken had to sell his house. He wrote the first six episodes of *Shortland Street*, including its most famous line, 'You're not in Guatemala now, Doctor Ropata' (for which he's had zero recognition), then, after understandably having had a gutsful of television, has since gone on to become one of New Zealand's most successful writers of fiction for children and young adults.

The veracity of Ken's intelligence was proven some weeks later, when John McRae, head of drama at TVNZ, brought me into his Centrecourt office to confirm that he wanted me to adapt *Verdict on Erebus* into a four-hour mini-series. John's rationale for using me was that, compelling as he'd found Mahon's book, he thought it might need to be dramatically interpreted by someone with a legal background. I was to take the book away, read it and report back.

When I did so, I told John that I wasn't sure there was a drama series in the book. *Verdict on Erebus* described Mahon's findings about why the DC-10 flew into Mount Erebus in November 1979. It was well written and compelling, but very technical.

John suggested that I sit down with the putative producer, Caterina de Nave, and script editor, Christina Milligan, and watch *The Dismissal*, the Aussie mini-series about Gough Whitlam's downfall. I think he meant it to be a kind of bonding session, but it didn't go well. After watching the tape, the three of us had a bite of lunch, during which Caterina announced that John McRae had told her something shocking Peter Mahon had said to him when they were discussing the television rights. When I asked her what it was, Caterina said she wouldn't tell me because it might 'colour my view of Mahon's character'.

I told her I thought it extraordinary that she would keep any-thing from me if we were to be working closely together. As the conversation developed she asked whether we should read the allegedly defamatory bits cut out of Mahon's book before publication. Caterina thought we shouldn't. I also found that alarming, given her willingness in an earlier conversation to look at top-level machinations and the like. She more or less indicated that we should stick to the book. I argued that we should try to get the whole story and only then would we know what could be left out. I told her I wasn't prepared to approach the project on a piecemeal basis; I found that suggestion perverse.

Christina backed me up and Caterina appeared to concede, somewhat. The exchange set alarm bells ringing for me. I felt that if I couldn't trust my producer to disclose everything to me, we were very soon going to find ourselves up shit creek. I got the feeling that Caterina was already feeling some pressure, or was anticipating it.

Perhaps as a response to that exchange, John recommended that I meet Peter Mahon and talk about it with him. So Caterina, Christina and I went round to Peter and Margarita's house in Brighton Road, Parnell and had a preliminary talk with him.

I was stunned by how emaciated Mahon was. The figure I'd seen a few short years before in the early 1980s, when he was Royal

Commissioner of the Erebus inquiry and all over the television news, was tall and athletic when seen striding in and out of the hearings, and, in close-up, had the penetrating eyes and saturnine jowls of an elegant bloodhound. But he'd since suffered a series of afflictions which Margarita laid at the door of stress over what had happened since the inquiry. Mahon had been weakened by influenza, had developed a viral heart condition and was fighting a cancer in his mouth. He was shrunken, his voice reduced to almost a whisper, and clearly not long for this earth. He spoke a little about what had happened to him since the inquiry, about Muldoon's rejection of his report and about his subsequent fight with the New Zealand government and judiciary. By the time I left his house, I knew what the series should be about.

I told John McRae that Mahon's quest and ultimate tragedy was the stuff of drama; that I wanted to go beyond the covers of the book and tell the larger story of how a Judge was commissioned by the government to find the truth – and what happened to him when the truth he found was unpalatable to that government.

John backed me, and so did Caterina, who now made all the right noises about how excited she was by the project and how much she looked forward to working with me. I think the initial blip was simply her trying to maintain the usual producer/writer power dynamic – knowledge is power, keep stuff back – and that she'd subsequently realised that on this project it was the wrong model. Every bit of information had to be sifted through and commanded by at least one intelligence, which had to include the writer's.

I told her, given the greater ambit of the project, that I wanted to call the series *Erebus, The Aftermath*. Caterina wasn't impressed; she said it would do as a working title and we'd think of something better before the series went to air. After the series went to air as *Erebus, The Aftermath*, Caterina remarked to me what a brilliant title she'd dreamt up.

The broadening of the story made the project a hell of a lot larger. *Verdict on Erebus* did not deal with Muldoon's rejection of the findings of the royal commission, nor did it deal with Air New Zealand's subsequent appeal to the Court of Appeal, nor Mahon's final appeal to the Privy Council. And although I had the confidence of youth, I must have had some idea of what I was in for because I made three critical demands of TVNZ.

Before I signed the commissioning contract, I insisted on reversing the usual writers' warranties, where the writer gives an assurance that none of the material is defamatory. I made the case that TVNZ, not me, would be supplying, via Peter Mahon's book or via original research, all the material the mini-series would be relying on and had the ultimate call on what went to screen. I was very worried that most of the characters in this drama were still alive and that some of them were highly litigious. I wanted to be indemnified against any defamation action: I was in no position to put my new family's meagre assets at risk.

Second, I insisted that the project have an independent legal adviser. The disquieting exchange with Caterina was still fresh in my mind and, unlike her, I thought if we were going to get nobbled, it would come from within TVNZ, not from outside. I knew that if we relied on the TVNZ in-house lawyers to vet the scripts, nothing would get through those cover-your-arse corporates, because they were paid to minimise risk. This was critical, because we ended up with Gary Harrison as our legal adviser. Gary had been Counsel

Assisting the Commission at the inquiry and brought with him a profound background knowledge of the whole matter – and a hell of a lot of courage, when it came to okaying the kinds of things we needed to be able to say.

The other addition to the team was also critical. Caterina and I had agreed that, given the larger story we now wanted to tell, we needed to generate a lot of our own research and interview as many of the players as possible, rather than just rely on the book or the evidence from the inquiry. We needed to know more about the people involved and find out what had happened to them since. I didn't see how I could do that sort of research and plough through the existing material – the book, 3000 pages of evidence and a lot of technical stuff on flying a DC-10 and whiteout. The answer, I thought, was a full-time researcher, who turned out to be the very capable Di Musgrave.

Finally, I asked for security for me and my family when the series went to air. The 1979 accident, when an Air New Zealand DC-10 collided with Mount Erebus in Antarctica, had killed 257 people, almost all of them New Zealanders. In a society so small that six degrees of separation are reduced to two or at most three, almost every New Zealander had some connection to someone who died that day. Since then, the Report of the Air Accident Inspector, Ron Chippendale, the Royal Commission of Inquiry, Prime Minister Muldoon's public rejection of the commission's finding, and the subsequent decisions of the Court of Appeal and Privy Council, had kept the ripples of concern and consternation fanning out through our very small pond, and ensured that many New Zealanders held very strong opinions. The whole business had also spawned its fair share of obsessives and nutters.

Even though I was desperate for a job, I was half expecting and hoping that TVNZ would baulk at my contractual demands, but they gave me everything I wanted and I had no option but to dive in, with John Keir's words ringing in my ears. Keir had produced a documentary about the Erebus inquiry and told me when I met him in the corridors of TVNZ that I'd 'never make a drama out of that'.

We did. It nearly wrecked me. I had the book and thousands of pages of evidence to edit down to four commercial hours, which were effectively two, because there was a lot of story to be told before and after the inquiry, which took up the central two hours. There were the Court of Appeal and Privy Council decisions to wade through and make sense of, as well as all the original research material we were generating. When I say 'we' I mean Di Musgrave, who interviewed almost all the major players. She spent hours with Morrie Davis, the CEO of Air New Zealand at the time of the tragedy, and spoke to many of the operational, briefing and navigation people within Air New Zealand. The only major ones who wouldn't speak to us were Chief Pilot Ian Gemmell and the Chief Navigator, Brian Hewitt. This last was understandable: along with the pilot, Jim Collins, Hewitt had been made the scapegoat, and had suffered enough.

The only interviews I did were those with Peter Mahon, because I'd made the initial contact and we seemed to get along. He spoke a little Italian and loved Dante. One of his quotes from *L'Inferno* was apposite to his experience of Erebus and has stayed with me:

> Where the instrument of thinking mind
> Is joined to strength and malice

Man's defence cannot avail

To meet those powers combined.

I did wonder how I'd feel if, at the end of all the research, I thought he'd been wrong. I like to think, despite developing a rapport with Peter and Margarita, I would have said he was mistaken if that was what I'd come to believe.

For some months I plodded on through the evidence, head down, arse up, not knowing enough to venture an opinion. This was before computers and word processors were common, and I ended up literally cutting and pasting, then dictating the first pass onto tape, which I would deliver round to Eve in Norfolk Street, so that she, sworn to silence, could type up something that looked coherent.

The truth began poking like the sun between the endless dark clouds of evidence. Paul Davison's grilling of Brian Hewitt was dramatic and proved something was seriously amiss at Air New Zealand:

> Davison: That is error or omission Number 10. Can you think of any other errors or omissions we should add to the list before going any further?
>
> Hewitt: No, I can't.
>
> Davison: . . . It's a woeful story, isn't it?
>
> Hewitt: It is not a good story.

Davison's bravura was reinforced by David Baragwanath, the unsung hero of the inquiry, who determinedly and inexorably

242

exposed the structure of a severely dysfunctional airline.

That corporate dysfunction stretched credulity when the airline's executive and briefing officers began giving evidence about whether they were aware that previous sightseeing flights had descended below 6000 feet, which the company said was the minimum safe altitude down in the Antarctic. These witnesses denied any knowledge of previous flights descending below that altitude, despite being shown prominent reports and photographs in newspapers publicising flights as low as 800 feet. Air New Zealand's own Director of Flight Operations had been a passenger on one such trip. The low altitudes had even been publicised in the airline's own newsletter. Yet Air New Zealand continued to deny any knowledge of such flights and insisted that Collins had broken this inviolable rule on the fatal flight. On one occasion, Mahon had an almost farcical exchange with one of the briefing officers, about the meaning of a phrase from the airline's own newsletter:

> Mahon: So in your view then, the phrase – 'As the DC-10 cruised at 2000 feet past Mount Erebus' – properly translated means – 'As the DC-10 cruised at 16,000 feet over Mount Erebus'?
>
> Anthony Lawson: I would have to assume that, sir.

After reading the evidence of the airline's executive and briefing officers, I told Mahon that it was clear to me that a) the witnesses were lying, b) they were lying in concert and c) to achieve that, they must have put their heads together before taking the stand. I think Mahon was relieved. He'd been watching my reported progress through the evidence with a wary eye, half believing, I think, that I would be overwhelmed or lose concentration.

I was sitting across the table from him at Brighton Road when he said, in his raspy, weakening voice, 'The orchestrator was . . .' and I didn't hear the name he articulated. I can't miss this, I thought, the orchestrator of the notorious litany of lies, just because I fear being rude or tiring the old man out, so I asked him if he would mind repeating it. 'The orchestrator,' said Peter Mahon, quite clearly this time, 'was Des Dalgety.'

Des Dalgety was a director on the board of Air New Zealand, and was also personal attorney to Robert Muldoon, on whose behalf he had fought various defamation battles. Muldoon was Minister of Finance, as well as Prime Minister, and was therefore Air New Zealand's shareholder, on behalf of the nation. Muldoon took huge pride in the airline, as if his shareholding were personal. He kept model planes in his Beehive office and saw Air New Zealand not just as the nation's window to the world but also as an international high-tech advertising banner. As shareholder, Muldoon would have been rightly concerned about insurance liability and about the deleterious effect on international perception and internal morale if the airline were found culpable for an accident that had claimed so many lives. A directive on strategy from Muldoon through Des Dalgety to Air New Zealand made a lot of sense, as did a reverse flow of technical information from somewhere in the airline's operational command about the tactics necessary to execute that directive.

The more I saw of Di's interviews with Morrie Davis, the less I thought he was a party to the decisions to obfuscate and confuse, to modify and manipulate, and find scapegoats who would clear the airline of culpability. I began to believe that Morrie was nothing more than a reliable mouthpiece for those who stood behind him, that he didn't actually know enough about the operations side of the airline to run such a sophisticated technical defence. I came to feel that Des Dalgety's point of contact into and out of Air New Zealand had to be someone or several people with detailed operational knowledge. I also believed that this subterranean flow of strategy and means of execution had probably started down on the ice, shortly after the recovery of the bodies and personal items of the aircrew.

Morrie Davis, like Muldoon and Dalgety, was of that tough-minded generation of men whose personalities were shaped by the Depression of the 1930s and the Second World War. They had the fierce pride of patriots, and regarded themselves as men who could do the right thing under pressure – and the right thing to do here was to circle the wagons around the national airline. If a few individuals suffered as a result, that was an acceptable sacrifice for the greater good.

As I plunged further into the research, the list of victims grew. There were the 257 people who died in the crash and their families and friends. The families of Captain Jim Collins and First Officer Gregory Cassin went through a special type of hell, as the Civil Aviation Authority (CAA) of the Ministry of Transport, in the person of Ron Chippendale, decided that they were pretty much entirely to blame. Muldoon made sure that Chippendale's report was published before the commission of inquiry began, making Mahon's chances of an alternative finding even more difficult.

Chippendale was one of the people I began to call 'the absolutists'. We met and interviewed a lot of them: they had a one-cause theory, to which they held hard, despite reams of muddying evidence. Having worked through it all myself, I understood the temptation to scream 'Enough!' and cling to something that seemed to make sense – as long as you then resolutely barred the door to any other truth that started to seep in under it.

Chippendale clung to pilot error, through hell and high water. Former senior Air New Zealand pilot Gordon Vette told me that Chippendale's logic was that if a Cessna is flying along and, for reasons of structural weakness or lack of maintenance, its tail falls off, but if, after the tail falls off and before the plane hits the ground, there's some procedure the pilot might have done but failed to do that might conceivably have prevented the crash, then the cause is pilot error.

It was the perfect example of the limitations of what Civil Aviation were asked to do – find the last action or omission that made the crash inevitable. And according to Ron's brief, that last thing was Collins' descent, while uncertain of his position, below the minimum safe altitude of 16,000 feet prescribed by CAA and Air New Zealand. Nothing else that Air New Zealand's navigation or briefing sections did before that had any bearing on the cause of the accident.

There were many other 'absolutists', including, as Mahon pointed out in his book, the Flat Earth Society. I got to hear from or about most of them.

Then there was someone like Maria Collins, the pilot's wife, who had more reason than most to hold to an absolutist line that blamed the airline and exonerated her husband. By the time we talked to her, she had had the benefit of seeing and hearing the damning evidence at the inquiry about the manifold and serious balls-ups by the operations, navigation and briefing sections of the airline. Yet though she told me, as others confirmed, that her husband Jim had been meticulous to the nth degree, she said that didn't mean he was incapable of making a mistake. He was human and she could have accepted that he might have contributed to the accident in some way. But it made her sick to her heart to watch Civil Aviation's attempts, seized on by the government and by the airline, to make her dead husband the sole scapegoat.

The other thing that particularly struck me was how many airline pilots were prepared to accept pilot error. Gordon Vette was very unusual. Most were like a Concorde pilot who gave evidence for Air New Zealand and was only too ready to put the blame on his colleague.

Vette told me that it made psychological sense that pilots wanted to believe that crashes resulted from other pilots making a mistake. It meant that if they didn't make mistakes, they were safe. If they could control their own actions, they could control the consequences. If the crash resulted from systemic mistakes within the airline, which then impacted on the flight plans and systems they relied on, these were matters beyond their control: things too dreadful to contemplate when you were sitting at the controls of an aircraft about to defy the laws of gravity, with 200 to 300 souls entrusted to you. Given the Concorde's later problems, maybe this pilot's fears were better founded than he knew.

There were many other victims as the aftermath grew. Gordon Vette lost his job at Air New Zealand as he fought a lonely battle to bring the dangers of whiteout into the arena. There was Hewitt, Air New Zealand's Chief Navigator, an abject figure who was thrown by the airline to the Paul Davison wolf at the inquiry.

Then there was Lloyd Brown QC, Mahon's close friend, who had been appointed senior counsel for the airline. Their long lunches with the de facto Danish consul were legendary. Mahon told me that he believed the government appointed him to be commissioner because it thought Brown could exploit their close relationship. Instead, it broke that relationship, utterly. Mahon was prepared to concede that at the beginning of his tenure, Brown may have taken at face value the material his client was serving up to him. But as the commission of inquiry developed, Mahon began hearing evidence that tested his credulity. More than that, he began to believe that the airline witnesses were lying in concert, and at that point he couldn't help but believe his old friend must be involved in briefing these witnesses to take the stand and lie.

At one point after the inquiry was over but before the Court of Appeal hearing, Mahon tried to put that bitterness behind him and resurrect their relationship, but was told by Brown that he didn't consider 'being seen with you in public would be consistent with . . . representing Air New Zealand's best interests . . .' Mahon wrote a short note back to Brown pointing out that in his actions as Royal Commissioner he'd been representing the interests of those 257 people who'd lost their lives on Mount Erebus. There was no further contact and Mahon never forgave Lloyd Brown. Neither did Margarita. Brown later wrote to her when Mahon was at death's door, asking Mahon to forgive him for whatever transgressions he thought he had committed. Mahon, by now almost completely isolated from all his former colleagues, still could not forgive Brown. A few years after Mahon's death, Lloyd Brown's car left the road to Piha, on a corner he was very familiar with, and he died in the crash.

Brown was not alone in his rejection of Mahon. Margarita told me that all but two of Peter's brethren from the High Court had disappeared into the woodwork of the bench when Muldoon attacked him. However, omitting to support Mahon when he most needed it was one thing; the actions of the Court of Appeal were quite another.

Air New Zealand appealed to the Court of Appeal against Mahon's findings, maintaining that their witnesses were denied natural justice in that Mahon had never warned them that he thought they were lying. (In that context, it's worth rereading the exchange quoted earlier between Mahon and Lawson, one of many where the Air New Zealand witnesses must have had a sneaking suspicion their credibility was in question.) The Court of Appeal agreed with Air New Zealand, finding that Mahon had reached his conclusions in breach of the principles of natural justice in that before describing Air New Zealand witnesses as being involved in a 'predetermined plan of deception' or 'an orchestrated litany of lies' he should have told them he was going to make those findings and asked them for their response before doing so. But, as Auckland University legal academic Stuart Macfarlane pointed out in his book, *The Erebus Papers* (a must-read for anyone who wants to be seriously informed about any of this), Mahon was in a difficult position: if he'd gone further than he did and challenged the witnesses, he might well have been castigated for bias, particularly given the attitude of certain members of that Court of Appeal.

The minority decision of the Court of Appeal by Sir Owen Woodhouse and Sir Duncan McMullen went further and was about as scathing of Mahon as legal decorum allows. I'd certainly never read a decision like it, where an appellate court, without rehearing the evidence, has said that the judge who did hear the evidence, who had sat there watching and listening to the witnesses day after day, had no grounds for findings on the credibility of the witnesses who appeared in front of him. 'It was a public announcement,' said Mahon to the *New Zealand Listener*, 'that I was unable to determine whether what I was told could be regarded as the truth.' To Mahon, that minority decision seemed personal and vicious and he was wounded to the quick.

I'd been a great admirer of Woodhouse, the architect of our Accident Compensation system. Whatever the faults of the ACC in operation, the wisdom, compassion and foresight of the Woodhouse Report that begat it is unquestionable. I'd also enjoyed his decision in *Kinney vs Police*, where some poor schmuck had been convicted of disorderly behaviour by a District Court judge after wading into an ornamental duck pond at the Botanical Gardens in Napier after a 'daylight festival of amplified pop music'. On appeal, Woodhouse decided that the appellant's decision to join the pond's usual inhabitants long after the crowd had departed hardly warranted such a conviction, given that an essential element of the offence was that it be upsetting to a reasonable bystander. Woodhouse dutifully attempted to find that innocent bystander and in the process reduced the prosecution argument to its logical absurdity. 'The ducks seemed unperturbed – they remained on the surface of the water with scarcely an increase in their rate of stroke,' he wrote. 'The attitude of the goldfish is unknown.'

As fodder for lawyers who wanted to inject a little erudite humour into their repertoire, *Kinney vs Police* ranked right up there with the famous case of the speculating vicars, authored by none other than Peter Mahon. In many respects Woodhouse seemed to be the one senior judge with the same literary bent and wit as Mahon. New Zealand's literary history is full of personal spats. If this was one of them, it had more consequence than most.

After the decision was published, the weekly newspaper *Truth* dropped a bombshell: two of the five judges on that Court of Appeal, the two who had authored the minority decision that had so upset Mahon, had close family ties with Air New Zealand. Sir Owen Woodhouse's daughter worked as a public relations officer for the airline, while Sir Duncan McMullen's son was a pilot. *Truth* also confirmed that Auckland lawyer Richard McGrane, who represented Air New Zealand during the Royal Commission of Inquiry, was a close friend of the McMullen family.

The Woodhouse connection was news to Mahon – he later said that if he'd known, he'd have objected. Mahon did, however, know about McMullen's connection to McGrane, and that he was a constant visitor to the McMullens' house during the inquiry, while he was third counsel to the airline, briefing the Air New Zealand evidence that Mahon disbelieved. Before the Court of Appeal hearing, Mahon had informed Sir Robin Cooke, the Acting President of the Court of Appeal, of McMullen's association with McGrane. Despite this, and his son's employment by Air New Zealand, McMullen insisted on sitting. As Mahon pointed out to the *Listener*, the convention for judges was well established:

> there's a rule that if you have a personal interest to the
> extent that a bystander may claim your impartiality is under
> strain – then the law is that the person should not sit. Think
> of the system of calling jurymen. Someone says: 'My sister

knows one of the witnesses.' Well, in those circumstances, they turn down jurors all the time.

Sir Duncan McMullen was also a member of the Privy Council at the time, but at least managed to keep his bum off that bench during the legal farce that followed.

Infuriated by Woodhouse and McMullen's attack, Mahon urged Attorney-General Jim McLay to appeal the Court of Appeal decision to the Privy Council. McLay insisted that if Mahon wanted to appeal he would have to do so in his own name: the Attorney-General had no interest in the appeal and would remain neutral. Mahon said he could not fund the appeal himself. The government tried to strike a humiliating deal, offering to fund Mahon's appeal if he forsook his judge's pension entitlement. In the end, Mahon got his appeal to the Privy Council four years after the Royal Commission. By that time he was too ill to attend the hearing in London. It might have been a blessing, because there was to be no satisfaction there.

The Attorney-General's neutrality seemed to vaporise in London. The Law Lords were advised by his counsel that 'the New Zealand Court of Appeal is inevitably better placed than your Lordships' and that 'the Attorney-General submits that the Court of Appeal's assessment should be given very great weight' and that 'it would only be appropriate for your Lordships to differ from [the Court of Appeal decision], if you are quite satisfied that it is manifestly wrong'.

The Privy Council's 'advice' reads like a decision that has been made on other grounds, an ex post facto attempt to rationalise that decision as law. It twisted like some legal contortionist to promote the airline's view and presented me with a huge problem in terms of how to render it succinctly yet dramatically. In the end I decided on a scene in Mahon's garden, where a tired and ailing Mahon attempts to summarise it for Magarita, with a kind of ironic fatalism:

> **Mahon:** The Privy Council is simply saying: one, that
> my analysis of the cause of the accident is brilliant and
> correct; two, that my analysis of the cause of the accident
> is incorrect, in so far as I give any weight to executive
> knowledge of low flying; three, that the Air New Zealand
> executives might well have been lying about their
> knowledge of low flying; four, that that doesn't matter
> because their Lordships don't consider low flying had
> anything to do with the disaster; and five, that because at
> the time they lied, the executives thought low flying *was* a
> cause of the disaster, it was quite understandable for them
> to want to lie.

In 1991, several years after the series was screened, Macfarlane's *The Erebus Papers* provided a comprehensive, damning summary of the Air New Zealand evidence to the inquiry, and also provided a detailed, meticulous, relentless dismemberment of both the Court of Appeal – particularly the minority decision of Woodhouse and McMullen – and Privy Council decisions, the most disturbing element of which, to Macfarlane, was the latter's 'economy with the truth'.

That Privy Council decision is so contorted that I'm left wondering if someone had a quiet word to their lordships that it was in the national interest for the Court of Appeal decision to stand. Whatever the motivation, it is clear that this decision protected the government and Air New Zealand, vindicated the Court of Appeal and totally destroyed Mahon's reputation.

To my mind, it also undermined the argument that the Privy Council should not have been abolished because it was a necessary curb to the powers of the state, providing an outside perspective and backstop to the New Zealand judicial process, immune from the wink-wink nudge-nudge suasion that New Zealand's establishment might bring to bear on a local court.

The project progressed, slowly but well, through 1986. We were a good team. Caterina got to grips with the unique nature of the project and was in her element. I called her, behind her back, the Whispering Sicilian, owing to her tendency to lower her voice in meetings. I was never sure whether it was a Muhammad Ali type power play – he would start whispering in press conferences so that everyone had to lean closer, almost in an attitude of piety if they wanted to hear the oracle – or whether she was naturally conspiratorial and just a little paranoid about anyone overhearing what we were up to. Probably the latter: we'd be chatting away in a lift about something quite banal, but as soon as anyone entered, she'd put a finger to her lips in a most obvious way and maintain an awkward cone of silence until the interloper had fled. But she was absolutely committed to the project and, like John McRae above her, fought tooth and nail for it.

Christina Milligan began as script editor, until she went away to do a producer's course and Philippa Campbell took over and brought fresh energy and an objective perspective to what we'd done so far.

Di Musgrave did all the front-line interviews and suffered for it: she, not I, had to face their anxieties and humiliation for hour after hour. And Gary Harrison was always there to give me context, to help me make sense of the huge deluge of material and to show courage in deciding what could be used. The only time he appeared to waver was when I wanted to use a phrase of Mahon's – 'a bunch of schoolgirls' – to describe the judiciary. Gary felt if that phrase was used, we'd never get a fair trial if we were ever sued. However, if we'd had a corporation lawyer involved, we wouldn't have had a story, as we were to find out soon enough.

Despite the team around me, I felt at times as if I was drowning in the sheer volume – and technical detail – of the material. To my shame, when Mary's mother died suddenly and unexpectedly, I tried to spend the morning of the funeral working, rather than supporting her. But, finally, I completed first drafts – way too long – of each of the episodes. From there, I thought, it was a just matter of trimming and fine-tuning.

As Head of Drama, John McRae had the power to buy properties and commission projects, so it wasn't until the final drafts were ready to go upstairs to be signed off that Allan Martin, the Director-General, really got a handle on what we were doing. He was, in the words of someone who was dealing with him at the time, 'shit scared'. He immediately advised the board of the dangers that could be facing TVNZ and them, perhaps personally.

We were told that, despite the presence of Gary Harrison, the scripts had to be vetted by one of the top defamation lawyers in the country, Tom Goddard QC, later a judge of the Employment Court. When Goddard read the scripts, he ruled out fully half the content as potentially defamatory, including the use of the phrase 'orchestrated litany of lies'. At the final hurdle, we seemed to be buggered.

But Tom Goddard didn't know that we'd kept meticulous source scripts, which recorded the origin of every bit of information, every scene and virtually every line of dialogue attributed to any character. When these were produced, he was taken aback. Gary and Caterina went through every one of Goddard's objections with him. Every item was reinstated, bar one, which I can't remember and can't have been important. We started shooting.

Peter Sharp had been asked to direct the series. It was a huge challenge for him to make the central two hours in particular visually interesting, which he did. Peter was terrified of Englishman Frank Finlay, who was to play Mahon, because he'd had an awful experience with the manic Patrick McGoohan on a film called *Trespasses*. But Frank was a wonderfully kind and unpretentious actor and made the perfect Mahon.

Despite Frank's impact, Ian Mune as Morrie Davis almost stole the show. Before the shoot began, Caterina warned me that Ian wanted to have a few words with me about one of his speeches. I wasn't keen, because Mune was notorious for wanting to re-write everything. But I had a weapon up my sleeve this time and told Caterina I'd welcome Ian's call, which duly came.

Mune was apoplectic about one speech in particular, where Morrie was on the witness stand at the Royal Commission. 'It makes no sense,' said Mune. 'In fact it's complete gibberish!' I told him I'd actually edited down that speech by a third from its original length in order to give it whatever coherence it now had. 'Well, I'm not bloody saying it!' stormed Mune. I said that was fine by me, but he should be aware that as long as he stuck exactly to the scripted speech, he'd be covered by TVNZ in any resulting defamation action. As soon as he changed it by so much as one word, and thus endangered the emphasis or sense of the whole, he was on his own and would have to be personally liable for whatever followed. The speech was word perfect on the day and Mune won the best actor award for that year. I did notice that I wasn't on his list of thank yous.

Once the show was in the can, Allan Martin and the board viewed it and again got spooked. This time, they called in Des Monaghan, the Controller of Programmes, and told him to find a way to stop the thing from going to screen.

I began to get worried again that we'd be deep-sixed, particularly when Caterina started making noises like 'I don't want to put the corporation at grave risk'. Eh? Now it was the producer's choice as to whether TVNZ actually screened the programme? Context is everything, but I was worried as much by Caterina's use of the producorial 'I' as the actual content of what she said. When the Queen uses the royal 'we' it's a matter of convention and deference – she really means 'I'. When producers start using 'I' when they should be using 'we', it tends to mean that they've seen the writing on the ceiling and want to ally themselves with a power dynamic somewhere above them. On the other hand, when they use 'we', it can mean that they're worried or anxious about what those powers above will think of our current endeavours and want to spread the load, or the blame . . . It's hard to say which is worse.

We were, again, extremely fortunate. Instead of stopping the series, Des Monaghan, a charming Irishman who had begun his career in TVNZ as a floor sweeper, became our guardian angel – an unlikely one, perhaps, for those who know him now as one of the hard-charging principals behind the Australasian production company Screentime. Des came across like a silver fox, but his boxer's nose with its broken, flattened bridge, hinted at some steel for a fight. He certainly had the credentials: he had a background in current affairs, having produced the hard-hitting *Gallery*, and, more importantly, was one of the few to have taken on Muldoon publicly and beaten him, back in 1982–83, over the film *Death of a Princess*.

The movie concerned a Saudi princess who was publicly beheaded in 1977 because she had engaged in an allegedly adulterous and politically unacceptable affair. When the film was about to be screened on British television, the Saudis threatened to destroy British business in the Gulf. They warned of sanctions. Similar tactics were employed to stop the film airing on American public television. The BBC and PBS refused to submit and screened the film.

When Des Monaghan purchased the film for screening on TVNZ, the Saudis brought similar pressure to bear on Muldoon, who accused Des of having no interest in the well-being of NZ, that by screening *Death of a Princess* Des was prepared to put the country's oil supplies at risk. Des sued Muldoon (represented by Des Dalgety) for defamation and was successful.

Meanwhile, the Broadcasting Corporation board, under the chairmanship of Ian Cross, author of *The God Boy*, crusading president of PEN and an ardent campaigner for the freedom of the press, issued a detailed critique of the film, which it had not seen:

> The corporation believes that there are valid grounds for the
> claim that it misrepresents and distorts the values of the way

of life it deals with and that conveying by fictional techniques generalisations about the whole legal and religious basis of Islam, the film is not reliable as a documentary and without real value as education or information.

This capitulation was not Ian Cross's finest moment, but a concrete demonstration of how intimidating Muldoon was.

A few years later, however, when Des and John McRae went to see the board and go into bat for *Erebus, The Aftermath*, Des knew what he was up against and he had some 'form'. Fortunately, Ian Cross was gone and Des held sway. Later, Des was told that his action in suing Muldoon over *Death of a Princess* might have had some bearing in persuading the powers that be that it would be easier all round to let the show go to screen.

Peter Mahon died on 11 August 1986, more than a year before *Erebus, The Aftermath* screened. I was glad in some ways that he was spared the burden of once more standing up and defending himself and his integrity against the likes of Morrie Davis.

The first episode went to air on Sunday night, 18 October 1987. On Monday morning, driving to the office, I heard Morrie Davis being interviewed on the radio, saying that, in writing the thing, I was 'dancing on the coffins of the dead'. He seemed to be claiming, by some self-appointed proxy, outrage on behalf of the victims of the accident. But the responses of families and friends of the victims were encouraging. They seemed upset not by the programme – they had completed their grieving years ago – but by being used by Morrie to whack me over the head. Several of them made it clear through the media that they were pleased to see an attempt to tell the whole story in a coherent way.

Right after Morrie Davis, Phil Recordon came on the radio to say, as chairman of the New Zealand Council for Civil Liberties, that he thought Morrie Davis had a case for being deprived of his right to tell his side of the story. I knew Phil from the '81 protests, and from the anti-tour case in '85, and rang him to tell him how disappointed I was. Had Morrie told him, I asked, that we'd spent more hours interviewing him than we did with Peter Mahon? No, said Phil, Morrie hadn't divulged that he'd talked to us.

There were other weird and wonderful reactions. Sean Brown, then a television journalist, did a review in the *New Zealand Herald* in which he said we should have had visual markers on screen to demarcate when a scene was based on research and when it wasn't. That response was typical of the Kiwi 'Don't tread on my patch, mate' mentality. If the likes of Sean, later a very effective and popular Head of News at TVNZ, had covered the story properly, I wouldn't have had a story. Besides, a journalist should surely have had enough understanding of the libel laws in this country to make that kind of frivolity with the facts out of the question.

Erebus, The Aftermath ran four nights in a row, from Sunday through to Wednesday and, despite my dancing on coffins, the series was a stunning success. It rated through the roof and one episode even outrated the network news on TV One, which was unheard of in those days. It was difficult, demanding television, yet people made the effort. The episode that rated highest was the one we were most worried about: where the action was locked into the claustrophobic inquiry room for the whole hour. So much for John Keir's dictum.

TVNZ was true to its word and provided 24-hour security around our house at John Street. I wasn't sure whether that was as a result of a threat they'd received or just part of the service. We had our phone unlisted.

It soon became apparent that though Morrie Davis complained to the Broadcasting Complaints Authority and to whoever would listen, no one was going to challenge us in court. It also became clear that the mini-series was about as complete a success as it was possible to have, almost exactly a year after the equally complete failure of *Whitemen*.

That spring, in celebration, we had a huge party in the back yard at 8 John Street. Hampo was at the door mixing margaritas for each guest as they arrived. Mary's Californian poppies in the gardens I'd pick-axed out of the asphalt were blooming around the melia tree where Caitlin's placenta was buried. She and her little mates were climbing it, swinging off the bough and dropping into the lavender bed. My mate Murray McIlwraith and his combo played jazz in the cavernous garage at the back of the property, where, rumour had it, the first Ponsonby bus used to run from.

When Mac and I had decided to go for it in London, back in '78, as jazz musician and writer, it had been an exercise in dogged optimism for both of us, because neither of us really believed that a career in either discipline was possible in New Zealand. Here we both were, nearly 10 years later, married with daughters and earning a living from music and writing. Okay, Mac was teaching music to make ends meet and was having to compromise musically by playing weddings and corporate dos, while I had ended up in television. But we were doing what we wanted to do and both felt very fortunate.

Erebus, The Aftermath was later screened by the BBC in Britain and by the ABC in Australia, to good reviews and ratings. It was repeated in both places, but was never repeated here. I heard that was part of the deal Air New Zealand did with TVNZ: if it wasn't screened again, the airline wouldn't sue.

Time has probably defeated it. Now it might look dated, the music portentous (it was brilliantly sent up at the time by *McPhail & Gadsby*) and the narrator a bit DJ-ish (my one regret is that I didn't have time to get rid of the narration), but at its heart, *Erebus, The Aftermath* was a seminal piece of New Zealand television.

It's my belief that Mahon got it between 85 and 100 per cent right, with the remaining percentage being possible pilot error. To achieve that kind of result in what was one of the most difficult, complex, emotionally charged and technically obtuse cases ever heard in this country was a feat any one of his brother judges might ordinarily have been proud of. They never articulated that. Peter Mahon began the inquiry as a respected member of that discreet and privileged inner circle. When he stood up to Muldoon he became a man of the people – and to his brother judges that seemed to make him the worst of men, a populist, in the same vein as his enemy, Muldoon.

It's easy to forget the atmosphere of fear Muldoon engendered. That a judge (not Peter Mahon) could tell me in all seriousness that Tom Scott, a political columnist, was the only effective opposition to the rampant MP for Tamaki probably shows how craven the New Zealand establishment was at that time. The National Party itself was part of this – they knew they'd let loose a demagogue, a rogue elephant, but instead of trying to rein him in, they were more intent on not being trampled. By standing up to Muldoon, Mahon attained a status that other judges had forsworn but probably secretly envied. But in 'going public', it was as if he'd renounced the secret rites of the judicial lodge. Judges cannot publicly defend their decisions, they tut-tutted. When Mahon explained that when he defended his decision he was acting as a royal commissioner, not a judge, it mattered not. They went after him with a will, at first using isolation and ostracism. But when Mahon was taken before the Court of Appeal and then went to the Privy Council, he gave his brethren a terrible power and put himself squarely in their sights. And both his learned colleagues and the government took their chance to put him on the rack.

There's an outward-looking New Zealand which is, as Michael King suggests in his celebrated *Penguin History of New Zealand*, 'good-hearted, practical, commonsensical and tolerant'. But there's also another, darker New Zealand, professionally inbred and introverted, which is rife with the base envy, territoriality, unspoken conflicts of interest and vicious feuds of an Appalachian valley. New Zealand society is so small that everyone presumes to know everyone else and imputes motive – usually the worst – to whomever is under attack. Usually the target is someone like Mahon, who has challenged the powers in some way, strayed onto someone else's patch, stuck his head above the dull parapet of convention or is simply perceived as having been too successful. Such a person becomes an affront to our egalitarianism. We mistake equality of opportunity for equality of result. We demonise them, then belt the living bejesus out of them . . . in as civilised a manner as possible, of course. Our history is littered with them. For the Peter Mahons, Te Maiharoas, Joe Karams, Titokowarus and Archibald Baxters, RIP New Zealand.

My immersion in the Erebus story made me aware that it had

generated many more victims than those who had lost their lives on the icy flanks of the mountain. There were the family and friends of the deceased. There were the family and friends of those who'd had the first hot finger of culpability pointed at them, the Collins and the Cassins. There were the Vettes who had tried to defend the pilots and lost their jobs. There were the Hewitts and Lawsons and others who had been the next ones thrown to the wolves in an effort to save the airline. There were those whose reputations or relationships had been compromised by the positions they had taken on either side of that oily line in the snow – the Ron Chippendales, Lloyd Browns, Owen Woodhouses, Jim McLays and many of the operations and briefing personnel at the airline, not to mention Morrie Davis himself. Beyond that, there were the absolutists and obsessives whose lives were blighted or ruled by what had happened on Mount Erebus. I was determined not to become one of them. I kept telling myself that it was just a job, and when it ended, if it ever ended, I would move on.

And finally it had ended. Only just.

I heard that Morrie Davis had tried to persuade Air New Zealand to sue TVNZ for defamation, so that he could piggyback on their case. The airline, thank goodness, could see that a defamation action would have thrown the whole case open to be relitigated. I would have been named as a defendant and lost another couple of years to Erebus. But Air New Zealand wanted to move on. So did I. Having seen how the aftermath of Erebus had continued generating victims, living and dead, long after the bodies were brought home from the snow, I was determined not to join that list.

I gave no interviews, lost contact with the likes of Margarita Mahon and Gordon Vette and did what freelance writers do. I got on with the next gig, which couldn't have been more different.

fifteen

Ghost Writers in the Sky

In 1984, the incoming Labour government had slipped the economic leash on the dogs of capitalism and Lange's little 'Polish shipyard' in the South Pacific almost immediately reinvented itself as a nation of entrepreneurs and miracle moneymakers. During '85 and '86, these economic shamans quickly became the rock stars of the new age, and names like Allan Hawkins and Bruce Judge and Colin Reynolds became as well known to the man on the street as any of the All Black stars of the time. They were the princes of paper palaces, built on an escalating vortex of public floats and corporate cannibalism.

For Kiwis inured to Muldoon's wage and price freezes, carless days and no Sunday trading, it was like being invited to a party where the buffet was share scrip and the drug of choice was greed. Your average Joe and Josie Blows started playing the share market either individually or in share clubs, following the dictates and soaring trajectories of the new gurus of lucre. Share prices ex divvy and p/e ratios became part of the lexicon, though these stodgy fundamentals were soon forgotten as certain shares started to defy the laws of economics and gravity. Almost everyone had an opinion on Equiticorp vs Chase, much the same as they would speculate on the outcome of a footy match. Most of the punters were about as well informed too.

There was even an element of patriotism involved, as Hawkins and Judge seemed on the verge of a leveraged takeover of Australia Inc and Michael Fay went after the America's Cup in Fremantle in '86 with *KZ7*, the fibreglass rocket, known popularly – and entirely appropriately for the times – as Plastic Fantastic.

There were confident Young Thrusters everywhere, making big paper money on the coat-tails of their gurus. They wore power suits and mirror glasses to match their corporate eyries, had premature jowls from long lunches and fine wines and were loud of voice and weighed down by their wallets. They called themselves brokers, arbitrageurs, mergers and acquisitions bankers, forex or futures dealers and/or had some sort of nebulous status within the divine circle of corporate sharks who were devouring each other, fuelled by speculative money from the public in return for share scrip which turned out to be about as much use as an IOU from a dero. But we didn't know that then.

Roy Billing was up to his elbows in it. His wife was the corporate secretary for Equiticorp and on the strength of their paper millions Roy and Suzanne had built an extravagant home up at Albany, which opened up to the view like a stage. There were lots of parties up there, fevered cross-pollinations of corporate wide boys with the mostly poor denizens of page and stage and screen. I remember seeing Maurice Shadbolt wandering around looking a bit dazed and confused, so I risked breaking the rule among writers and asked him what he was working on? An Apple Mac, said Maurice, preserving the code.

Along with Circa's Grant Tilly, Roy had been the first and definitive Tupper, back at Theatre Corporate in '80, and had subsequently made the role his own in a number of other productions. When I burned my Junior All Black jersey in '81, Roy was there holding the matches, while Mary held the diesel. He'd been a prime mover in Working Title Theatre until he got frustrated with the hopeless ideological hand-wringing and lack of business acumen. It must have been hard watching our theatre group bumble its way towards trying to set up 'professional' productions for peanuts, while through Suzanne he could see glimpses of corporate nirvana, where millions were made by swapping paper.

The worlds of rough impoverished theatre and corporate pirates didn't really meet, and soon Roy and Suzanne were estranged. Roy went through agonies, some awful and dark, some funny, at least in retrospect. He told me about waking up one morning, terribly hung-over, cramped and hot, with some shaggy hairy form damn near suffocating him. It was the matrimonial red setter, and when he poked his head out and opened his bloodshot eyes to the dawn, he found that his abode for the night had been the dog's kennel.

Dean Parker had been watching all this 1980s capitalist shenanigans and excess with the sceptical eye of an old socialist. I'd got to know him a lot better since working on *Roche* together. We'd been involved with the Writers' Guild and Working Title and he had invited me along to pre-season practice at Grey Lynn Park with the Halt All Racist Tours (HART) soccer team.

Before that, when we'd lived out west, I'd been playing social soccer for a team of psychiatric nurses from Oakley, as it then was. I couldn't tackle and I couldn't head – they weren't skills which transposed from rugby – but I still had a bit of pace and could bend the ball with either foot, so I ended up on the wing or as striker. It was great fun and a way of getting out of myself at the end of a week spent in my head.

For me, the hardest thing to get used to about social soccer was the level of verbal abuse. Every week, there'd be little guys with strong accents dancing around calling me variations of a fucking cunt – a big fucking cunt, a dirty fucking cunt, a filthy fucking cunt, a great fucking cunt, a fucking fucking cunt, a cunt of a fucking cunt. When I played rugby, before television and touch judge got into the scrutinising act, you gave or got one warning, which more or less said, Try that again and you're dead. And if you did, you were, as near as damn it. They carried you off.

So in my first game of soccer, as the curses rained, I was expecting mayhem to break out at every moment, but nothing much happened, except on one occasion, which was the single worst incidence of violence I ever witnessed first hand on any sporting field. On that occasion, my striking partner, a psychiatric nurse, had a bit of ongoing niggle with an opposing defender. Towards the middle of the game, he saw the defender flat on his back, helpless, and ran 10 metres to kick him full in the face. It looked like he'd had plenty of practice. The victim went into convulsions, but luckily, there was the odd nurse or two on the field and they seemed to know what to do. What they did to the perpertrator, I don't know; I sent myself off and never went back.

The HART team was much more sane, and interesting. Even

Tim Shadbolt, incumbent Mayor of Waitemata, turned out for us occasionally. By this time he was a bit heavy of bum and slow of foot, though he'd just been voted the Sexiest Man in Auckland by *Metro* readers. He used to complain about how the sexiest man in Auckland couldn't get a naughty with his wife. I'd met Miriam Cameron a couple of times. She had a socialist intellectual background and when she left Tim a couple years later, he seemed to lose his compass and never had quite the political acumen and edge he'd had while Miriam was at his side.

Over a beer after a HART game, I told Dean about Roy Billing's predicament and how, extrapolated, I thought there was a great story there – the clash of worlds, Art and Money, how just as Roy had got a glimpse of the rich man's club he was summarily ejected.

Dean in the 1980s must have been a bit like Bertolt Brecht in the Hollywood of the 1930s, fascinated and repulsed in equal parts by what was going on around him. The 1980s were a bad time for Marxists – it seemed the only Marx anyone had heard of was the guy who buzzed Eden Park with a Cessna in '81. Dean had a bit of the hard-line Romeril about him, but his asceticism was defeated by a liking for the odd drink, a passion for Liverpool FC, a rollicking sense of humour and a huge nose for gossip. Roy's adventures seemed to fit with a story and some characters Dean had already started thinking about. 'Love & Money' was born.

Dean and I had collaborated closely on storylines for *Roche*, but once we got to commissioned drafts, those scripts were the separate preserve of each writer. 'Love & Money' was different – we were writing it together, and to begin with we didn't know quite how it was going to work. I was terrified we'd be sitting at the same computer, farting and picking our noses as we agonised over each word. Who would actually do the typing?

Dean was probably as terrified as I was, but he said nothing and we just organically and very quickly got into a system that seemed to work. We'd discuss characters and moments, note down narrative beats, then take a sequence each and go away and develop it into a storyline. Who got which sequence to write up depended to some extent upon who'd come up with what and who could see it most clearly. We'd cut the different sequences together, talk about them some more, then each go back and rework the whole thing. This involved rewriting each other's work, clearly an opportunity for problems. Maybe Dean can remember some problems doing this, but I can't.

One of the reasons this template worked was my admiration for Dean's writing. No one wrote more seductive 'big print', or 'directions' or 'action'. All three terms are misnomers in my opinion – I never use caps for 'directions' because it makes the script look like a starter's prep for new entrants. 'Directions' is unfortunate too, because most directors regard that stuff in the same way as a Neapolitan regards a red traffic light – as an indication of what he might do if he can't come up with a better idea. And 'actions' doesn't cover the multitude of tasks the non-dialogue bits convey. They might set a scene atmospherically, they might place it in a landscape, they might contain critical choreography for both the actors and the camera (who sees what and when), and they should offer huge clues as to tone and style. 'Action' also confuses: sometimes when it's used, particularly in theatre, it describes character dynamics. The non-dialogue words in a script are prose, and most of the prose in Dean's scripts was worthy of an audience far beyond the directors, cast and crew who would ever get to read it.

He was also one white man who could jump. Narrative beats are like stepping stones across a river: they have to be spaced just right so that you can get safely to the other side. Too wide apart and you risk falling in; too close together and you're chicken-stepping, repeating yourself too much and not travelling at the optimum pace. If you ask the audience to jump too far between beats, you lose them, while if you give them chicken steps, you bore them rigid. Neither Dean nor I believed in the theoretical absolutists like Eisenstein and Mamet, who maintain the cut is everything. The cut itself, the jump, should precipitate something of interest – whether the juxtaposition is ironic, or deliberately obfuscatory or comedic. At his best, Dean could pump the jumps and lift the story.

He was also an interesting, cynical and funny bugger to be around. He knew a lot about all sorts of things, from the origins of trade unionism to our literary history. He had the instincts of a social historian, but with a very mischievous eye to go with his nose for gossip.

These last two character traits had given rise to 'The New Zealand Bedside Literary Companion', Dean's unpublished and probably unpublishable compendium of the most salacious and scurrilous gossip about New Zealand's literary icons: Frank Sargeson caught masturbating, Lauris Edmond, Maurice Shadbolt, Fiona Kidman, James McNeish, Roger Hall and, dredging the literary pond, Greg McGee. No one, it seemed, was safe, particularly after they kicked the bucket, or were unwise enough to tell a dodgy story in Dean's presence.

The best known of these involved Barry Crump and Dean's

next door neighbour in Vermont Street, Peter Varley. Peter was an old queen from stage and screen whose claim to fame was that he'd played Vanity (under the stage name Alba) in *Bedazzled* and had been fucked or sucked by some amazing names in his time. Which was very definitely past. When I knew him, he was in his 70s and the sight of him sashaying down Ponsonby Road or John Street in his cut-off denims with his balls nearly spilling out over his gnarly old legs got plenty of attention as Ponsonby gentrified itself through the 1970s and 1980s. Mary used to feel sorry for him, struggling down John Street with his bags of shopping, and would bring him in for a cup of tea, then give him a ride home. Until he turned up with a jar of Vaseline as a birthday present for Oli, her beautiful son, just turned 13.

Peter told Dean that many years ago he'd been at a party across town with a number of celebrities, though they weren't called that then. Peter got bored and let it be known he was about to go. Barry Crump said he was heading back that way; did Peter want a lift? Peter said that would be very kind. When they pulled up outside Peter's little flat, Peter thought, in true Sir Edmund spirit, 'Nothing ventured, nothing gained,' and asked Barry if he wanted to pop inside for a cup of tea or coffee. 'I would, thanks Peter,' said Barry.

Peter was stunned, though very excited, but as he headed for the front door, with Barry following, he was assuaged by doubts as to whether Barry knew what he was up to? Could Barry Crump be that innocent? Perhaps he was such a Kiwi bloke, thought Peter, that matters like that never crossed his mind. Perhaps he did just want a cup of tea? But as Peter inserted the key in his front door, a large masculine hand descended on his shoulder and a deep Kiwi voice said, 'You will be gentle with me, won't yer, Peter.'

When Peter Varley passed away some years later, Dean wrote an obituary for a Sunday paper and, ever mischievous, mentioned in his by-line that he was Peter's literary executor and was working through his diaries, with a view towards putting together a biography of Peter Varley's life, times and lovers. Within hours a major literary figure was on the phone to Dean threatening to sue if he was mentioned in the upcoming biography. That call was followed shortly after by a blokey icon of a director who admitted sheepishly that Peter had taken his 'cherry' and said, 'You've gotta understand, Dean, in theatre back then, there was only one way of getting ahead.'

Since the 'Love & Money' screenplay seemed to be happening, we thought that although Roy's predicament was just the spinning-off point for the story, Dean and I had better check it out with him before we got too far down the track. We did. Roy might have been down, but he was still the consummate professional. 'Sure,' he said, 'as long as I get to play the lead.'

With that squared off, Dean and I needed a producer and took the idea to Chris Hampson, who was also a mate of Roy's, and whose own travails had given him a particular empathy with the story. Hampo had separated from his wife Ruth a couple of years before and, though it was amicable, the separation seemed to engender something akin to a death-wish in him. He'd begun dressing in black, and with Nehru collars, rimless glasses and razor-cut grey hair, he looked increasingly like a defrocked Jesuit with a slight whisky problem. His habit of blessing people in Latin as he left the room, and signing off his letters and faxes 'Yours in Christ, James M Liston, Bishop of Auckland', heightened the liturgical impression. I'd taken to calling him Vicar, and though I'd managed to dissuade him from driving us into the Clutha in flood, various other accidents and incidents had closely followed that one.

Just after the Clutha incident, during the filming of *Illustrious Energy*, Hampo insisted on driving me down from Clyde to my parents' place in Oamaru. The Clyde production base was in the Dunstan Hotel, just across the road from Oliver's Restaurant, created by Fleur Sullivan. Fleur, now celebrated for her own wharfside restaurant at Moeraki, wanted us to take a chair to her parents, who had a house in the lee of the Duntroon bridge.

On safe delivery of the chair, Fleur's father rewarded us with a spot. Fine, except that we'd also stopped for spots at the Lowburn pisser (to say goodbye, as it was about to be drowned in Lake Dunstan), Omarama (to be convivial with my sister who taught school there) and Kurow (because Hampo was feeling thirsty and it had a pub). We made it to Oamaru safely and after a spot with Dad I thought that was it, that Hampo was staying the night. But against our entreaties he insisted on plunging on – he had a friend in Dunedin.

I got a call from the Roxburgh Hospital the next morning. Hampo had finished his assignation in Dunedin and decided to try getting back to base at Clyde because bad weather was threatening to close off the routes back to Central. He'd, quite conveniently, come to rest against a tree outside Roxburgh Hospital and had a badly smashed nose.

Later in the year, he had another accident in the Bay of Plenty, this time without benefit of alcohol, and I volunteered to drive him down to court at Tauranga to lose his licence. I'd never driven Hampo's beloved old '73 Porsche before and thought, as we charged down the motorway, that the steering was a bit heavy.

Hampo told me that it was the result of the lack of power steering, and assured me the steering became lighter as you went faster, so we did. We charged on, up the Bombay Hills and down the other side, until we were slowed by a line of traffic. As I braked, the front left wheel fell off and we arced slowly into the ditch at the side of the road. We completed the trip to Tauranga by rental.

When Hampo lost his licence for a period it was some relief to his friends, in that it closed off one avenue of damage. But his experience contributed to his fascination with Mike McGuire, the central character of 'Love & Money', and his descent into desolation and dissipation. In an effort to get some development funding, Hampo took the project to an outfit called Mirage, which was Don Reynold's Cinepro (*Trial Run*, *Illustrious Energy*) rolled into Larry Parr's production company (*Constance*, *Came a Hot Friday*, *Bridge to Nowhere*).

Mirage was filmdom's perfect expression of the 1980s. There was, as Wesley had said in *Came a Hot Friday*, money to be made and The Don and Larry were just the lads to make it. Mirage's plan, as far as I could ascertain, was to make a television series based on the movie of *Came a Hot Friday*, shoot a movie, Larry's adaptation of the dodgy and dangerous M. K. Joseph story *A Soldier's Tale*, and on the back of that anticipated double whammy success and their combined back catalogues, float Mirage to the public and count on the public's voracious appetite for shares to make huge amounts of money. It was no more nor less than any number of other would-be entrepreneurs in many other industries were doing.

Larry's background was as a producer, but, of course, he really wanted to direct. We never saw Larry at Mirage. He was in France, finally getting to direct. We saw Don, looking increasingly desperate as the filming in France went way over budget. It seemed to me that while Don regarded Mirage as a vehicle to get public investment into film, and into his pocket, to Larry Mirage was simply a vehicle to finally realise his dream of directing *A Soldier's Tale*, a story he'd been entranced by for years.

Came a Hot Friday had been a great domestic success without ever quite cracking it internationally. It was rumoured that an American distributor had bought it and had agonised for six months over how to cut the trailer. The problem was Billy T. James, playing the Tainuia Kid. Despite great performances by Peter Bland and Phil Gordon as Wesley and Cyril, the two peripatetic small-town con artists, Billy stole the movie. The problem there was that the Tainuia Kid was a minor character with not a lot of screen time. That bothered the international distributor and audiences but didn't bother Kiwis, who flocked to a movie that had a wonderful over-the-top confidence, almost theatricality, engendered by the director, Ian Mune.

Despite the '86 disaster of *Bridge to Nowhere*, Mune was a very bankable element. He'd given *Friday* a great sense of adventure, energy, pace and humour, so it made sense for Hampo to ask Mune if he'd like to direct 'Love & Money'. Mune was definitely interested and it seemed to make sense because Dean and I were also working alongside him on another project for Mirage.

Because *Came a Hot Friday* had been such a hit domestically, Don and Larry thought it would be criminal not to exploit it further by turning it into a television series. That way, they could correct the 'faults' of the movie and make the series more about the Tainuia Kid. Ian Mune would, of course, direct the nine episodes, and Ian and Dean and I were to write three episodes each.

After *Erebus, The Aftermath*, the *Came a Hot Friday* scripts needed light relief. The characters were established and fun to write and it was wonderful not to be constrained by 'the facts'. It was back to real drama where, if we found a dramatic problem, we invented our way out of it or around it. The only problem was Mune.

Roger Donaldson's wife Melvine had told me at one of the awards functions that she thought Mune was potentially a more talented director than Roger, but Mune couldn't decide what he wanted to do – act, direct or write. In his notes to Dean and me on our drafts for the *Came a Hot Friday* series, the sub-text was that he could do better himself. Dean was accustomed to that from his experience with Mune on the movie; I wasn't. Fortunately, Mune had been contracted to write three scripts himself, and when he finally delivered a draft, late, it completely undermined his lamentations about our scripts. Thereafter, Ian's notes were more respectful, at least with the *Came a Hot Friday* scripts.

'Love & Money' had another major problem: the climax of the movie depended on a share market crash, and in those halcyon days, no one at Mirage felt that was a credible scenario. Dean and I felt we needed some heavyweight back-up about the possibility that the share market could crash. We thought the man to go to was Brian Gaynor, a financial analyst I knew through Paddy Finnigan.

Hampo, Dean and I met Brian for lunch at Rick's Café at the Victoria Park Market. Brian listened to our predicament and didn't laugh us out of court. In fact he told us that anyone who had any doubts that the stock market could crash spectacularly should read J. K. Galbraith's account of how it happened in 1929, because in his view nothing had changed. He felt that few of today's speculators knew their history. If they did, they might be a hell of a lot more wary about where they were putting their money. In summary, he told us that the crash we'd written about in our movie was eminently, if not imminently, possible. That was July of '87. Money was still raining from the heavens . . .

Mary and I had bought quite a few Equiticorp shares on the back of Roy's enthusiasm for them before his marriage broke up. Mary wanted to replace the crappy kitchen at John Street and wasn't as impressed as I was with the paper profits. After talking to Brian Gaynor, I gave in with bad grace, sold all the shares, then watched with some annoyance over the next six weeks as the bandit builders started ripping apart our kitchen at huge expense while the Equiticorp shares kept rising.

During that buoyant time, Dean and I had also been approached by an Australian producer, a guy called Trevor Lucas, whom we immediately rechristened Bruce Spielberg. He had caught an episode of *Roche* while in New Zealand on business and reckoned it would adapt perfectly to Oz. Bruce had a number of things going for him: he was a ginge, he loved our show and he was prepared to offer us money.

We sent over VHS copies of the show so that Bruce could show his backers, and he came back to us with an offer for Australian rights for the existing scripts. Under the generous TVNZ conventions of the time, the rights had reverted to Dean and Simon and me. Bruce wanted to rename the show (and the family) 'The Furys' and run the trucking firm out of the working class part of Balmain. He also wanted Dean and me to write further episodes, so that the first series would be 13 episodes, and thereafter we'd have first dibs on a second series and, of course, continuing devisers' royalties (along with Simon).

The more we found out about our Bruce Spielberg the more we liked him. He'd become involved with a late incarnation of Fairport Convention, a ground-breaking British folk-rock band of the 1960s and 1970s and had married the lead singer, a tortured nightingale called Sandy Denny. They had a daughter, then when Sandy died in '78 after a cerebral haemorrhage, Trevor returned to Australia with his daughter.

Trevor seemed to have the right contacts and to know what he was up to. Dean and I tried to affect a degree of professional scepticism in the face of these potential riches, but when the contracts arrived, they were veritable works of art, and we finally knew we were onto a winner, particularly since Trevor's letterhead glinted in the sun, outshining even the gilded artwork of Mirage. There were separate option, assignment and writing contracts and when Dean and I saw them, we signed them with alacrity, sent them back and waited with palms raised for the Big Spondoolies to fall from the sky. I think we posted them back to Sydney in September of '87.

In late October, instead of raining spondoolies, the sky fell in. The share market crashed spectacularly – and terminally for most of the rock star entrepreneurs. They were soon in sackcloth or jail. The climax of 'Love & Money' was suddenly prescient and thoroughly credible. Particularly so, unfortunately, for our aptly named producer, Mirage, which had floated on the New Zealand Stock Exchange on 31 August 1987.

Within a few short months of the share market crash, Mirage's first film, *Queen Street Rocker*, bombed, followed down the box office gurgler shortly after by *A Soldier's Tale*, which meant a loss of $12.1 million for the first year rather than the forecast profit of $2.3

million. Even worse, Mirage's debenture holder was none other than Equiticorp, now a rapidly falling star. Equiticorp needed every dollar it could lay its hands on and in June '88, when Mirage couldn't meet Equitcorp's and BNZ's demands for repayment of its debentures, Equiticorp placed Mirage in receivership. Mirage's 10 months between floating and sinking might still be a record for the New Zealand share market. As Mirage went up in flames along with the rest of the ephemeral paper palaces, there was still a chance that 'Love & Money' might have been rescued from the debris, but there was another problem.

The storyline had evolved somewhat from its origins in Roy's traumas. Dean and I were working out some things that were important to us. Children. By that time, Dean had a son, Emmet, and I had Caitlin and Guy and Oli, and we'd seen a lot of 'modern' fragmented relationships. We wanted to look at our central character's estrangement from, and ultimate reconciliation with, his first born.

Mike McGuire's journey in 'Love & Money' was similar to that of Bill Murray's in *Broken Flowers* – backwards through past wives and lives, looking for connection and redemption, but fucking things up anew as he goes. Unlike Jim Jarmusch's movie, our screenplay had some warmth and humour (and certainly wouldn't have had Bill looking endlessly off camera towards the director, wondering if he'd missed hearing 'Cut'). And instead of finishing in a metaphorical cop-out at an intersection after an encounter with a young man who could have been his son, or a drifter with absolutely no connection, or a passer-by who had accidentally wandered into shot, our man finds some sort of redemption by reconnecting with his son by his first marriage.

That redemption was a big problem for Ian Mune. Hampo, Dean and I were summoned to his goat stud at Stoney Creek, Kaukapakapa, for a meeting. The goats were very expensive Angoras, all drugged so that they'd come into heat at the same time. They looked slightly bewildered, perhaps feeling something rising in their waters, but not entirely sure what. They weren't to know, but the bottom was also falling out of goats.

Mune told us that Mike reconnecting with his son was 'the booby prize'. Mike had to get the girl. What girl? we asked. Mune said Mike had to woo the last wife back, the young corporate whiz-kid who'd precipitated Mike's journey back through time by kicking him out.

That made no sense to Dean and me: this guy, who'd been married three or four times and made a mess of each relationship and not been a father to his children – his solution, his enlightenment, was to get back with the childless corporate bimbo? And what, bring more children into the world? Mune was adamant – he'd worked in Hollywood and knew about such things. Mike had to get the girl. I got the goat and walked out.

Pain and confusion for Hampo as producer. The writers, who had moral ownership, were revolting. The director, who was the only bankable element in the director-driven world of film, was saying 'Them or me'. The production company, which had legal ownership, was in the process of being liquidated . . .

'Love & Money' floundered about for a while until, with the passage of time, everyone involved realised it wasn't floundering, it had foundered. And it took its place on that growing shelf of the unproduced. With the benefit of hindsight, that was a pity, because it anticipated a whole slew of popular movies about fathers and sons and families in general and would have hit the screen about the same time as the likes of *Parenthood*, which came out in '89.

And, of course, the share market crashed in Sydney too. Bruce Spielberg was no longer returning calls. In fact his phone seemed to be disconnected. Months later, Trevor Lucas resurfaced and was terribly apologetic. His big money backers had gone to the wall. Yes, we had signed contracts with him, but what could he do? He had no money and no backers. Indeed, what could we do? We liked Trevor, appreciated his tragic history with Sandy Denny and sympathised with his predicament. Trevor had done his best and it had fallen over, through no fault of his. That just seemed to be the way it went in this business. Dean and I wished him well and said we hoped that, maybe if things came right, we could still pull off The Furys of Balmain. Things never came right for Trevor. He died of heart failure a couple of years later. I kept his contracts for a long time. I've never seen anything quite like them.

It was an era built on greed and dreams, which metamorphosed into paper palaces of inflated share scrip. Dean and I had written a television series based on a movie that was close to Dean's heart, and a screenplay that was close to both our hearts. But they were paper too, and burned with the rest of the edifices.

It's interesting how fondly I remember some of the screenplays that never got made. Is that because they never got made? What I've increasingly come to remember about most of the ones that got made are the compromises and fights and fuck-ups, whereas others, like 'Love & Money', still live in my mind as vital and vivid and untrammelled. They're also still mine. Once they're made and out there, whether they're loved or hated, feted or kicked and abused, they're part of the ether, ghostly constructs from the past, with just the odd one still showing something of a shimmer from time to time.

Both Dean and I took a while to recover from the demise of 'Love & Money' but at least, thanks to Mary, there was a new kitchen at John Street, and we had Roy's downward trajectory to keep our merely creative losses in perspective.

Roy and Suzanne had borrowed against their Equiticorp shares to finance the fabulous house. They didn't want to cash in the shares because they were appreciating by the day, whereas the mortgage principal was fixed. Within the space of a week in October the shares became virtually worthless, while the mortgage, of course, kept its value. Instead of fighting for his share of the matrimonial assets, Roy was being pursued for his share of the matrimonial liabilities.

At that point, the thought of trying his luck in Hollywood looked like a good idea. But to the Americans, Roy looked like a Mexican with a very unusual accent, and they had lots of Mexicans who could do an authentic Mexican accent. It wasn't quite the acting he'd intended to be doing, but Roy took the hint and did what Mexicans in Los Angeles do – got non-green card work washing dishes in a restaurant and, just to rub in his fall from grace, cleaning up locations trashed by film crews.

Roy eventually made a fine career for himself in Australia, starring in movies like *The Dish* and *Rabbit Proof Fence*, but for several years after the '87 crash his occasional visits home were fraught. On one of these visits, Mary and I bought his microwave (a luxury item back then) and we had to pay him quickly in cash. When I met him in Ponsonby Road to effect the transaction, Roy was wearing mirror shades and a big hat and quickly whipped me into a side street before I showed him the money. He said his creditors were after him and couldn't know he was in town. In a bizarre twist, his principal creditor was none other than Equiticorp, the model for the rapacious corporation of 'Love & Money', for whom Roy's ex-wife still worked.

Mirage may have been perfectly named, given its fate, but Don and Larry had at least seen the future. They, and Roy, along with farmers and workers and many others in our society, were all painful indicators of not just a rewriting of the economic rules, but a completely new script for New Zealand Inc. Most of us still couldn't see it, but it rapidly became clear that it was a production that wouldn't be denied.

sixteen

Abandon Hope All Ye Who Enter Here

Seismic aftershocks from the '87 crash rippled through '88 and beyond. While Mirage and its mortally wounded debenture holder Equiticorp bickered with the receiver over the carcass of Mirage's assets, 'Love & Money' convulsed a couple of times, as it went through what seemed a circular process of rewrites, and finally died.

I began to feel like a pilot in a storm, looking for an aircraft carrier to land on so that I could take on some fuel and sustenance, but every time I attempted to land, I couldn't quite catch the hook.

I almost made a safe landing on a vehicle for Billy T. James, a fish-out-of-water comedy film called 'The Duke', wherein Billy inherited a duchy in England. John Barnett of Endeavour Films was producing it with Rob Whitehouse. I didn't really know Barney at that stage, but I'd heard he was a hard man with the money, so I steeled myself for a tough contract negotiation.

Uniquely, in my experience, most New Zealand writers for film and television don't use agents. I'm not sure whether writers here don't earn enough money to want to pay an agent's commission, whether it's just because the industry – and writers' part in it – is so young, or whether historically, because a writer's remuneration was set in concrete in the days of award rates, there was no advantage to be had by employing an agent to negotiate for you. Certainly, that's no longer true, even if it was true then.

When, as President of the New Zealand Writers' Guild during the late 1990s, I would tell the American, Canadian and British screenwriters that in New Zealand we sat down direct with producers to negotiate contract fees and terms, they were horrified. They couldn't see how the primary creative relationship between a producer and a writer could survive such hard-arsed face to face confrontations over money. When they put it like that, I could immediately summon up a number of examples in my own career where my creative relationship with my producer had been compromised because I had to be my own advocate when it came to the contract. But the death of the creative relationship between producer and writer wasn't the only problem.

Writers generally are not the most secure and confident species, and are often not accustomed to talking turkey, particularly when it comes to putting a monetary value on their own services. I didn't have that problem – I always found talking about money a hell of a lot easier than writing. Even so, and as egotistical as I might be, I still found it difficult to put a value on myself, and I developed some negotiation strategies which helped me, and which I shared with other writers through the guild.

The most obvious one was to pretend that I was a lawyer who was acting for a third party, who happened to be me. That wasn't as easy for those writers who didn't happen to be ex-lawyers, but other strategies for objectifying the process were useful for all writers.

I would tell writers never to get into a situation with a producer where they had to put a monetary value on their own services, because they'd inevitably undersell themselves. I encouraged them to get the producer talking about the budget, because, being producers, they would most often talk it up in order to sell the project. Once the producer puts a figure on the budget, the writer can begin objectifying the process more, start talking about the rule of thumb percentages for scripting – usually between 2.5 and 5 per cent of the overall budget. That way, the discussion is about percentages, and the writer isn't having to advocate his or her own value in intimidating tens of thousands of dollars. And the writer can then steer the discussion towards *what a good script is worth to the project*, rather than what the writer is worth. Most producers will have to agree, particularly to a writer, that a good script is central to the success (if they don't, the writer has a clear signal to get out of there) and once they've done that, then it's just a matter of mutual agreement that a really good script is surely worth whatever paltry percentage of the budget you're going for. The writer will have, of course, worked out before he or she goes in there – particularly if, like me, he got 24 per cent in School Cert maths – what the likely budget will be and what the dollar value of the various percentages are.

So when I went in to negotiate with Barney over 'The Duke', I was well prepared for what I thought would be a really difficult meeting, partly because I knew they were planning this to be a largish budget movie with international appeal and I didn't think they should pay me any less than they'd expect to pay an English or American writer. As it happened, the meeting went very differently from what I'd expected. Barney wanted to talk about what he'd been reading and watching, books and movies and television here and overseas, and proved to be an extremely well-read and well-travelled individual. I remember thinking that if I ever needed a partner for Trivial Pursuit, Barney would be the man. He seemed reluctant to even talk about money, and in the end it was me who felt obliged to bring the subject up. I did my thing and walked out of there with verbal agreement for a contract worth $100,000. I was very pleased with myself, even though much of the fee was deferred, down the back on the never-never, payable if and when the thing went into production. In April, after some more discussion about percentages of deferrals, which went up from 30 to 40 per cent, I signed the contract, perhaps the first of that magnitude for a New Zealand writer.

One of my first missions, after some preliminary meetings and discussion of the concept, seemed a bit extra-curricular, but given the size of the contract I'd signed, I would have been quite happy to hang upside down and fart a sonata if they'd asked me to. So when they suggested I go and see Billy T. to get him excited about the project, I agreed.

By this time, Billy T. James was about as big a star as we had ever had, and he had the accoutrements to prove it: a big black sports car with shaded windows, flunkies who procured for him whatever he wanted and a lifestyle 'ranch' out at Waimauku, where I went to meet him.

Billy was cordial enough, but from the look of him, I didn't fancy my chances of getting him excited about anything, beyond his next takeaways of food, drugs or alcohol. He looked bloated and depressed, his great limpid brown eyes devoid of any spark and, despite the odd hovering flunky, he seemed quite isolated. The house was freaky, festooned with guns of all vintages and descriptions. It was a pretty desultory conversation. The only time Billy got excited was when he grabbed one of the pistols and started waving it about like the Tainuia Kid reincarnate. I pretended to be enthusiastic, but was grateful when I drove out of there.

'The Duke' seemed in a hell of a rush – the deadlines were unrealistic for a quality screenplay. I don't know whether the producers knew something I didn't, but the next time I saw Billy was in hospital later that year, when he was recovering from a heart transplant. 'The Duke' was always going to be tied to Billy's fate. He seemed much better for a while, but died of a heart attack in '91, precipitating an unseemly fight for his corpse between relatives who had perhaps struggled to get a piece of him while he was still alive.

Meanwhile, back in the staid but comforting world of television drama, Caterina de Nave had told me that TVNZ was keen to do a follow-up to *Erebus, The Aftermath*, because it had been such a success. Given how close TVNZ had come to being sued by Morrie Davis, I was never sure how far up the hierarchy this enthusiasm went, but after seeing the realities of independent production houses up close through my involvement with Mirage and Billy T.'s vehicle, the security and stability of the TVNZ Drama Department looked inviting. I had done some preliminary research for another mini-series about a signature moment in New Zealand's recent history, and I was keen to test TVNZ's enthusiasm.

On 3 January 1988, David Lange was quoted in the *Dominion Sunday Times*:

> 'We have never developed in New Zealand a person of undoubted pre-eminence who somehow stands apart from the political. You can get it in the States, you can certainly get it in the UK. People who, like Rothschild, were not contaminated, if you like, by the political process, but who were sort of repositories of the national wit, wisdom and wealth.' Mr Lange believes that there may be one such dynasty burgeoning in New Zealand – that of America's Cup notable, Michael Fay.

Like a lot of Kiwis, I'd become fascinated during '85 and '86 by the hype and glamour and patriotism whipped up by *KZ7* in Fremantle, by the way the nation became galvanised by the campaign and by the way the whole thing ultimately fell to pieces on the water against *Stars and Stripes*, despite the 'Plastic Fantastic' *KZ7* being in all probability the fastest boat. Somehow Michael Fay's entrepreneurial mana had survived it all to get a tickertape parade down Queen Street on the team's return from their big choke – and a big rap from David Lange.

By late '87, Fay was gearing up for another challenge for the America's Cup which, like the Anzus snub to the US, had all the appealing elements of the New Zealand flea biting the arse of the American elephant: Fay had challenged in a J boat of huge dimensions and was fighting the Americans' refusal to accept through the New York courts. Once again, Fay was portraying himself as a man with a national vision and his inspirational motivational speeches, centred around doing it for New Zealand, had become almost Churchillian – 'New Zealand rules the waves, but we are not going to let San Diego waive the rules.'

At about this time, Mary and I were invited to dinner at Susie McGillivray's flat down on the rocks at Brett Avenue, Takapuna. Susie was a friend from Otago University days, a farmer's daughter from Waimarama in the Hawke's Bay. A physiotherapist, she was an attractive combination of elements – beautiful, sporty, yet earthy and maternal – and was one of Fay's earliest recruits for the team. When the Fremantle challenge materialised, she gave up her practice for a year to go to Western Australia. Just weeks before the finals, Susie had been quite publicly cut from the team and had to return to Auckland to pick up the pieces of her life and work.

Late that evening after dinner, she began telling us a little of what had happened to her in Fremantle – and her story sounded a hell of lot more interesting than any of the material I'd seen reported in the media here by the journos who flew to Perth courtesy of sponsors' junkets and freebies, the ones Susie described as going up to Fay's office 'like roosters' and coming back down 'like bantams'.

I was fascinated by Susie's description of the divisions and paranoia that developed in the team over the course of a long and demanding campaign. Everyone from Michael Fay to the lowliest grinder passed through Susie's little physiotherapy cubicle in the spartan surrounds of the Portuguese Fishing Club, where she lived with the rest of the team. Her gender – she was also the only woman in the team, apart from the cooks – and her primary role meant she had constant one-on-ones with both management and crew and became a confidante to most of the men in an increasingly divided campaign. Her detailed picture of life inside the hermetically sealed base seemed wonderfully dramatic and yet of a very human scale.

A couple of days later, I rang Susie to thank her for the dinner and asked her if I could interview her on tape to see whether her inside story had the makings of a mini-series for television.

Many of the issues Susie talked about, like the conflict between Fay and skipper Chris Dickson, the power struggle between the man who had the money but no knowledge of sailing and the man who had that knowledge, but was immature and insecure, were confirmed later in the year by Alan Sefton in his book *The Inside Story of KZ7*. But they were dealt with pretty sketchily and from a consistent point of view: Sefton clearly knew not only where his bread had been buttered in the past but who was going to be running the dairy in the future. Michael Fay came across as the font of all wisdom and Dickson as someone with huge talent but debilitating faults which, ultimately, led to mistakes on the water that blew the challenge.

On my reading of Sefton's book, Fay seemed to have played no part in the chain of events that led to the loss, yet Susie told of a group of young men – most now household names – who were clearly the best crew out there in the early and middle stages of the campaign, but who were worn down by isolation, unrelenting performance pressure, stress and division. It was clear that it was Fay who set the tone and made the big decisions, particularly over personnel, some of which, like the belated appointment of John Adshead, were disruptive.

The conflict between Fay and Dickson forced Fay off the dock, but he was saved from being an impotent figurehead by Dennis

Conner's allegations of cheating, fomenting the whole 'plastic fantastic' controversy that gave Fay the international spotlight he clearly relished. But, according to Susie, as he became the public face of the New Zealand challenge, he was losing control of the people at the cutting edge, the *KZ7* crew.

Susie's story about the build-up to the final of the Challenger series with Dennis Conner was marked by Fay's gradual loss of control, by Dickson's retreat from brash arrogance to fears about what the pressures were doing to him psychologically and by the pre-eminence of a team of young men who had been under Fay's unrelenting performance demands for 12 months or more, and who eventually cracked when it mattered most.

The series was lost when Dickson and his super-crew made two foul-ups in the last race. Twice they were on the point of overtaking Conner: they blew the first when they couldn't get the gennaker down cleanly and they blew their last chance when Dickson steered *KZ7* into a buoy rounding the last mark. While New Zealand rejoiced in being able to take on the big boys and come so close, Fay was livid and unforgiving. Even as he and Dickson rode down Queen Street in a Mercedes convertible to an unprecedented reception by the New Zealand public, both knew that Dickson would never again skipper a Fay boat.

I was fascinated by what was driving Michael Fay. He seemed to have been bitten by the same bug as Sir Thomas Lipton, Peter de Savary and Alan Bond before him. But I suspected from what I'd read about Fay, and from what Susie had told me of him, that deep down there were other drivers.

Was he just a frustrated sportsman who was now rich enough to buy himself a team he could play for? In Fremantle he had earnestly tried to complete the physical programmes done by the team: he had reportedly loved the sequestered military environment he had created at the Portuguese Fishing Club and had moved out reluctantly when his wife and kids arrived in Perth. His dream was to be on the boat, to be out there, one of the boys, maybe even at the helm as the boat took the gun to win the cup, but there was no way that would be realised as long as the race was decided in 12-metre boats. The positions were too specialised and demanding and he was too old and no yachtsman. Somewhere there, the seed of the idea to take the cup out of the realm of 12-metre vessels might have germinated: to challenge in a huge yacht that had the grandeur of history and required a huge crew, among which a man of middle age and limited yachting experience could 'hide' and realise his frustrated sporting aspirations without prejudicing the boat's speed.

In 1988, through the courts in New York, Fay forced the elephant to turn and confront the flea – and he appeared to have won. On the day the judgment was delivered Capital Markets, Fay Richwhite's public investment vehicle, jumped 25 cents in a falling market. This almost symbiotic relationship between the yachting and his business also interested me. Fay and his partner, David Richwhite, whom I knew from Otago University, ploughed a hell of a lot of money and time into the America's Cup challenges. Was there a quid pro quo there?

That challenge in San Diego was still to be played out when I took a proposal to TVNZ Drama Department. It was for a mini-series based on my research with Susie. I briefly outlined what Susie had told me on tape about the reasons she was cut from the team, and I told TVNZ that it needed more research and was dependent on Michael Fay agreeing to tell his side of the story, which, crucially, still needed an ending: triumph or tragedy.

The Erebus accident had been a national tragedy, but the drama *Erebus, The Aftermath* became a tragedy only when its central character, Peter Mahon, died, and only in so far as his death could be linked to the humiliation, stress, rejection and isolation he had suffered as a result of his quest for the truth. When I presented my America's Cup proposal to TVNZ, I was clear that the ending had still to be written, most probably by Michael Fay. What would become of his challenge in the monstrous J boat? Would he be defeated and discredited? Would his obsession for the America's Cup have an unfortunate effect on his banking business? What would become of this man who, according to David Lange, was a national icon?

I felt sure that San Diego later that year would provide something suitably dramatic, triumphant or tragic. In the event, it was neither. 'San Diego believe they can defend the Cup in a windsurfer or a surf ski,' thundered Fay. 'A hot air balloon seems more appropriate.' It turned out the only hot air was coming from Fay who, later that year, when he'd duly taken his place on his monstrous boat, had his pants pulled down by Dennis Conner in a catamaran, which made it no contest.

Beyond that, Fay's obsession with the America's Cup seemed to bring him no ill: it was no impediment to his and David Richwhite's lucrative buying and selling of national assets like Telecom, BNZ and New Zealand Rail; it delivered him a knighthood and made him a citizen of the world. A world to which he escaped when Winston Peters' Wine Box Inquiry began ferreting about in his financials. His departure, along with Doug Myers, Craig Heatley and some of the other heroes of New Zealand Inc, who had encouraged the government to get out of business and 'leave it to us', was hardly triumphant. And though Lange's comment that Fay might become some sort of repository of 'the national wit, wisdom and wealth' became risible, there was certainly no tragedy in that, either for Fay or New Zealand.

The tragedy lay in the opposite direction. Susie McGillivray finally found her man, Simon Carr, an erudite and funny Englishman who had become marooned here with Simon Walker after touring with the Oxford Union debaters. Simon wrote a witty play, *The Every Weather Girl*, which was produced a couple of times, then took Susie back to London, where he's now a columnist for the *Independent*. Susie and Simon had a son, Alex, but within a very short time Susie was diagnosed with cancer and after fighting it to the last, she died at her home at Waimarama in 1994.

Long before Fay's challenge in San Diego proved that my story had no ending, and long before I got an official rejection letter in early '89 from Brian Bell, Head of Drama at TVNZ – 'As you know,' wrote Brian, 'the Drama Department is winding down' – it was apparent that the great TVNZ Department of Drama aircraft carrier was in trouble.

Through '87 and '88, whenever I went into Centrecourt, there was a feeling that the Drama Department had been somehow hollowed out, and that the energy which used to buzz through the place had leached off somewhere else. Brian Bell was courteous and enthusiastic – his great dream was a series based on Maurice Shadbolt's *Strangers and Journeys* – but there was the smell of doom about the place and Brian looked more and more beleaguered and impotent, manning the helm while something bigger and better was being assembled somewhere else. I was shortly to find out what that construction was, but had no idea that the Drama Department had already, by '88, effectively been decommissioned and beached and that Brian's view from the bridge was of a dry dock, where the rusted shell and innards of the department were about to be cannibalised or purloined for scrap.

In '86, Julian Mounter had been appointed the new Director-General of TVNZ. This had come as a huge surprise to Des Monaghan, TVNZ's Director of Programming and Production, who had applied for the job and had been assured by various people on the BCNZ Board that it was his. When the official announcement was made, after a last-minute change of heart or directive, Des was understandably disappointed – he was later told that his prospects for promotion had been stymied by his temerity in suing Muldoon for defamation. He was also dismayed, because he'd met his new boss round the international television traps and was pretty sure they wouldn't see eye to eye. Some of it was probably personal antagonism, but there was also a clash of vision and philosophy which meant that the board's choice of Mounter was to have far-reaching implications for TVNZ and for New Zealand television generally.

Mounter was promoting an all-commercial model for TVNZ, while Des believed that TVNZ should not turn its back on the public service element in its channels, that as long as it was owned by the community through the state rather than by commercial shareholders, it had a duty to serve the totality of that community with considered, intelligent programming that would cater for specific interests at least some of the time. Des wasn't against commercial broadcasting, but he advocated diversity of choice enhanced by a well-funded public service option. Through the rest of '86 and '87, TVNZ's Director-General and Director of Programming and Production were at odds over the future course of TVNZ, which might have explained, if I'd known, my feeling that the Drama Department was adrift, wallowing, about to founder.

Going back to my journal, looking for some insights into what I was thinking and writing at the time, is a disappointing exercise. My entries seem obsessed with money – and the word that keeps reappearing is 'overdraft'. What I should tell the bank to get it extended, when the next cheque might land in the bank to reduce it, and when I might have an excuse to present another invoice to someone. And, increasingly, stuff like this – 'My knees have gone wobbly and I've seldom been so depressed about my chances of making a living out of this industry . . .'

By the latter part of '88, two other projects, a telemovie with the working title of 'The Final Test', which I was writing with Dean Parker, and another docudrama about the aftermath of the '84 election, which I was helping Tom Scott with, had both been either stalled at TVNZ or turned down. 'Time to take stock,' I wrote in my journal. 'Prospects of immediate cash flow are dire . . .'

Within a few short months of signing a contract for $100,000, I was struggling for survival as a professional writer. Since 1980 I had determinedly described myself in my passport as a writer, not a short story writer or a playwright or a screenwriter, and in '88 I tried to deliver on that description by diversifying.

Philippa Campbell, my script editor from *Erebus, The Aftermath*, had told her husband, Simon Wilson, of my fantasy to be a sports writer. Simon, chief sub-editor at the *Listener*, called my bluff and

I began a fortnightly sports column for the magazine. I could write what I liked, so I ranged across the sports, doing pre-season features for cricket and rugby, and a piece on Sugar Ray Leonard, urging him to retire, which he completely ignored. And I did a piece on steroids, using Broochay, the guy I played with in Italy, as a reference point. I finally tracked him down in California, where he'd married an American air hostess (as they then were). I asked Broochay how he was doing, whether there'd been any ill effects from the steroids. None at all, he said, then told me that he could hardly jog and had trouble losing weight etc., etc. So I asked him about another notorious side effect – the disappearing penis. Hang on a minute, said Broochay. Next moment, breathing into the phone was one of those soft seductive American female voices, assuring me that Bruce's penis was still right up to the job in hand. I was grateful for the lack of videophones.

It was a relief to be working in prose and doing stuff that was finished in a day and published almost instantaneously. Simon Wilson was the man who had penned the play that ran at The Depot to replace Mervyn Thompson's. I wanted, on Proc's behalf, not to like Simon, but he proved to be erudite, earnest and likeable. The sports column was soft yakka and good fun, but it was also clear that there wasn't a real living to be had there. 'Saved financially this month,' reads my journal for October, 'by two unexpected cheques – from a production of good old *Foreskin's Lament* in Wanganui by the amateurs and from Victoria University Press (for publishing royalties on my plays). I'm owed a grand by the *Listener* for two columns and a feature. There is nothing else in prospect, there is nothing else I can conjure up.'

To add to the financial pressure, Mary's job as a counsellor at the AMAC abortion clinic also came to an end in controversial circumstances.

In August of '88, Mary appeared on the cover of the *Listener*, going head to head with Bert Potter, blowing the whistle on Centrepoint's control of the clinic. Centrepoint was a commune espousing the dodgy doctrines of Potter, a former pest eradicator who had an idiosyncratic take on sexuality, one that seemed to appeal to the middle class and middle-aged, particularly those who had missed out on 'free love' and the Swinging Sixties.

In the *Listener* article, titled 'Very Peculiar Practices', Sandra Coney detailed how the AMAC abortion clinic had been set up as a charitable trust in the 1970s by a group of altruistic pro-choice advocates who wanted New Zealand women to be able to have abortions legally and safely at a clinic with the highest medical standards. By 1984, AMAC had survived a decade of concerted attempts by the anti-abortion lobby to shut it down, from legislation to attempted arson, but the original trustees had been worn down to just three, and they made the terrible mistake of appointing two Centrepoint people to the trust, Dr Keith McKenzie and Sue Brighouse, and allowing another, Dave Mendelssohn, Brighouse's husband, to take over the accounts. The Centrepoint connection was through one of the original trustees, Anna Watson, Mendelssohn's sister.

From that point, AMAC became a cash cow for Centrepoint, which had fallen on hard times in the early 1980s. In '86, the original AMAC premises, the old Aotea Hospital in Ranfurly Road, Epsom, were sold and new premises purchased, using only half the sale proceeds from Ranfurly Road. Between '85 and '87, as detailed by Coney, Centrepoint spent nearly $2 million. The new premises in Dominion Road included a counselling room exclusively for Centrepoint use and effectively became the town base for the commune. The AMAC recovery and waiting rooms would also be used at night for Centrepoint massage and sexuality workshops.

Mary had felt disquiet about Centrepoint's increasing influence for some time. Staff meetings were run like Centrepoint groups. Whenever vacancies came up for counsellors, Centrepoint personnel filled them. Most of them were inexperienced, with no commitment to abortion. Some were entirely unsuited and one was so out of her depth that the operating doctor refused to allow her back in theatre.

Despite this, Centrepoint immediately accredited itself as one of the approved providers of upskilling courses for AMAC counsellors, providing another source of income for Centrepoint and putting pressure on non-Centrepoint counsellors like Mary to do their mandatory annual courses at Centrepoint. Mary resisted, having heard stories about the two- and three-day courses out at Albany, but finally agreed to do the bare minimum, a two-day course where she didn't have to stay overnight. It turned out to be an experience that gave her no reassurance about Centrepoint's ability.

As a warm-up to the days' activities, everyone had been encouraged by the instructor to share a 'personal issue'. When the first personal issue was shared by one of the guys on the course, the instructor said it was 'bullshit'. This guy replied that the instructor's reaction was unduly harsh and subjective because he was 'going off' with the instructor's wife, who was also on the course. There was a long silence as the instructor looked at his wife: clearly, this was the first he'd heard of the arrangement. The wife looked angrily at her lover. The lover shrugged and said that she'd told him she was going to tell her husband. This seemed to prompt the wife's memory – she reminded her husband that she had indeed told him of this new element in her life, but he'd 'forgotten' (clearly an easy thing to slip the mind at Centrepoint). The husband instructor maintained he hadn't known and therefore couldn't have been unduly prejudiced in his judgement of the lover's personal issue, which was still, therefore, bullshit. Which certainly cleared that up. Until it was the wife's turn to share a personal issue. Her issue was that she didn't mind being 'blown' by other women, but whenever she was blown by her husband, the instructor, she was scared he was going to bite her on the clitoris and couldn't relax. I doubt if the previous exchange with her husband would have reassured her. But her problem precipitated a similar issue in another man on the course, which he felt compelled to share: he didn't mind having the blackheads on his nose being popped by other people, but he really hated his wife doing it – why was that?

Enlightenment on the blowing and the blackheads didn't seem forthcoming, though they stuck at it for two days. Some of the Centrepointers told Mary the place was 'heaven on earth', but to Mary, the only true 'outsider' on the course, it felt more and more like a prison, with her featuring on the menu as fresh meat. The 'single' men would come and sit down with her during the breaks, talk animatedly for five minutes, maybe seven, then ask if they could 'show her around'. When she told them she'd already seen everything and gave them the message, they demonstrated how very cool and emancipated they were by giving her the cold shoulder thereafter.

As they gained confidence and control at AMAC, the Centrepoint counsellors there began talking openly about sexually stimulating their children – called 'blowing'. The last straw for Mary was when she saw a tearful woman and her partner being ushered out of the Centrepoint counselling room by a senior counsellor, who was also a leading light at Centrepoint. This counsellor told Mary – in total breach of confidentiality – that the woman's six-year-old daughter had complained that the partner, her stepfather, had been touching her genitals in the shower, and she didn't like it. The counsellor told Mary that she'd advised the couple that this sexual contact was 'only a problem for the child if it was a problem for the mother'. In other words, the distressed mother had been told that if she came to terms with it, so would her daughter.

At a staff meeting, Mary raised her concerns about the independence and integrity of AMAC. She said the trust had been set up to provide a comprehensive service for women in a politically delicate area. She asked why all the trustees were from Centrepoint. She asked why every vacant counselling position went to a Centrepoint person. She said that if the public suspected that AMAC was being run as a revenue-earning offshoot of Centrepoint, that would be huge ammunition for opponents of abortion. She said that Centrepoint should lose its paranoia about the outside world and start employing counsellors from outside. She suggested that half the trustees should step down so that other trustees independent of Centrepoint could step in. She told them that she'd be prepared to put her name forward as a trustee and a couple of the non-Centrepoint doctors (the certifying consultants) would too. Lorna Winn, the manager of AMAC, cried and said the Centrepoint trustees would not step down. Then her deputy,

Barbara Kingsbury, stepped in and tried to turn it into a personal spat between Mary and Lorna.

This was classic Centrepoint gobbledygook. Whatever problem you had about an act or omission by them was actually your problem, not theirs. They would listen politely while you explained that, for instance, a floor littered with empty tubes of KY jelly from the previous night's sexuality workshop wasn't a good look when you ushered a woman into the room for abortion counselling. When you'd finished your explanation, they'd smile the smug smile of the enlightened, look you deep in the eyes and ask, 'What is it that you're not getting?' It was never about the issues; it was always turned back on the person raising the issue.

Sure enough, when Mary raised these issues at the staff meeting, Kingsbury told Mary she seemed angry and had a personal problem. She said there was something Mary wasn't getting and asked what it was. She then asked Mary and Lorna Winn to imagine they were each other and give each other a hug, presumably so that 'Mary' could reconnect with 'Lorna' and 'Lorna' could forgive 'Mary' for her 'angry outburst'.

As a result of that ineffectual staff meeting, Mary invited non-Centrepoint staff to our house at John Street in April of '88, to discuss what to do next. Sandra Coney, award-winning journalist and a former counsellor who knew the history of AMAC, was also invited and a letter was drafted to the trust, setting out their concerns. One of the main tenets of the letter was the conflict of interest for the trustees between Centrepoint and AMAC, which resulted in bizarre practices like the clinic's autoclave sterilisers being used for packs of materials required for goat embryo transfers on the Centrepoint stud farm.

The points made in the letter were basically ignored. Instead, one of the two doctors who had attended that meeting was told there were other doctors ready and willing to step in, if he had problems. And at the next staff meeting, Winn did a little exercise where the staff were asked to consider whether their unmet needs might be better met in another job. Winn said the staff would be asked to come in to her office during the following week and discuss whether they were happy in their jobs and whether there was some other career they might prefer. Dr Keith McKenzie was, unusually, at that meeting. He was a foundation member of Centrepoint and had distinguished himself in the past: in Coney's article, she quoted a senior counsellor who recalled McKenzie saying of a client who had been raped twice at a rock festival that 'she was the type who would be raped'. Another ex-counsellor was furious when McKenzie turned to a rape victim during his consultation and said, 'Don't be surprised if this happens to you again. It's been found that some women attract this kind of thing.'

At the meeting, McKenzie pronounced himself pissed off, especially at the person 'initiating' the dissatisfaction. Everyone knew McKenzie was referring to Mary, and the non-Centrepointers, who had resolved they should be dealt with as a group, not as individuals. So when Winn asked Mary to come in to her office and discuss her job, Mary refused and began considering her options.

Two of the doctors from the John Street meeting who had promised Mary support, to the point of withdrawing their labour, were now equivocal: both, like Mary, had a longstanding commitment to pro-choice and felt that their obligations to women patients came first. Though I was upset by their decision and regarded it as a triumph of hypocrisy over Hippocrates, Mary had worked for over a decade in the cause and was more understanding of their position. Shortly after, the operating doctors were given their first rise in years. I was reasonably close to one of those doctors and our relationship has never recovered.

Mary felt obliged to continue alone and expose how the AMAC Trust had become a cash cow for a misogynist group of child abusers. In May of '88, Mary resigned from AMAC, so that she could contribute freely to Sandra Coney's exposé in the *Listener*.

As a result of the *Listener* article, the Attorney-General referred the whole matter on to the Solicitor-General for investigation. The Solicitor-General talked to the Abortion Supervisory Committee headed by a woman called Heather White, who had spent a night at Centrepoint and pronounced herself 'impressed with what a group of middle class people can do when they pool resources'. Perhaps it was felt that exposure of Centrepoint's control of AMAC would be a huge setback to the abortion cause: whatever the reason, nothing was done and it took Sarah Smuts Kennedy and other victims of Centrepoint misogyny and abuse to finally force the state into action.

In 1992 Dr Keith McKenzie was convicted of indecently assaulting a minor and was struck off the medical register. Dave Mendelssohn was convicted of indecently assaulting three minors and sentenced to four years in prison. Bert Potter was sentenced to seven and a half years in prison after being convicted of indecently assaulting five minors, some as young as three and a half years old. These days of reckoning, however, were in the future and no help to Mary or me in '88, when she lost her job.

Dean Parker, my writing partner from *Roche*, was also out of work and had gone back to writing graffiti to relieve the tedium of perusing the situations vacant columns. His authorship was easy to spot. The graphics were shite, but the message was clever. After the Queen Street riots in '84, 'Loot Now While Stocks Last!' had appeared on Dean's favourite site, the AEPB building at the bottom of John Street, just up from his house in Vermont Street. In '86, the US was putting the heat on Labour's anti-nuclear stance, with lots of help from Jim McLay, the Leader of the Opposition, who had an American wife, Marcia. 'MarC.I.A says Hello Sailor!' wrote Dean. Then, when poor old Jim took a stand against Aids, Dean thought he looked a bit camp himself and wrote 'Don't Take Blood From Jim McLay!'

By the latter part of '88, Dean had found a new billboard, a fresh writing pad. Holmdene, the double-storeyed Georgian palace at 195 Ponsonby Road, just across from Prego restaurant, had just been fulsomely renovated. Typically, given the paranoia that new money and gentrification had brought to Ponsonby, the pièce de résistance was a high, freshly plastered stucco wall which now ran the length of the section, guarding the palace from the street. 'Abandon Hope All Ye Who Enter Here!' sprayed Dean, right along the new wall.

The first tenant of the renovated palace was an outfit called South Pacific Pictures, run by none other than Des Monaghan. His offsider was big Don Reynolds, miraculously risen out of the ashes of Mirage, proving not for the first time nor the last that he was more Phoenix than Icarus. No one was terribly sure just what South Pacific Pictures was, at first. It seemed to have the backing of TVNZ, yet the Drama Department was still operating, after a fashion.

We gradually realised, as the TVNZ Drama Department formally bit the dust and 'wound down', that we were on the verge of a new era, that South Pacific Pictures *was* the Drama Department, with many of its bits and pieces and lots of new bits, reconstituted as an 'independent' production house but with the inordinate advantage of operating capital and overdraft facilities guaranteed by the deep pockets of TVNZ.

There were various rumours going around as to how this state of affairs had transpired, that it was an inevitable consequence of the 1986 State Owned Enterprise Act, or that it was the dastardly scheme of Julian Mounter, who had brought some funny ideas with him from Britain. Both of those elements were factors, but not in the way any of us guessed at the time. The truth about the birth of SPP, now the privately owned powerhouse of New Zealand television production on the back of series like *Shortland Street* and *Outrageous Fortune*, not to mention movies like *Whale Rider* and *Sione's Wedding*, was much more bizarre: the idea arose directly out of the clash of vision between Mounter and Monaghan and first saw the light of day among the deros and street kids of the Grafton cemetery, just across K Road from the old Sheraton Hotel.

By early '88, Des could see the writing on the wall for public service television, and the message bore an uncanny resemblance to Dean's graffiti. It had become clear to Des that he had lost the battle for the retention of any public service element in TVNZ and Mounter's full-bore commercial model was going to be implemented. In the face of that bleak prospect, Des didn't want to stick around. When, during a meeting at the Sheraton Hotel, Des told the board of the Broadcasting Corporation of New Zealand, at that time the overseeing body for an SOE comprising both Radio New Zealand and TVNZ, that he was looking for pastures new, the board immediately called Mounter in and gave him a last-ditch directive to find a way to make Des stay.

Des and Mounter left the Sheraton and wandered across K Road to the Grafton cemetery where, among the flotsam and jetsam of society, they walked round and round in the sunshine, as they talked round and round the problem. They were getting nowhere until, finally, Mounter stopped and asked Des: in an ideal world, if he could have anything – anything – he wanted, what would it be?

Des knew better than most that TVNZ was about to become a very different beast. As the full commercial model was implemented, much of the work previously done in-house would be outsourced to independent contractors, and as a result, within a year or two, there would be massive redundancies among TVNZ staff. Drama would not be immune. Des thought he could see a way of having his cake and eating it – get out from under Mounter, make drama independently of TVNZ, away from its hardening creative arteries, yet with access to its huge financial resources. He told Mounter he wanted an independent production house backed to the financial hilt by TVNZ.

Done, said Mounter, and they crossed back to the Sheraton to tell the board. Done, said the board, who later proved how pleased they were by giving Des a better remuneration package to run this new 'independent' production house than they'd given the new director-general to run TVNZ. So it came to pass, perhaps appropriately, through personal antagonism, frustration, compromise and pay-off, that the new giant of domestic television production was born, ready to take advantage of an imminent change in the rules.

Des christened this new entity South Pacific Pictures Ltd, and it was duly registered as a company in July of '88. But Des never got to enjoy the fruits of his passion: shortly after registering his new baby, he learned that the BCNZ board was going to be disestablished. TVNZ and RNZ were to become separate SOEs, which meant that, come '89, Des would have to report to Mounter, not the BCNZ board. Even his new baby couldn't reconcile Des to that fate. In September '88, he abandoned it and took a job with the Seven network in Australia, and was on his way even as Dean and I were invited to a meeting at the new Ponsonby Road premises of SPP.

In one of the huge rooms at Holmdene, still smelling of new carpet, Don Reynolds and Ross Jennings, another refugee from the TVNZ Drama Department, explained that they had to quickly get SPP up and running as a viable production entity, and that meant getting product out into the international marketplace. To begin with, they wanted to concentrate on product which New Zealand had a track record – kiddults. Series like *Hunter's Gold* were the one generic New Zealand television product that had sold consistently well overseas, so they wanted Dean and me to come up with series concepts for kiddults. If we were interested in doing that, they'd put us on a retainer for three months. Three months! From where we were sitting, looking at the situations vacant columns, three months seemed like an eternity of financial security . . .

Neither Dean nor I had ever written kiddults before, but what the hell, necessity was the mother of invention and we told ourselves that we could use the SPP retainer as a way of subsidising more 'serious' pursuits. Ross was pretty forthright: he explained to us that any satisfaction to be had from the kinds of projects they were talking about would be derived from working as a team. In other words, there'd be no creative satisfaction to be had from actually writing the kind of programmes they wanted to make. Maybe they were worried that Dean and I were pointy-heads and fancied ourselves as Artists. Not with our overdrafts.

The paint on Dean's graffiti along the wall was barely dry as we walked out through the gates of Holmdene with our contracts in our pockets. We didn't know it at the time, but those contracts were also front-row tickets to a new era of television drama, the commercial model, Mounter's full Monty, which would make what I'd experienced so far look like a group hug. I'd often been told and just as often repeated to others the adage that conflict was the essence of drama, but thus far I had taken it to refer to the action between characters on the page or screen. In this new era which was now upon us, whether we were ready for it or not, the off-screen dramatic stakes often seemed higher than any on screen, and at times Dean's invocation of Dante would come to seem like something more than a hell of a good joke.